Imagined Nation

ENGLAND AFTER BRITAIN

Imagined Nation

ENGLAND AFTER BRITAIN

Edited by Mark Perryman

Lawrence & Wishart
LONDON 2008

Lawrence and Wishart Limited
99a Wallis Road
London
E9 5LN

First published 2008

British Library Cataloguing in Publication Data.
A catalogue record for this book is available from the British Library

ISBN 978 1 905 007 73 8

Text setting E-type, Liverpool
Printed and bound by Biddles, Kings Lynn

Contents

Acknowledgements

The idea of this collection occurred to me at the launch of Billy Bragg's *The Progressive Patriot* organised by Philosophy Football. So thanks to Billy for writing a book that reignited a lot of my thinking and extended it beyond my mental touchline.

It is, however, on away trips following England to World Cups and European Qualifiers that a lot of my thoughts on English national identity have been developed. It is in these foreign spots that you get a much better sense of what England looks like. At World Cup 2006, thanks to Ian and Thea Ward in Frankfurt; Frank Weniger and Antje Schuetze in Munich; Juergen and Simon Jakobi in Nuremburg; Claus Melchior in Munich; Mark Swatek and Marianna Evenstein in Cologne; Uli Hesse-Lichtenberger and Sabine Lichtenberger in Witten; Karin Ernst and Ansgar Schäfer in Oer-Erkenschwick.

While cheering on England in far-away places an imaginative range of fan-friendly events are organised by supporter groups – effectively putting into practice the virtues of a soft English patriotism, full of pride without the prejudice. It is this experience more than anything else that convinces me of the absolute necessity to reimagine what England might become. Thanks therefore to those who have helped out. At World Cup 2006 Antje Hagel from the Offenbach Fans Projekt, Frankurt Bembel Bar, Beverley Taylor in Munich, Maccabi Munchen, Herbert Schroeger and the Munich 1860 Supporters Projekt, Peter Schuengel from EDFF in Dortmund, Beate Weisbarth and the Elsa-Brändström Realschule in Cologne. And for help on the way, we thought and believed, to qualifying for Euro 2008: the British Embassy, Brian Taylor and Vladimir Stojcevski in Skopje, the British Council and Sasa Dupor of UKMI in Zagreb, the British Council, Maccabi GB, Football 4 Peace and Bnei Sakhnin FC in Israel, the British Council and the British Embassy in Tallinn, the British Council in Moscow, the British Embassy and *Ballesterer* in Vienna. However none of this fan-friendliness in the name of England would happen if it wasn't for the involvement of the fans themselves. Too many to mention but a special thanks to traitor in black Dave Beverley, person with the sponge Lizzie

Hart, team captain Dan Scott, managers Ade Alleyne, Simon Fawell, Stuart Fuller and Dave 'Chopper' Hancock plus stalwarts of each and every initiative, The Judge, Jess Mortimer and her mum, Paul and Lynda Lamkin, Grant Madden, Fred and Howard Thompson. Without your participation and example not much of what I think and write about Englishness would make very much sense.

Various individuals and bodies have supported my endeavours towards a positive England over the past two years. In particular Hajra Alibhai, Jeremy Bell and Andy Battson at the Foreign Office, David Bohannan and Martin Gooday at the Home Office. Simon Johnson, Phil Smith, Andrin Cooper, Sarah Gillett, Harpreet Grewal and Nicola Jones at the Football Association, Karl Pechatscheck and Katja Wostradowski at the Goethe Institute in London, Rosemary Hilhorst of the British Council in Portugal. And for recording the antics of our soft English patriotism on film, with only over-long interviews with yours truly spoiling the finished product, Gregg McDonald. Of course neither myself nor any readers should hold any of this respectable lot responsible for what I get up to, and write, but your support is much appreciated all the same.

Students and staff on the Sports Journalism degree at the University of Brighton where I teach part-time are often an unwitting test-pad for my latest thinking on national identity. Your responses are always most welcome and necessary, even when I remain in disagreement. My business partner on Philosophy Football, Hugh Tisdale, endures my obsession with the English Question with impressive fortitude and on more than one occasion has turned it into the makings of a fine T-shirt for fellow soft patriots to wear (one of which inspired this book's cover design).

Sally Davison has been a patient and conscientious publisher. If there were more outfits with the solid political commitment of Lawrence and Wishart, less of the idealism some of us fondly remember as the founding basis of the left might have melted into thin air over the past eleven years. Fran Davies has put up with my ideas to produce a fine cover.

Home and away one person more than any other puts up with all I do, write, even wear, towards this soft patriotism. For Anne Coddington my imagined nation isn't another country, it has become part of our relationship. For better or worse? Only she can answer that one.

Mark Perryman
February 2008

Introduction

The first three terms of a Blairist-Brownite Labour government have been constitutionally dominated by devolution. Whilst the English at the outset of this process mostly took a take-it-and-leave it attitude, the impact in Scotland, Wales and Northern Ireland has been much more profound. So much so that in May 2007 nationalist parties became a central part of government in each of these parts of our once united Kingdom.

Thus Gordon Brown finally became Prime Minister just as Britain appeared to be entering an irreversible drift towards some kind of separation. Although the time scale remains uncertain, any idea that the moves towards devolved power will be reversed is an untenable position – whichever party wins the next Westminster General Election. Yet Brown seems to be seeking to reinvent himself as the 'Bard of Britishness' (in a wonderful phrase from Tom Nairn).

Thirty years ago Tom Nairn was a lonely voice on the left in his argument about the Break-Up of Britain, and the democratic potential in bringing an end to the Union. Now it is Brown and his party which appear the lonesome ones when they urge us all to run a Union Jack up the flag pole in the face of the much greater appeal of identities framed by our English, Scots, Welsh or Northern Irish belonging. 'British Jobs for British Workers', Brown demanded, in front of a huge Union Jack backdrop at his inaugural Labour Conference as prime minister in 2007. This was an appeal to the most backward, defensive and narrow version of national identity, wrapped in a flag that increasingly lacks the unifying appeal he is so obviously seeking. One wonders how often Brown has been out canvassing back home in his constituency of Kirkcaldy and Cowdenbeath, urging voters to fly a Union Jack out of their window to celebrate their 'Britishness', or stuffing Labour Party leaflets adorned with the same flag through letterboxes. Just what kind of response would Gordon get if he tried?

Instead of retreating into a sour-faced jealousy of our Celtic neighbours who have achieved something denied to the English – a measure at least of independence and difference from the one-flag-fits-all politics of the Union – the English would do better trying to learn from our nearest, if not always dearest. It is time to embark on a process founded on engaging with what England might become, rather than what it once was. Not just a St George Cross to stick out the car window and a national dress of bri-nylon football jerseys, but the beginnings of shaping some kind of state of independence out of these summer tournament bursts of ninety-minute nationalism. This is what *Imagined Nation* sets out to do.

Mark Perryman argues, in the book's opening essay, that it is time to move on from a simple celebration of the enormous, friendly and increasingly multicultural flag-waving parties that take place at major football, rugby and cricket events, to consider the connections between these eruptions of Englishness and a broader cultural, social, and political emergence of Broken-Up Britain. This is in part a response to a critique by Beatrix Campbell. Speaking at a discussion of Billy Bragg's book *The Progressive Patriot*, Bea questioned the centrality that Mark and others award to football in re-imagining Englishness: 'By aligning football with national identity you are ignoring the fact that football has been connected with some of the worst things in English history. It's a mistake to think that national culture is defined by football. What is it about the insecurities of masculinity? Why would anybody want to think that football should define in any way at all the new English sensibilities?' England and football have certainly been responsible for some of the nastiest expressions of English patriotism, but they have also contributed to moments of a popular, inclusive, multicultural Englishness. Yet Bea's point is essentially correct: if football is all we've got, what kind of nation do we imagine England might become? *Imagined Nation* seeks to uncover other resources of hope for an England after Britain.

The contributors to this book take a variety of viewpoints on whether or not an independent England is a likely or likeable option. But all agree that some kind of break-up is underway. Andrew Gamble opens the first section of the book, 'A State of Independence', by cataloguing the current constitutional inconsistencies. He argues that it is this discontinuity between the current version of devolution and common-sense democracy that is most likely to create the momentum towards change. Also in this section Graham Macklin provides a vital insight into the BNP today, which is seeking to mobilise support around this momentum by defining national identity not only racially, but as the frontline against both immigration and Europe. This, of course, is an option not limited to the far right: such defence-mechanism politics is resorted to by a much broader constituency. And if we fail to engage with these arguments they will almost certainly come to define Englishness on their own terms – of insecurity in the face of difference. Rupa Huq finds something positive to sustain any challenge to a rightward-moving Englishness in the most surprising of places – suburbia. From behind the chintz curtains through which Terry and June and Margot and Jerry once peered there have also emerged the punk Bromley Contingent of The Sex Pistols and Siouxsie Sioux, *Bend it like Beckham* and Zadie Smith's *White Teeth*. Spaces and places are sites of both resistance and change, and suburban England is now in the frontline. Stephen Brasher also detects many places where the picture is different from the stereotype – seaside seats which are rock-solid Labour, a tradition of rural trade-unionism, and an English Labour vote that sustained not only the 1945 landslide but also the 1997 result. It can't be assumed that English votes for English laws will always be Conservative votes.

Billy Bragg is a vocal supporter of all that good Englishness might represent. He's written songs about it, and will turn his concerts into a communal think-piece on the subject given half a chance and his mug of tea. And instead of cluttering up the bookshelves with a ghost-written biography, he took the trouble to write a book on the subject, *The Progressive Patriot*. Billy opens the second section, 'Little England', with a constructive response to the flak he has had to take since writing his book. He argues that England will be a new nation, though of course with an ancient history; tradition is important but so is the process in which those traditions are identified, dusted down, or put to one side to be refashioned and reinterpreted for today and tomorrow. Billy provides an insight into how this process might help us emerge as something more than a quaint theme-park for tourists and hotel chains. Richard Weight and Julia Bell develop this theme in their essays in this section. Our history and language isn't simply constructed out of an imperial and martial legacy, though it is pulled into different shapes by these past episodes, and migration and colonialism add layer upon layer to the story. The full English isn't to be found by trying to locate a pure, deep English – a task which is thankless and futile. It is the mix, the impurity, that is so distinctive. Ben Carrington contributes a keynote chapter to this section, drawing on his work on the sociology of sport. He reflects on the events of 2005, when within 24 hours of London being successfully voted an Olympic host city, the capital was devastated by the 7/7 bombings. The celebratory flag-waving in Trafalgar Square was replaced by anxieties of cohesion and an enemy within. Can the integration that sport supposedly fosters help us to understand the motivations of suicide bombers? Ben's chapter is a powerfully argued exploration of the contours of race, examining how our innocent pastimes and guilty pleasures are criss-crossed by definitions and experiences defined by practices of integration, assimilation and separation.

The book's next section, 'Home Truths from Here, There and Everywhere', looks at England from a variety of geographical perspectives. Gerry Hassan details not just Scottish nationalism and devolution, but their likely contribution to influencing England's own independence campaign. His scenarios for possible future developments make compelling reading for those still unconvinced that the changes of the last decade will lead inexorably to a different future. David Conn considers what a resurgent Englishness might mean for a North that has always been suspicious of a metropolitan London and southeast. Will one disunited Kingdom be simply replaced by another? Anne Coddington reviews the *Folk Archive* of artists Jeremy Deller and Alan Kane to provide some possible answers to this question. *Folk Archive* is a cultural practice founded on giving voice and visibility for all that makes us different through foregrounding the contribution of people actively engaged in producing contemporary 'folk art'. Their archive is an effective challenge to representations of England as just the politics of another brand value. The final contribution to this section is from German journalist Markus Hesselmann, who has an eye for what is that makes us different – and appealing!

The closing section of the book aims to think about England's future, dreaming or otherwise. Paul Gilroy records a journey from the hate-filled *Rivers of Blood* speech made by Enoch Powell in 1968 to the hope Paul sees all around him in modern England. Hopes not yet fulfilled, but with a presence that makes them increasingly hard to ignore. The chapter by Daniel Burdsey is similarly circumspect with its optimism. Englishness remains immersed in definitions of nation and culture out of whiteness. Waves of migration have impacted upon this, sometimes provoking a response that opens up what we imagine England might become; but this conversation is too often closed down before it has begun. This is a debate whose outcome is not yet determined, but its importance remains crucial. Nicola Baird locates Englishness in a different, though related, political space. The rubric of Green politics is basing our preservation of the local in our commitment to the global. Does this offer us a different way of settling national and international loyalties, to their mutual benefit? A green and pleasant England – a patchwork of particularities – is one route to Jerusalem; and perhaps it has the potential to merge the progressive and the patriotic. Andy Newman argues that broken-up Britain must be accompanied by a new imaginary for an English left. In considering the processes of devolution and their eventual outcome on England, he revisits some of the debates that have deterred or encouraged the left in England when it comes to considering its own version of a national-popular democratic politics.

More than thirty years ago, Tom Nairn argued in his magisterial *The Break-Up of Britain* that the left should take seriously the democratic inconsistencies of our United Kingdom. Twenty years after the book's publication Scotland and Wales voted yes in devolution referendums; the Scottish Parliament and Welsh Assembly followed, and shortly afterwards self-government for Northern Ireland was restored. But England was left out of this constitutional settlement. Tom's short postscript to this book invokes one of the great cultural icons of Englishness, Shakespeare's Henry V, to remind us of some of the resources we can depend upon, as well as some that we should ditch, in the process of becoming England after Britain.

Imagined Nation is a much-needed start on making a wide variety of political connections between a popular affiliation with Englishness and a political expression for the emotional investment that so many share. The authors don't underestimate the difficulties in such a process, but most recognise its crucial importance. The collection offers a series of starting-points for a soft patriotism – one that is open and inclusive, and hard to take for those who favour hate and prejudice. Its aim is an England which will be for all, after a Britain that was always for some.

Becoming England

Mark Perryman

28 March 2007, halftime score Andorra vs England, 0-0. A little bit of footballing history. It's the first time this tiny principality (pop 71,000; registered footballers 736 – all amateurs) has trotted off to their dressing room after 45 minutes against international opposition with no goals conceded. If there was a low-point in England performances under manager Steve McLaren this was probably it. Fortunately, in the second half a pair of goals from Steven Gerrard and a last-minute toe poke from David Nugent meant England finished the game as easy, if not particularly worthy, winners. But the score remains at one-nil to the micro-states of Europe when it comes to the trappings of nationhood. An anthem, their own head of state and a government of sorts can all be claimed by the countries such as Andorra, Liechtenstein and Luxembourg, as well as newcomer Montenegro. OK, Liechtenstein's national anthem may share the same tune with *God Save the Queen*, but the words are proudly their own: 'High above the young Rhine lies Liechtenstein, resting on Alpine heights. This beloved homeland, this dear fatherland.' Hardly going to be confused with ours is it? But then that's the point. Who, in this instance, is us? Is a football, rugby and cricket team (plus Wales) really all we have to call England? And why, when the stands are full of a nation's passion, are we lumbered with singing a song we can't even call our own?

Over the past decade Englishness has been characterised by two parallel, yet intimately related, developments. The emergence of a popular English national identity formed around support for the England football team, accompanied by the unfolding break up of Britain. It is the connections between these two factors that provide a key starting-point to answering the questions posed by the possibilities of an England after Britain.

The Blair years saw a decade of England qualifying for every tournament going, with English Rugby World Cup and Ashes victories, plus the 2002 Manchester Commonwealth Games. But they were also witness to what threatens to become the irreversible separation of a once United Kingdom into four nations. Scotland has its Parliament, with Scottish Nationalist Alex Salmond now proudly reigning as First Minister. The Welsh have a slightly less impressive Assembly, presided over by Labour's Rhodri Morgan, thanks to a coalition agreement with the party of Wales, Plaid Cymru. And No Surrendering DUP is ruling in Stormont, the historic seat of devolved Northern Irish Government (though they have to endure Sinn Fein's Martin McGuiness as deputy, perhaps the basis for expectations that a United Ireland can't be more than a generation away). All this adds up to nothing much short of a political earthquake. Yet in England, as historian Eric Hobsbawm once memorably remarked, 'the imagined community of millions seems more real as a team of eleven named people'. [1]

COMMUNITIES AND VILLAGES OF OUR IMAGINATION
Benedict Anderson has set out some key definitions to explain his description of the nation-state as an imagined community:

> ... *Imagined* because the members of even the smallest nation will never know most of their fellow-members, meet them or even hear of them, yet in the minds of each lives the image of their communion ... It is imagined as a *community* because, regardless of the actual inequality and exploitation that may prevail in each, the nation is always conceived as a deep, horizontal comradeship.[2]

Anderson's definitions are peculiarly appropriate to any imagining of England after Britain. The connections we share will largely be imaginary: the era of texting, facebook and myspace may have put us more in touch than ever before, but the grand narrative ideas that once would have mobilised a class behind one unitary idea are fragmented, remnants of a fast disappearing mass political culture. Englishness offers one opportunity to become a collective noun once again – a 'we' where most of the time 'me' is our lot.

England after Britain will also bid a perhaps not very fond farewell to GB and UK, and the process will undoubtedly be driven by Scotland, Wales and Northern Ireland. As their separation from the unity of GB continues, England will come to define itself too. No longer part of something that calls itself Great, or United, the danger might be that we choose to retreat towards exclusion, fortress Little England. How we imagine our community will in large measure determine that outcome: blood and soil, an unwelcoming land distrustful of all things foreign, or an England of communities in the plural, connected and contributing to an England in-the-making, not ready-made. It was this latter vision that musician Simon Emmerson sought to conjure up, under the banner *Imagined Village*, on his 2007 album and tour. He explains: 'It's not about authenticity, it's about identity. I'm not interested in people listening to this record searching for authenticity. But there's a lot of identity there. That's what multiculturalism is about – not losing your identity in some beige soup, but standing up and saying, this is what I am, I'm rooted and I'm English.'[3] Bold acclamations of Englishness, musical or otherwise, are listened to with foreboding by some, but since 1997 and the devolution referendums of Scotland and Wales, what is increasingly obvious is that this imagined community of England is in the process of construction. My argument is that we need to engage with this process rather than allow it to be dominated by the nationalist right.

KEEPING THE FLAGS FLYING

A key moment when questions about the building blocks for a new England become most apparent is when the England football team qualify for a World Cup or European Championship. News reporters are dispatched to account for the sudden flurry of flag-waving, the business pages analyse the surge in sales for any product with Three Lions attached, while the tabloids helpfully provide a cut-out-and-keep St George Cross. Meanwhile the quality papers' columnists ponder on the meaning of this upsurge in English nationalism.

As World Cup 2006 approached, Mark Lawson in the *Guardian* spotted a curious political symmetry: 'David Cameron seems to view the World Cup as a chance to position himself at the head of a non-barmy army, displaying both street credibility and a brand patriotism that is not scarred by either war or border controls.' As for Gordon Brown: 'His sudden cheering for a football team his native culture requires him to despise is a way of positioning himself as a leader acceptable to the English.'[4] In the *Observer* Jason Cowley was less bothered by the posturings of the political class; he was more interested in what all this flag-waving meant in the nation's pubs and living rooms. 'These manifestations of soft nationalism – the flags, the plastic hats, the silly songs – are largely benign, little more than a release from the mundane, an expression of commonality and mutual interest.'[5] As England's tournament ended Brian Appleyard in *The Times* was admirably certain of what the past few weeks represented: 'Let us be exact, the fans and players of all colours, creeds and classes are saying, this is England – or, more commonly, Ingerland – not Britain. We, the English, are a people'.[6]

In the *Daily Mail* Stephen Glover observed the political conse-quences for the Union of all this draping ourselves in St George, comparing today's England fans to those who once witnessed our sole lifting of any silverware. 'In 1966 they thought of England when they thought of Britain, and hardly distinguished between the two. Now their successors who frantically wave and display the St George's flag are plainly thinking only of England, and celebrating their Englishness rather than their Britishness.'[7] From 1996 to 2006 a decade of tourna-ments not only inspired our nation to keep those flags flying; it also produced a lot of pondering about what this might mean. The consen-sus, by and large, was that England was imagining itself once again as a nation, and rather liking the idea.

LEFT, RIGHT, ON THE MARCH

But some critics remain, and from opposite ends of the political spec-trum. The Socialist Workers Party (SWP), though a small group, has considerable influence in such campaigns as Unite against Fascism and Love Music Hate Racism, where they consistently oppose what they regard as a destructive flirtation with Englishness by rival sections of left opinion. The SWP's National Secretary Martin Smith takes Billy Bragg to task for his 'progressive patriotism':

> Anti-racism, multiculturalism, trade union activity. My argument is really simple. This has got nothing to do with being English. It's got everything to do with solidarity, with socialism and the international struggle. That's a completely separate thing. You can be just as proud of this in France, in Latin America, in China, in Japan. They are traditions we share. They are international traditions. They are the complete oppo-site to questions of patriotism and the country where you come from.[8]

This is one-dimensional Marxism at its worst, purporting to be ultra-radical but in effect betraying a wilful conservatism. Of course there is a credible philosophical position committed to one world free of all borders and flags. But to pretend this is a majority point of view within the working class, or that any identification with the country you come from is necessarily reactionary, results in a dangerous retreat from poli-tics. It ends up as a denial of the particularity of national cultures; any credence given to such particularity is denounced as exclusivist and discriminatory, and the whole world reduced to a mishmash of platitu-dinal oppositions.

A much more sophisticated argument from the left is offered by Mike Marqusee, author of a brilliant book on the establishment's stranglehold on English cricket, *Anyone But England.*[9] Ahead of World Cup 2006 Mike urged those of us who would be cheering for England not to pretend that everyone in the country would be doing the same:

> Millions of people in England will not support the England team. None of them should be required to camouflage or justify their own forms of partisanship or indifference. Most importantly, not being keen on the England football team does not make anyone less English, less a full and equal member of the community, than anyone else. The challenge during the World Cup will be securing space and respect for this diversity of partisanship.[10]

Sure, there are some who wear the Three Lions on their shirt as a badge of intolerance. But it is a strange kind of left miserabilism that denies the human capacity to mix our partisan support for England with the popular internationalism of global football. When England played Jamaica in their final warm-up match before the World Cup, my friends Jos Johnson and Roy Cole turned up at Old Trafford in a rather special kit they had tailored themselves. They had sewn the front half of their England shirts to the back half of their Jamaica shirts. As Jos explained, on this day he had two teams, two countries, two heritages and cultures to support. In the run-up to World Cup 2006 round North London, where I live, I spotted plenty of cars flying St George out of one window, and the flag of Trinidad and Tobago, our Group opponents in Germany, out of another. And when England drew Israel in our Euro 2008 qualifying campaign, the Hassidic Jews who run the grocery store opposite my home became overnight Israel fans. The same experience repeats itself from community to community, tournament to tournament. Our national identities, including the English, have acquired a welcome flexibility. Nationalism and internationalism co-exist for many, and it's time the leftist moralisers wised up to the change.

But it's not just leftists who are fearful of all this football-fuelled flag waving. From the Right Max Hastings warns of the change the revival of St George might represent:

> We have always known the Welsh don't do much soccer and the Scots hate cricket, but that was not the point. The Union Flag was the national symbol of England and Britain, which were understood to be interchangeable. I hope that English nationalism does not mean that in the future we shall favour the flag of St George over that of the Union, other

than in football competitions. This country has done such great and wonderful things under the old flag, that it will be a national tragedy if our national symbol is eclipsed.[11]

Jealous of the increasingly independent politics of Scotland and Wales, Hastings and his sympathisers can't comprehend this lack of a desire for a Union that they still see as belonging to England. And so they are forced to downplay the bi-annual waving of St George as a merely temporary interlude, for football but not very much else. And the best way to ram home this point is to assure us that the events of the weeks that precede England's sad and inevitably trophyless retreat from an international championship are just another hyped-up media phenomenon representing all that's wrong with modern society. Stewart Steven in the *Mail on Sunday* bemoaned all the excitement that followed England's unexpected defeat of Argentina at World Cup 2002.

> Football hysteria is part of the dumbing down of culture. I'm not here talking about even the lower elements – the daft, aimless football chanting which we hear these days at night in nearly all our city centres. No. It's the way otherwise intelligent people can get together in the pub or office and talk absolute nonsense for hour upon hour. Men talk less and less about politics or books, or cinema or anything actually requiring a little effort or a little learning. They are diminishing themselves. Football seems to drive even sensible people nuts.[12]

He just didn't get it, did he? Beating Argentina really means something in the history of our football nation – though we know, of course that it is not more important than world peace or stopping climate change.

The political and media classes never have the humility to stop and ponder why a 1-0 victory may have more emotional purchase than a clash at the Westminster dispatch box or a carefully-crafted leader column. Could it have something to do with the interchangeable ideologies and labels of a frankly meaningless middle ground? Perhaps football, draped in St George, gives to a fair sprinkling of England a sense of belonging and well-being that party-politics so patently fails to provide.

LOVE IS IN THE HERR
There is nothing quite like the England vs Germany rivalry, hopelessly confusing two World War victories with our never-let-them-forget World Cup victory too (though it was followed by more defeats than most of us would care to remember). Germany has a particular place in

the imagination of English nationalism, and matches between the two countries take place against the background of ancient rivalries, memories and stereotypes from on and off the pitch. Thus before the 2006 World Cup in Germany there was one headline after another about those beastly Germans' preparations for the forthcoming England fans' 'invasion'. The *Sun* front page, 16 December 2005 – 'BRITSKRIEG: Germans buy tanks to control our fans' – set the tone for the tournament build-up. A month later, 27 January 2006, the *Sun* front page led with: 'HANS UP! German cops over here to nick World Cup thugs'; on 9 February it was 'DON'T MENTION THE WALK: German cops will jail fans who goose-step like Fawlty'. Four weeks later, on 9 March, in another front-page screamer, a 1966 World Cup hero got it in the neck: 'GEOFF WURST: England legend to promote Germany'. And in April the theme was continued: 'FOR YOU ZE SNORE IS OVER: England fans' bed ban'.

The January story about the German police at English airports happened to be printed the day after I chaired a LondonEnglandFans forum where the proposition was first explained by the British police. Their German counterparts would be present at all major departure points, enabling them to phone through to Germany that no special precautions would be required because every travelling fan had been properly screened. An idea loudly applauded by all the England supporters present. And when the Mayor of Nuremburg, on a Home Office World Cup preparation visit, dropped in on our fans forum, he answered a question about England supporters travelling to his city without tickets by saying 'You're all welcome, with or without tickets, however many'. The fans were banging the tables, the applause almost deafening. In other words, there was another way of relating to the Germans, and one, it turned out, that was shared by most English fans. What's more, thinking about Germany in a different way meant being English in a different way.

With this kind of friendly German reception, once the tournament began the *Sun* had to change tack. The Germans didn't hate us, and most of us didn't hate them either. On 17 June, the *Sun* front page proclaimed 'LOVE IS IN THE HERR: England fans best, say Germans'. In the summer of 2006 there was a story in the 400,000 England fans who travelled to Germany and found ourselves made welcome. The antipathy – often bare-faced loathing – that we had stored up against the Germans for decades wasn't returned in kind. And at the World Cup party most of us put all that unwelcome history to one side and just got on with joining in. When we got lost on the way to the stadium, the Germans couldn't be more helpful with their directions, leading a few of us to guiltily ponder whether we would have been as accommodating to them back home. We hung our flags up, turned a sort of pasty red in the sun, ate an unhealthy amount of *Sauerkraut*, and appreciated the warm regard in which we were mostly held. Germany made it through to the semi-finals after England had already exited the tournament, and the measure of the change underway could be gauged on the Englandfans' web-forum, as post after post, began with 'I never thought I'd say this but ...', and went on to declare how much they hoped Germany would win that night.

It would be reckless to pretend that everyone shares this appreciation of the softer side of our passion for England. As I stepped out of Frankfurt train station a mob was gathering across the street at O'Reilly's – ironically an Irish bar. I could hear the strains of 'No Surrender', followed by verse after verse of 'Ten German Bombers'. But most of us spent our time in Germany learning that being friendly is far more fun than being feared. As the defeated German team trudged round the pitch after they had lost their semi-final to the eventual World Cup winners Italy, the German fans sang, defiantly, 'You'll Never Walk Alone' – the Anfield Kop's – England's – fan anthem. (And being well-organised Germans, it was in word-perfect English.) No greater compliment could be paid to the warmth and generosity of the English at their best.

When England failed to qualify for Euro 2008, the po-faced commentators couldn't have been happier:

> The news that England are coming – England, with their travelling army of good-time boys, the red-faced, singlet-wearing, oddly middle-aged bruisers with their bum-bags and white ankles and insatiable appetite for tray after tray of fizzy lager, ensconced volcanically in the cafes and bars of your sleepy market town – has sent a chill through the hearts of successive rural European communities. So good news for Europe, then. We're not coming.[13]

The author, football fanzine writer Barney Ronay, had not taken the time to check the FIFA and UEFA official reports on World Cups 2002 and 2006, and Euro 2004, when England fans were singled out for their friendship, passion, and commitment. Nor was he content with this particular indulgence in the snobbish stereotypes that England fans are so well used to. He also decided he'd have a go at supporter-led efforts to transform the ways of England fans:

> Carrying on a grand British colonial tradition, the English football fan travels abroad not just to fight you, but also to proselytise at you. A new

breed of friendly, culturally aware England fan has mobilised in recent times. So even more good news for Europe. They won't even have to engage in a ceremonial exchange of goodwill pennants with us.

For Barney, as for so many critics determined to have nothing good to write about Englishness, hopeful developments in English fan culture are of no real interest. Yet since Euro 2000, when England came close to being expelled from the Championship for crowd trouble, thousands of ordinary fans have taken responsibility for our reputation, deciding that all this couldn't be allowed to be drag on any further. The impulse was patriotism – the shame we were forced to feel by those wearing the same shirt, flying the same flag. The context was internationalism – since away games involve travelling overseas; our reputation was at stake as much abroad as at home. We have made a conscious effort to think about how Englishness is connected to supporting the national team – and, yes, that does sometimes include the swapping of 'goodwill pennants'.

At the start of the Euro 2008 Qualifying Campaign in Macedonia, our overweight and unfit fans team was advertised as an 'England XI', taking on the ex-pros of the current Macedonian Cup-Winners in front of a crowd of 500 Skopje locals. They couldn't believe we'd make the effort, or how awful our team was! This was neither middle-class, nor do-goodery. It was do-it-yourself Englishness, engaging and open and authentic – not a celebrity-driven photo opportunity – reflecting the core as well as the diversity of our support. If you really think this is 'colonial' Barney, I'm not sure you've read any decent books on the British Empire. Our Englishness is shaped by these exchanges every bit as much as what we give in return – not what colonial means according to most definitions. Thousands were involved in the course of the qualifying campaign, and our last away trip to Vienna in November 2007 featured a snowbound fans match and party with our Austrian hosts. Two days after England lost to Croatia and failed to qualify for Euro 2008 – the day Barney's article recorded that huge sigh of relief on behalf of tournament hosts Austria and Switzerland – I received an email from *Ballesterer*, a Viennese fanzine (the sort of outfit Barney started his career with). 'Our St George is flying half-mast outside the office today', reported editor Reinhard Krennhuber – their way of showing that many Austrians were disappointed that England, team and fans, would not be going to the Championships.

THE UNITED KINGDOM AND THE BARD OF BRITISHNESS
In June 2007 one of the Labour government's favoured think tanks, The Opinion Leader Forum, published a report, *It's the Taking Part*

that Counts: The Role of Sport in Strengthening British Values. The purpose of the research was fairly explicit, to present the 2012 Olympics as an opportunity to reinforce these values in the specific context of Britishness. There is of course an awkward contradiction here. The most popular team sports are played mainly by different formulations of the 'home' nations. And individual athletes, too, are increasingly thought of in terms of where they come from: Andy Murray is surely Scottish first, British second; while Tim Henman was always the Tiger Tim of middle England. Some might transcend this – Lewis Hamilton and Ricky Hatton perhaps – but not enough to outweigh the sense that sport symbolises our broken-up Britain. Labour's think-tankers were having none of this:

> Sport is one of the most powerful tools available to policy makers seeking to entrench the best of British identity. In its elite and mass forms it reaches into the lives of many millions of people. In the run-up to the 2012 Games, with their focus on children, children are going to be increasingly involved with sporting activity that is explicitly British rather than English, Scottish or Welsh.[14]

The political agenda is pretty obvious, the emphasis on re-education of Scots and Welsh children wayward in their national affiliations vaguely Maoist in inclination. There is no recognition of the cultural and political inclinations that have coincided over the past ten years to foster an increasing identification with England, Scotland, Wales or Northern Ireland, rather than GB. The Olympics is the number one global sporting event, and the Olympics Team GB have been markedly more successful over the years than any of our home nations' football teams. But the bunting, flags and open-top buses for the medal-winners just don't have the same passion and broader significance of those other sporting contests, football in particular – which better represent where GB is heading. Near neighbours yes, one nation no. Olympic 2012 might be on the wish-list of Gordon Brown to put it all together again, but the signs are that sport is simply reflecting (and sometimes leading) tendencies that are heading in the opposite direction.

Like most male (and some female) politicians, Gordon Brown trades on his football fandom as having some worth in terms of political capital. And as a lifelong Raith Rovers fan, active in promoting the club's Supporters Trust, Brown has more claim on some real affection for the game than the tennis-loving Blair. But in the past few years Brown's commitment to the Union has stretched to breaking point his credentials as someone who understands the cultural impact of football. He fooled precious few England fans, and impressed even fewer Scots, with his carefully managed watching and cheering of England in the 2006 World Cup. In November 2007 Gordon fondly remembered the Home Internationals of his youth.[15] But he obviously wasn't at Hampden Park in November 1999 for the Euro 2000 play-off between Scotland and England, or at Wembley for the return leg a few days later. Sometimes ugly, and frankly impossible to ignore. England vs Scotland couldn't do more to convince anyone that we're separate nations.

Tom Nairn, who originated the 'Break-up of Britain' thesis in 1977, following an earlier SNP break-through, returned to the argument in 2006 to dub Gordon Brown 'the bard of Britishness'.[16] Nairn described the Prime Minister's political trajectory from editor of *The Red Paper on Scotland* to tireless campaigner on the need to save Britain:

> Brown, 'the Party man' who took flight as a left-wing prophet, was to end up as today's strident UK nationalist. The Scottish Icarus felt his wings melting away even as he assumed office, and understood how the ungrateful way of this world might grant him almost no terra firma to return to. None that is without the restored or reconstructed 'greatness' of Britain. Hence service of the imperial state-inheritance, and improvement of its estate with minor changes was the sole way forward. Or so dour realism seemed to indicate. A specific combination of Party vanity and self-confidence made him feel he could take the monster over. Unfortunately, it worked the other way round. The antique inheritance took possession of him. The result was a chain of compromises that have transformed him into the fulsome bard of Britishness.[17]

It would be quite wrong, of course, to personalise these issues, or to suggest that Brown has executed this turn simply to appeal English voters who might desert him as man of the Manse. After all, New Labour, almost from its outset, has form on this subject.

In 1997, a matter of months before Scotland and Wales each voted in referendums for devolution, Demos, another think tank favoured by the patronage of Labour ministers, came up with the bright idea to 're-brand Britain', without a single mention in the 72-page report that we were in the process of devolving, if not yet separating, into four constituent parts. The breathless enthusiasm for all things bright, British and Blairite in the face of this awkwardness leaps off the page: 'Its position has stabilised as a major industrial power and political power. It is bursting with the energy and excitement that young countries enjoy. Britain is now ready for its spring, a period of renewal and increased self-confidence.'[18] Five years later, after the establishment of a Scottish Parliament and Welsh Assembly, and moves towards devolved government in Northern Ireland – not to mention all those irksome St George Cross flags in 1998, 2000 and 2002 – these changes did not seem to have registered with the author of these remarks, Mark Leonard. In 2002, now elevated to the Directorship of yet another Labour-patronised think tank, the Foreign Policy Centre, Mark was writing: 'We define Britishness according to values rather than unchanging institutions or a single religion, and celebrate Britain's global links, its openness to other cultures, its democracy and its creativity.'[19] All impressively modern-sounding, go-ahead and cosmopolitan, but determinedly ignoring the biggest shake up of Britishness in the three hundred years since the Union.

In June 2007 two of Brown's ministers, Ruth Kelly and Liam Byrne, co-authored a discussion paper for the Labour Party's Fabian Society, *A Common Place*, which, it can be safely assumed, closely reflected the prime minister's own thinking. In a curious combination of examples the ministers asserted the robustness of British identity: 'Whether it is supporting British athletes at the Olympics or worrying about Britain's role in the world – including where and how to deploy young men and women in combat – Britishness continues to retain considerable power.' And then they came up with such jolly japes as a British day – not a holiday, mind you, more the sort of opportunity we've all been waiting for to tidy up our neighbourhoods: 'A focus for residents to get out and do something together could act as a powerful motivator for action in many communities up and down the country.' Wow, if that's his ministers' idea of a national celebration, is it any wonder that Gordon is thought of as a tad dour? Never mind, though, there is at least in this document, at last, the recognition that there does exist a contradiction amongst all this road-sweeping in our Union Jack jackets. 'The shift is not dramatic, but the trend is clear – more of the English now than a decade ago feel more English than British.'[20] So what do Byrne and Kelly conjure up for us? – 'Regional Select Committees, and a revival of Local Government'. Hardly enough to take the wind out of all those flags is it? Nationhood might be a bit on the old-fashioned side for politicians who like to style themselves modernisers, but can't they at least notice that tarting up the Town Hall isn't going to begin to satisfy this popular impulse.

The 'bard of Britishness' had launched his campaign to be prime minister at the start of 2007 with a keynote article in the *Daily Telegraph*:

I am not alone in believing that a stronger sense of patriotic purpose would help resolve some of our most important national challenges, make us more confident about Britain's role in Europe and the world, and would help us better integrate our ethnic communities, respond to migration and show people the responsibilities as well as rights that must be at the heart of modern citizenship.[21]

But there is no compelling narrative here for the Union. These are all perfectly sensible social-democratic objectives – but they are currently being pursued rather better by the new governments in Edinburgh, Cardiff and Belfast than they are by Brown's lot in Westminster. This is an argument for a progressive patriotism – which could just as credibly be wrapped in a St George, Saltire, Dragon or Shamrock. The Union Jack cannot be justified on these grounds alone

PLAYING THE ENGLISH IDENTITY CARD

As the May 2007 Scottish Parliament elections approached, Gordon Brown and Labour's Scottish Secretary Douglas Alexander co-authored a Fabian Society pamphlet, *Stronger Together: The 21st Century Case for Scotland and Britain*, reasserting the Union as 'a message to the world' that 'nations of different traditions and identities can live harmoniously and prosper with a common purpose'. It is not particularly clear to me that the Union is the best way of sending this message, but there is a further problem here: English identity does not get a mention. The theme was set by the cover, two kids with their faces painted, one with the Scots Saltire and the other with the Union Jack. St George didn't get a look in. In foregrounding their case for the United Kingdom, Labour Unionists effectively have to deny England any existence. In their pamphlet Brown and Alexander argue that 'Working with our nearest neighbours is one of the keys to our success', but they have nothing to say about England, Scotland's nearest if not dearest neighbour.[22]

The imagining of what England might become is in train precisely because our 'near neighbours' are engaging in the process of separating themselves. And this has moved way beyond simply backing another football team. Indeed, if this continues as the main source of identity for the English, we will remain trapped within a state that Pat Kane has described (in discussing his fellow Scots) as 'cartoon national resentment, rather than confident and coherent national aspiration'. Pat puts a case for neighbourliness that the English would do well to listen to: 'An England finally liberated from its post-imperial, big-power angst, and able to display its creativity and diversity in a European and world context, would be a wonderful and challenging neighbour – surely the noblest outcome of the Break-Up of Britain.'[23] In other words, in defining a nationalist politics for three states on one island, mostly speaking the same language and with significant chunks of our culture and history in common, we can learn from each other at the same time as we entrench our separation. The two are not in contradiction. The contradictions that exist are entirely the product of unionism. When he was the Tory Shadow Minister for Higher Education Boris Johnson used to rant about Scottish students not paying university tuition fees. In an article headlined 'Are We All Equally British?', he challenged Gordon Brown: 'How does he think it contributes to "Britishness" eh? What's that doing for the spirit of national cohesion, the precious sense of UK identity that forms the centrepiece of his spine-cracking speeches?'[24] The point is so obvious that it cannot have occurred to Boris. It is true that Scottish policies since devolution have generally been more equitable than Blair, Brown or Johnson might have favoured. But none threaten the English in any sense. The point is simply that Scotland has had the opportunity to make this choice, while England has not.

In 2006 a Democratic Audit report on the strength of the British National Party (BNP) in England showed latent support for a Far Right BNP/UKIP voting bloc to be as high as 23 per cent of the electorate. The report argued that this level of support indicated that the BNP could no longer be seen as marginal (though it could not be regarded as a mainstream party, as it was not able to contest more than about one in six seats at a general election).[25] After the 2007 local elections *Searchlight* magazine came up with a lower figure, but it was still frighteningly high. Over 742 wards contested the BNP averaged 14.6 per cent of the vote.[26] These levels of support lead to entirely warranted concerns about this brutish and hateful party that trades on one particular version of nationalism. However, in opposing the BNP some get too easily wrapped up in a wholesale disavowal of any merit in popular identification with England.

Joseph Harker, writing in the *Guardian*, expressed this position more sharply than most as he recorded his response to the St George Cross flags, following the local elections and as World Cup 2006 approached:

> I've been looking at the drivers of these flag-waving vehicles, and – OK, I admit this isn't exactly scientific – half of them are in white vans, and the rest are white, male, tattooed, pot-bellied 35 to 55-years-olds: exactly the type I've been seeing on TV for the past month complaining about

'our houses going to the asylum seekers'. I can't tell if these drivers come from Barking and Dagenham, where the BNP gained 11 seats, but that borough is just a short drive from where I live, so who knows?

Joseph is identifying a problem here, but in overstating it he effectively hands over a huge chunk of electoral ground to the BNP. Of course, if you invest a part of your identity with where you come from, there will always be the inclination to exclude those who don't, and so he is absolutely right to worry that 'the BNP leaders are secretly smirking every time they see the flag'.[27] Every single time the BNP appear on the TV or in the papers, there's always a St George Cross being waved or worn. Their identification is absolutely clear. But it is a contested identification – or at least it should be. The BNP want St George to represent exclusion, an unwelcome mat for all those it decides don't belong here. If we deny ourselves the potential to offer an alternative representation of patriotism to the BNP's, their support will remain unchallenged around this key issue, a large electoral bloc that could potentially determine the outcome of England after Britain.

Nobody wants to conscript Joseph and his fellow-doubters into a flag parade, but it is reckless to presume that all those who have joined this happy band of St George Cross wavers are signed-up members of the BNP. This is the politics of do-nothing and despair, the opposite of the broad, popular and engaging challenge the BNP should face. This article attracted a huge amount of postings on the *Guardian* website, some revealing the racist presumptions it was warning against, but most just indignant, amazed that their support for England could be interpreted as support for the BNP. The next day the letters page carried a response from Unmesh Desai, founder of the militant anti-racist Newham Monitoring Group, and a left-wing Labour councillor: 'I am not worried at all about the number of St George's flags flying from cars right now. These flags appeared well before the May 4 local elections and bear no correlation to that BNP success. People of all colours have been flying the flag, which the politically correct left, by default, had allowed to be hijacked by the far right.'[28] Unmesh was right; giving up our capacity to shape the symbols and experience of national identity is to leave ground empty for the far right to dominate.

DON'T MENTION THE SCORE

As World Cup 2006 in Germany approached, the hopeless confusion of situation-comedy history and the serious matter and memory of the Nazis could scarcely be avoided. To deny this history would mean we had little to say about our national identity. Not mentioning the war can be just as problematic as turning it into another football chant. Our aim was therefore to make an intervention that remembered the war in a different way, and recognised the Germans too as anti-Nazi. When German fan groups came to London to meet our England fan groups we therefore cautiously made a proposal. In the period between England's final group game and a probable second round game in either Stuttgart or Munich, huge numbers of England fans would be based in southern Germany, not far from Dachau, the first of the Nazi Concentration Camps. Instead of pretending that none of this had happened, out of some misplaced effort at polite conversation, we dived straight in. What would the German fans think about laying wreaths with us at Dachau, the day before both our teams should, all things being equal, be playing a crucial World Cup game? The point was that we should do this together. The response couldn't have been more positive. At Dachau the coachloads of England fans were joined by German fans from Hamburg, Frankfurt, Berlin, Dortmund, both Munich clubs, and a group from Poland. The Jewish community sports group, MaccabiGB, had heard of what we were planning and also enthusiastically supported our efforts. Our wreath was a huge St George Cross made up of hundreds of red and white carnations. Some find it curious that a national flag should be chosen as a way to mark the memory of the holocaust. Isn't Dachau a memorial to what happens when a nation turns first on its own citizens, and then on citizens of other states, in the cause of racial purity, of nationalism? My response as I laid that wreath was to quote the words carved into the statute on the edge of Trafalgar Square to Edith Cavell, the nurse executed by the Germans in World War 1. I must have cycled past that statue hundreds of times but every single time those words have had a meaning for me: 'Patriotism is not enough. I must have no bitterness or hatred for others.'

In Stuttgart the cheap-shot patriotism of 'Ten German Bombers, and the RAF from England shot them down' was on parade, complete with 'Fly Spitfires' polo shirts in the style of the 'Fly Emirates' logos. The lives of others, lost in the defeat of fascism, had become just another joke. Why let history get in the way of a bad song? The following June, England played Estonia in Tallinn, where World War Two remains a contested memory: statues which for some are tributes to a hated occupier are to others symbols of sacrifice and unforgettable bravery. Tallinn's Museum of Occupation and Fight for Freedom, opened in 2003, doesn't offer reconciliation as a solution to this difference of opinion, but it does suggest an explanation. A panel in the foyer caught my eye:

The loss of memory and gaps in memory are dangerous for a people. Put a different way, the preservation of historical memories helps to strengthen the identity of both the people and the state. Regardless of what the past has brought (happiness or mourning, honour or shame) it merits being remembered. The past can't be removed from memory.[29]

We cannot, should not, forget the holocaust and Germany's part in it. But this is a past which we share: we can bear witness, respect the memory, together.

It is of course a curious form of patriotism that mistakes 4-2 at Wembley for the sacrifice and valour of two world wars. If we can situate a popular English patriotism in a space that helps us all understand and respect the difference between these two ways of identifying with one's country, while having the capacity not to be trapped by history, we might have the beginnings of a new England.

MULTICULTURAL ENGLISHNESS

To a much greater extent than arguments over Scottish, Welsh or Northern Irish identity, debates about Englishness are dominated by the question of race. Immigration, for the right, is their frontline in any defence of Britishness. A.N. Wilson in the *Daily Mail* marked the Queen's birthday with these regrets: 'It would be a bold person who stood up and said that the reign of Elizabeth had been Britain's most glorious period. For it is my sad belief that her reign is the one in which Britain effectively stopped being British. The chief reason for this is mass immigration on a scale that has utterly transformed our nation.'[30] As the break-up develops there will undoubtedly be powerful tendencies towards defining Englishness against immigration and Europe. Yet to presume that there is an unstoppable shift towards exclusion instead of inclusion suggests a profound lack of confidence on the part of an emergent English progressive patriotism. The combination of Englishness and migration is virtually indivisible; driving a wedge between the two would therefore be immensely difficult for the right if the left could only engage with both parts of the mix.

Recent large-scale migration has largely been from within the EU, and some Eastern Europeans have begun to suffer from prejudices similar to those endured by their predecessors from the old British Empire. This is linked to the wider little England rejection of English identity as European. Those who demonise the recent arrivals from Poland and elsewhere usually connect this to a more old-fashioned form of racism. They long for the days when England could be imagined not only as nothing to do with Eurrope, but as all-white too.

However it is now almost impossible to imagine England without black and Asian people as an integral part. From pop to politics, cuisine to music, fashion to business, the black experience is now intimately interwoven into the fabric of English daily life, in a way that is not so obviously the case in Scotland or Wales. Attempt to remove black people from England's racial landscape and you remove one third of the capital, between a fifth and a third of the football team, most high street restaurants and a huge number of successful businesses.[31]

The overwhelming proportion of all people of black or ethnic minority origin in Britain live in England – 45 per cent in London, with the next highest concentration the West Midlands, where it is 13 per cent. A little over nine per cent of England's population is of black or ethnic minority origin, compared to 2.2 per cent in Wales, 2.1 per cent in Scotland and just 0.75 per cent in Northern Ireland.[32] This is a significant differential, and one whose representation should be another subject of contestation. When we track the emergent popularity of the St George Cross flag as a potential symbol of our multicultural Englishness, this is the contest we are observing. A team, flag and nation for all, or only for some? There are those who parade their Englishness as a barrier to a new nation. And those who celebrate inclusion as a core value of the England that we seek to build – not in denial of our imperial and martial past but in recognition of, and opposition to, its worst excesses. In this sense the flags we fly, the shirts we pull on and the teams we cheer for are part of our interpretation, as individuals and communities, of the connections that bind and separate us. These are complex and contradictory, rarely uniform. As a shift away from insularity gathers pace, an opposition that resists such a process also emerges. But it is remarkable that this period of an unfolding emergence of Englishness as an identity has been accompanied by ever-increasing numbers of black and Asian football fans identifying with England. Does that mean an end to racist discrimination, abuse and assaults? No – and who in their right mind would make such a claim? But it does indicate that in our imagined England inclusion and identity are not the polar opposites that some presume. A place we can call multicultural England is emerging, with a pride in what makes us different – without that there's no basis of nationhood – but proud, too, of our differences.

TAKING DOWN OUR PARTICULARS

Stuart Hall has pinpointed the competing pressures that globalisation exerts on nationhood, arguing that there is a tension between capitalism's transnational imperatives and its tendency to develop the nation-state and national cultures. He sees this as 'a contradiction at the heart of modernity', one that has given nationalism and its particularisms 'a peculiar significance and force at the centre of the so-called new transnational global order'.[33]

This 'peculiar significance' is constantly ignored or underestimated by politicians and commentators who treat the global imperative in shaping politics and economics in isolation from the rising appeal of the local. Opposition to the effects of market-led globalisation is frequently underpinned by values that combine locality and environmentalism: not necessarily exclusively 'English' values, but ones that may have particular English expressions. A sense of place and identity can anchor the connections between local and the global. We can be friends of the earth our home is built on, the park where our kids play, the fields where we'd like our food to be grown, and the hills where we walk the dog. But Friends of the Earth too, living as we do in a planet under threat of environmental destruction and the impending devastation of climate change. A nationhood grounded in particularity suggests neither a hierarchy of difference nor the classification of those that do or do not belong. Instead we value what made England and recognise that this is an unfinished process, a work-in-progress. Sue Clifford and Angela King have pioneered a new way of thinking through and acting out this commitment to English particularism: 'the forces of homogenisation rob us of both tangible and invisible things that have meaning to us; they erase the fragments from which we piece together stories of nature and history; they stunt our sensibilities and starve our imaginations.'[34] As we piece together this imagined nation called England out of the wreckage of broken-up Britain, there could be a temptation to retreat into an unchanging past, a theme park for an old country. Of course the processes of history have shaped our particularities of custom and culture, landscape and diet, sense of place and faces we recognise as our own. But history isn't just about the past. It has a present and future too. A new England will take shape out of a modern separation as well as ancient origins. In our contestation with those who see this process as justifying brutish exclusion and the codification of authenticity, we would do well to incorporate Blake's vision of a green and pleasant England. Blake's Jerusalem was both unmistakably English and universal in the ambition of its values – and it's not a bad tune for an anthem either.

MY IMAGINED NATION
Does England exist solely in our imagination? Only if we believe that politics is founded solely on reality. Extinguish ideals and vision from political discourse – as the ten years of Blair-Brown have threatened to

do – and imagining a new country becomes something with little or no purchase on the mainstream politics. This, in large measure, is why the the main political parties are so incapable of engaging with this debate.

Wembley, 13 October 2007. A group of England fans are meeting up hours before the kick-off for the game against Estonia. We are going to lay out tens of thousands of red and white plastic bags – we call this 'Raise the Flag'. And when *God Save the Queen* begins, supporters will hold up the bags we've laid out on their seats to form a huge St George Cross. An imaginary fiction of our nation. Today three of our regular helpers, Yasir, Nahid and Hajra, have had to drop out. The early morning start was too much for the three of them after all the celebrating the night before of Eid, the Muslim festival that marks the end of Ramadan. Not an excuse I once thought I'd hear from England fans crying off from helping to Raise the Flag. But this is the England I dream of. Nahid and Hajra in their Hijabs beside me in my bobble hat. The flags get put away after the match, but the fantasy land we like to call England is taking shape, and changing too. Granted, not all would share in my dream of an England for all. But there is a space in which we can establish some kind of common purpose as Scotland, Wales and Northern Ireland take their leave. A purpose that combines all our yesterdays with some of our tomorrows, drenched in symbolism, entirely dependent on popular identification. Raphael Samuel described this mixture: 'Nation is a symbolic complex, with a multiplicity of discrepant meanings at any given time and ruptures over time that are far more significant than the continuities.'[35] It is the stuff of politics to construct those meanings, unpack those ruptures, maintain in good repair the continuities we favour, junk the ones we don't. Stephen Duncombe has called this kind of process the re-imagining of politics: 'a politics that embraces the dreams of people and fashions spectacles which give these fantasies form – a politics that understands desire and speaks to the irrational; a politics that employs symbols and associations; a politics that tells good stories.'[36] Our imagined community has its eleven named people, and millions more too. The process of imagining all of this as a nation has begun. It is an irreversible process, but with uncertain outcomes. Welcome to England.

NOTES

1. Eric Hobsbawm, *Nations and Nationalism Since 1780*, Cambridge University Press 1997, p143.

2. Benedict Anderson, *Imagined Communities*, Verso 1991, pp6-7.

3. Tim Cumming, 'Village People', in *Songlines Magazine*, December 2007, p27.

4. Mark Lawson, 'Three Lions, Who's King?', *Guardian*, 9.6.06.
5. Jason Cowley, 'The Cup that Rules the World', *Observer*, 11.6.06.
6. Brian Appleyard, 'It's not about Football. It's Bigger than That', *The Times*, 2.7.06.
7. Stephen Glover, 'I grow more fearful that devolution will lead to the break-up of Britain', *Daily Mail* 15.6.06.
8. Martin Smith, 'Can Identity Politics help us Fight the BNP', speech at Marxism 2007 conference, 6.7.07.
9. Mike Marqusee, *Anyone But England*, Aurum Press 2005.
10. Mike Marqusee, 'Anyone but Ingerland?', *Red Pepper*, June 2006, p22.
11. Max Hastings, 'England Stirs', *Daily Mail*, 10.6.06.
12. Stewart Steven, 'Victory! But look what we're losing', *Mail on Sunday*, 16.6.02.
13. Barney Ronay, 'Goodbye to All That', *Guardian*, 23.1.07.
14. Opinion Leader Forum Report, *It's the Taking Part that Counts*, Opinion Leader Forum 2007, p23.
15. Quoted in Andrew Porter, 'Brown backs Home Nations 2008 Tournament', *Daily Telegraph*, 23.11.07.
16. Tom Nairn, *The Break-Up of Britain*, Verso 1981.
17. Tom Nairn, *Bard of Britishness*, Institute of Welsh Affairs 2006, p10.
18. Mark Leonard, *Britain: Renewing our Identity*, Demos 1997, p72.
19. Mark Leonard, 'Living together after 11 September and the rise of the Right', in Phoebe Griffiths and Mark Leonard (Eds), *Reclaiming Britishness*, Foreign Policy Centre 2002, p xi.
20. All quotes from Ruth Kelly and Liam Byrne, *A Common Place*, Fabian Society, June 2007. Available free from http://fabians.org.uk/publications/freethinking/kelly-byrne-commonplace-07/.
21. Gordon Brown, 'We Need a United Kingdom', *Daily Telegraph*, 13.1.07.
22. All quotes from Gordon Brown and Douglas Alexander, *Stronger Together*, Fabian Society 2007, p27.
23. Pat Kane, 'Ninety-minute Patriotism', *Comment is Free*, 19.6.06, see www.guardian.co.uk.
24. Boris Johnson, 'Are We All Equally British? Not if Brown has his way', *Guardian*, 12.6.07.
25. Peter John, Helen Margetts, David Rowland and Stuart Weir, *The BNP: Roots of Its Appeal*, Democratic Audit 2006, p28.
26. Dave Williams, '2007 BNP overview', *Searchlight*, January 2008, p16.
27. Joseph Harker, 'Flutters of Anxiety', *Guardian*, 18.5.06.
28. Unmesh Desai, Letters page in the *Guardian*, 19.5.06.
29. Museum of Occupation and Fight for Freedom, Tallinn, Estonia, see www. okupatsioon.ee.
30. A.N. Wilson, 'A Stranger in her Own Country', *Daily Mail* 3.11.07.

31. Gary Younge, 'On Race and Englishness', in Selina Chen and Tony Wright (Eds), *The English Question*, Fabian Society 2000, p113.

32. All figures 2001 census, see www.statistics.gov.uk/census2001.

33. Stuart Hall, 'Our Mongrel Selves', *New Statesman*, 19.6.92.

34. Sue Clifford and Angela King, *England in Particular*, Hodder & Stoughton 2006, p xiii.

35. Raphael Samuel, 'Cry God for Maggie, England and St George', *New Statesman*, 27.5.83.

36. Stephen Duncombe, *Dream*, New Press 2007, p9.

A union of historic compromise

Andrew Gamble

The result of the May 2007 elections for the Scottish Parliament gave the Scottish National Party one seat more than the Labour Party, far short of an overall majority, but it allowed the SNP to declare a historic victory, and after a short delay Alex Salmond was duly installed as First Minister. The Welsh Assembly elections, also in May 2007, left Labour as the largest single party in Wales, but without enough seats to govern alone it was forced to enter a coalition for the first time with Plaid Cymru. In 2007 devolved government was also restored in Northern Ireland following agreement between the Democratic Unionists and Sinn Fein to share power.

These events mark a new phase in Labour's 1998 devolution settlement, ushered in by the Scotland Act, the Government of Wales Act and by the Good Friday Agreement. The constitutional landscape of the UK was changed, almost certainly irreversibly, by these early actions of the Blair government, since it is hard to imagine the political circumstances under which any future government at Westminster could seek to recover the powers which have been devolved. But the full implications of these changes have been muted up to now because Wales and Scotland have both had Labour dominated administrations since the first elections in 1999. Both had been willing to co-operate informally with the Labour government at Westminster, while devolution in Northern Ireland had been stalled by deadlock between Sinn Fein and the Democratic Unionists over the issue of the decommissioning of IRA weapons. The big questions have been put on hold. Whether the devolution settlement establishes a new long-term and stable form of territorial government for the United Kingdom, or whether it is a transitional phase towards more radical change, such as an explicit federal constitution, an English Parliament, or even the break-up of the United Kingdom altogether, with Northern Ireland being absorbed into a united Ireland. Will Scotland and eventually Wales become independent of England, and Britain cease to exist?

The constitutional reforms which the Blair government enacted after 1997 general election were presented in a piecemeal, often haphazard fashion, and their wider implications were played down, but cumulatively they have begun to transform British politics. Critics point out that they have created many new anomalies and problems, but the process of change unleashed by the constitutional reforms is still in its early stages, and the existence of these anomalies is already producing pressure for further changes. It may be some time before a lasting settlement is achieved, but the British political system already feels very different compared to when Margaret Thatcher left office in 1990.

The most radical of the reforms, and the most far-reaching in its implications, may turn out to be the devolution of powers to Wales, Scotland and Northern Ireland. The three devolutions are not the same, but what they have in common is the recognition that the old form of the Union had become untenable, and required renegotiation. This was most obviously true in Northern Ireland, where the eruption of conflict again in the late 1960s quickly led to the suspension of Stormont, the imposition of direct rule from London, and a long bitter sectarian conflict. The eventual agreement between Sinn Fein, the Democratic Unionists and the British and Irish governments did not end the British connection, but did acknowledge the legitimate interest of the Irish Republic in the affairs of the North, and the need for a power-sharing devolved government to reflect the complex pattern of loyalties and identities within the two communities.

The change was least marked in Wales. The Welsh Nationalist party, Plaid Cymru, has always been relatively small and its vote regionally concentrated. Large numbers of English have settled in Wales, and the country has never had the same kind of independent institutions, such as its own distinctive legal and educational system, to express its sense of nationhood which Scotland enjoyed. The 1997 referendum approved the setting up of the Welsh Assembly only narrowly (50.3 per cent to 49.7 per cent on a 50 per cent turnout). The operation of the Assembly and the Executive has received much criticism in Wales over its cost and its ineffectiveness, particularly from those groups who had opposed the setting up of an Assembly in the first place, but there has been no move to abolish it. Instead there has been more pressure, led by Rhodri Morgan, the First Minister, for more powers to be devolved to the Assembly. This was partially realised in 2007 with the grant of extended powers to the Assembly to initiate legislation in areas approved by Westminster, and the prospect of ultimately gaining the same legislative powers as the Scottish Parliament, after a further referendum.

Scotland has seen more dramatic change. The majority in the 1997 referendum which approved the setting up of the Scottish Parliament was substantial (74.3 per cent in favour, 25.7 per cent against on a 60 per cent turnout) and much more decisive than the Welsh result, and the powers that were devolved were more far-reaching than those given to the Welsh Assembly. Devolution represented the settled will of the Scottish people in a much clearer way than in Northern Ireland or Wales. For the first two sessions of the Scottish Parliament Labour retained its dominant position, although because of the PR system it could not command a majority on its own, and formed a coalition with the Liberal Democrats. The Lab-Lib coalition began exploring its powers and gradually distinctive Scottish policies began to emerge. But because Labour was in office in both Holyrood and Westminster the relationship between the two was generally harmonious. With the May 2007 success of the SNP in becoming the largest single party in the Scottish Parliament, a much more significant phase in the devolution settlement has opened. For the first time there is a different party in office in Edinburgh than in Westminster, and in Alex Salmond, the SNP have a leader with the tactical skill to exploit the position to the full. The SNP is a long way short of an overall majority in the Parliament, and could not persuade other parties to join it in a coalition, but it has taken over the government.

All these events confirm the gradual unravelling of the old Union state. The United Kingdom was from the outset a multi-national state, organised along unitary rather than federal lines. The different nationalities continued to exist, but there was a single sovereign Parliament. In practice this unitary state was not very centralised. There was a great deal of administrative devolution, particularly to Scotland. But this was administrative devolution to a Scottish Office, presided over by a UK cabinet minister. Different parts of the UK were given special status and treated differently, but none of this was a matter of constitutional right, rather it reflected a mixture of political expediency and established custom and practice.

It is this customary unwritten constitution, resting on a set of political conventions and political understandings which has now been ruptured beyond repair. The relationships between the UK government in Westminster and the devolved administrations has been put on a statutory basis, and more legislation will inevitably follow, defining the limits of each jurisdiction and setting up mechanisms for resolving disputes. There is no longer a single government of the UK, and this means that the devolved administrations will be keen to maximise their powers, and push for their extension into new areas, especially when one of the nationalist parties holds office. The politics of devolution has already created a new dynamic in British politics, one which is unsettling for the established Unionist parties. Devolution cannot be reversed, and has become part of the context in which all parties have to work.

THE WEAKENING OF UNIONISM

The fracturing of the old British unitary state has been accompanied by a marked weakening of Unionism. The British state has been fractured before, most notably when the Irish Free State was established in 1922 with jurisdiction over the whole of Ireland apart from Northern Ireland, at the end of the Irish War of Independence. But traumatic though that event was it actually strengthened the forces of Unionism in British politics, particularly in Scotland and Northern Ireland. The situation today is different. The Union is not threatened by immediate secession, but by a slow withering of support for the Union from within. Significant and apparently increasing minorities no longer want to be part of the UK, or are indifferent to it, and the English are becoming more restive too. At one time most Britons thought of themselves as both British and English, British and Scottish, British and Welsh. Now increasing numbers reject the British label or give it a lower priority. Gordon Brown has argued repeatedly that: 'A Britain founded on both the devolution of power but also on a partnership which brings us stability, co-operation and mutual support is the best way of expressing the aspirations of the Scottish and British people'.[1] But although these sentiments still resonate with a significant section of both Scottish and English opinion, Britishness is no longer the unifying force it once was. Gordon Brown's constant need to include references to Britishness in his speeches is in reality a sign of its waning power.

The reason for this is not hard to find. The British state was always a political construction based on the supremacy of England but offering the other nations partnership or incorporation into this larger political entity – the United Kingdom. What held it together were a number of interests, values and institutions, including the Monarchy, the Protestant religion, the British Empire, the British armed forces, and later the British welfare state. Britain was always a political project which offered significant advantages and opportunities to those who chose to be part of it. In particular many Scots from the earliest days of the Union seized the chance. The end of Empire meant the disappearance of the project which for so long had defined Britishness and British institutions. The new union with which the British began to get involved with, the European Union, was very different from empire. Britain was not dominant within it, and many of the member states had populations as small as or even smaller than Scotland and Wales. Ireland became a full member at the same time as the UK, and enjoying equal status in the EU became an important factor in improving relations between the two states, and relaxing the tensions of the past. The Empire was a *British* project in a way in which the EU was not. Indeed many saw the EU as the denial of Britishness, and the beginning of the end of an independent British state.

The other grand project which attempted to fill the void of Empire was the special relationship with the United States. Many in the British political class believed that only a close association with the United States could deliver both security in the post-war world and the continuance of the kind of liberal and open global economic order which had for so long been the goal of British policy. Britain could no longer be a dominant power, but it could be a close partner and ally of the dominant power, and in this way have some insider influence. This policy has been followed by all British prime ministers since 1940 with greater or lesser enthusiasm. Edward Heath was the least enthusiastic, and fell out with Washington by refusing an American Request during the Yom Kippur War to use its British airbases to resupply the Israelis, and also indicating that Britain would in future react to American proposals on transatlantic relationships after, not before, consulting with its European partners. But this new policy did not outlast Heath, and the traditional close relationship with the United States was resumed by his successors, if anything becoming even more pronounced. In Thatcher and Blair Britain has had two long-serving leaders who have made the relationship with the United States the cornerstone of their foreign policy. Margaret Thatcher in proposing a toast to Ronald Reagan in 1985 stated: 'The joint common sense, which is an essential part of our common heritage, has led (our) two Governments to resolve their differences and to work constructively together for our common purpose. Our joint interests prevailed, and I know they will continue to prevail. There's a union of mind and purpose between our peoples, which is remarkable and which makes our relationship truly a special one'.[2] Tony Blair in his famous speech to the America Congress in July 2003, shortly after the invasion of Iraq, concluded with this ringing declaration: 'Destiny put you in this place in history, in this moment in time and the task is yours to do. And our job, my nation that watched you grow, that you've fought alongside and now fights alongside you, that takes enormous pride in our alliance and great affection in our common bond, our job is to be there

with you. You're not going to be alone. We'll be with you in this fight
for liberty. And if our spirit is right, and our courage firm, the world
will be with us.'[3]

However in recent years British public opinion has become much
more critical of the United States and its role in the world, and resents
the perception that British governments are prepared to be subservient
to US interests. The Iraq war and its aftermath has placed a great strain
on popular support for continuing a close relationship with the United
States in security and defence matters, and military interventions. This
division in public opinion about the United States makes it hard for the
special relationship to become a new British project to replace the
Empire. Hostility to it is particularly marked in Scotland and in Wales,
especially over such issues as the Trident naval base at Faslane on the
Clyde, and British participation in US led wars. The attachment of the
UK government to the US relationship does not strengthen the Union,
but threatens to weaken it still further.

The decline of the British Empire and the failure of more recent
external projects to fill the void have contributed to the decline of the
brand of Unionism associated with the Conservative party. The old
battle cries of constitution, empire, and property are heard less often.
The intensely British patriotism which Unionism inspired at its height
has dissipated. The Scottish working class Unionist tradition has
become a pale reflection of what it used to be. Fifty years ago the
Conservative and Unionist Party could still win a majority of the
Scottish seats at the 1955 general election. In 1997 they could not win
one. Conservatism Unionism has been destroyed as a political force in
Scotland. It was always much weaker in Wales, while in Northern
Ireland the historic alliance between Ulster Unionism and the
Conservatives ended when direct rule was imposed in 1972. It has
never been rebuilt. The result is that the Conservatives have lost their
ability to be a broad coalition spanning all four nations in the United
Kingdom, with significant support in Scotland. They have become
predominantly an English party, with their electoral strength concentrated in the South East and South West of England. The Union
remains an important symbol for Conservatives, and no Conservative
Leader has yet publicly questioned it. But while the party is unable to
rebuild its strength in all parts of the United Kingdom, the
Conservatives are no longer credible advocates for the Union, and the
minority in its ranks which favours putting England first will grow.
Simon Heffer, a vigorous advocate of the case for English separatism
argues that the English must be allowed their say: 'The English deserve
their referendum, too, on whether they wish to remain in any sort of

Union with the Scots'.[4] Former prominent Scottish Tories like Michael Fry likewise now argue that independence would be best for both Scotland and England.[5]

The other two principal Unionist parties, Labour and the Liberal Democrats, have retained significant support in Wales and Scotland (they never contested elections in Northern Ireland), but here too there are signs of weakness. The Liberal Democrats were consistent advocates of devolution and decentralisation, but Labour was always much more divided over the issue. Many in its ranks, including Neil Kinnock, who feared what it might do to the unity of the United Kingdom. Kinnock in the 1970s said devolution could be the obituary notice for the Labour movement. The early attempt to get devolution in the 1970s, supported by elements in the Conservative party, foundered on the implacable opposition of a sizeable part of the Scottish Labour party. The threshold that parliamentary opponents managed to impose for the referendum to be valid nullified the majority voting in favour. Margaret Thatcher's 1979 general election victory then killed off any immediate prospect of devolution.

What revived the devolution cause in Scotland was the opposition ignited by the Conservative government in Westminster led by Margaret Thatcher pursuing radical policies to reorganise the British economy and the British state. A majority in Scotland had not voted for the Thatcher government, but Scotland now found itself subject to the changes Thatcher was determined to introduce, and in the case of one of the most controversial policies, the community charge (poll tax), the policy was first tried out in Scotland. One of Thatcher's unintended legacies was a greatly strengthened movement to devolve powers to Scotland and Wales. There remained doubters on the Labour side. It was Scottish Labour MP Tam Dalyell, who first posed the 'West Lothian question', the fact that under devolution as MP for West Lothian he would be able to vote on English matters in the Westminster Parliament, but would have no say in the same matters affecting his constituents. Labour opponents of devolution thought that it would be an unstable halfway house and that it would soon extend to full independence. They warned against upsetting the existing constitutional status quo, and above all the power of the UK Parliament to take decisions on behalf of all citizens in the UK. This view was shared by many Conservatives and articulated by John Major and Michael Forsyth among others. They thought devolution would lead straight to independence. Supporters of devolution, however, who were also Unionists believed the opposite. They argued that devolution would kill off Scottish and Welsh nationalism, because it would take away the grievances on which nationalism fed. It would therefore preserve the Union not destroy it. Whatever might be said about these two positions they could not both be right.

Devolution has also posed problems for Labour Unionism because of its impact on the welfare state. If the Empire had been the great project of Conservative Unionism that proved the value of the British state to its citizens, the great Labour project was welfare. The unitary British state was a useful vehicle for rolling out universal welfare programmes to all British citizens, and aiming for common standards and entitlements across the whole of the UK. This was practical citizenship, and made being a British citizen worthwhile. Many in Labour's ranks had always been opposed to the Liberal enthusiasm for decentralisation of services and political power, precisely because it would mean unevenness of service provision and the establishment of a postcode lottery, undermining the uniformity which only a centralised and unitary state could provide. Whatever the disparities in practice, the principle of equal provision was a clear one, and made British citizenship worth having.

The devolution settlement threatened this aspect of Britishness because it devolved responsibility for most welfare state matters to the Scottish Parliament and the Welsh Assembly. It attempted to limit their discretion by keeping tight hold of taxation and therefore absolute levels of expenditure, but there was doubt about how long these restrictions could be held, and the devolution of executive responsibility still allowed significantly different welfare priorities to be established. Citizens will increasingly associate their welfare benefits with the legislature and executive which is responsible for determining the policy. In the case of England this remains the Westminster Parliament, but in the case of Scotland and Wales it is now the Scottish Parliament and the Welsh Assembly.

With the disappearance of the Empire, and the devolution of control over major parts of the welfare state to the new devolved assemblies, two of the key planks that sustained the British state and a wider sense of Britishness had been dismantled. It was hardly surprising that politicians like Gordon Brown who still strongly believed in the Union should start stressing Britishness, the common values that bind all the citizens of the UK together. Feelings of Britishness still remained strong, and there are many important British institutions, including the monarchy, the armed forces, and the BBC. But Parliament itself has noticeably lost some of its authority and pre-eminence after devolution. Many of the reformers welcomed this, but it undoubtedly makes the case for the Union harder to sustain.

THE NATIONALIST CHALLENGE

The formation of a minority SNP administration in Edinburgh is the first serious test of devolution not because it means there will be an early referendum on independence – the pro-Union parties in the Scottish Parliament can block any such attempt – but because for the first time the parties in office in Westminster and Holyrood are no longer the same. This was bound to occur sooner or later under devolution, but it came rather sooner than expected, and at a particularly awkward moment for the Labour party, facing a transition to a new leadership. Labour faces an uphill struggle to hold on to its vote in many marginal seats in the South of England against a reviving Conservative party, but to have any chance of holding on to power at Westminster it also has to keep the support of its heartlands, and in particular Scotland. At the 2005 general election Labour won 41 of the 59 Scottish seats.

If it had been the Liberal Democrats or the Conservatives that had emerged as the largest single party in Holyrood, at a time when Labour controlled the Westminster Parliament, there might well have been tensions, just as there have been frequent tensions in the past between Westminster and some local authorities when different parties have been in control. What is novel about the situation in Scotland after the 2007 elections is that for the first time a party which opposes the present constitutional basis of the UK has taken control of one of the devolved institutions. This opens a new era in UK territorial politics. The SNP will use its position to present the case for independence, hoping it can create a momentum which will prove unstoppable. Its opponents hope to show that the way the SNP administration behaves will discredit the case for independence. However much politicians of all parties, pro-Union and anti-Union, declare they intend to work together for the greater good of Scotland, the reality will be rather different, since on the central question of the Union, they interpret the national interest so differently, and this is the lens through which all other political issues will be viewed.

A long war of position is now in prospect during which all the parties in the Scottish Parliament will seek to act so as to maximise their long-term support in the electorate and to wrong-foot their opponents. As the governing party the SNP has the initiative. It has the greatest opportunities and also faces the greatest pitfalls. It has to demonstrate it can govern competently within the constraints of the devolution settlement, at the same time proving that having an SNP government makes a significant difference. This will be hard to do since the SNP is a minority administration, and has to build alliances with other parties to get any measure through. The SNP needs to create a new political dynamic so that eventually it can win sufficient seats in the Scottish Parliament to call a referendum, but the polls indicate that there remains a clear majority in the Scottish electorate against independence. Scottish voters are not yet convinced that independence is viable, and offers tangible advantages over staying in the Union.

The SNP might therefore seem to be in a weak position, but in office it has played its hand well and gained some tactical advantages. Although there is no prospect of the SNP getting key parts of its manifesto through Parliament, the possession of office has allowed SNP ministers to raise issues with symbolic significance for the future of the Union, by contrasting the potential of a sovereign Parliament with the constraints of devolution. The SNP would no doubt prefer to keep debate permanently at this level. This will not be possible, and the danger for the SNP, as with all incumbents, is that its ministers may became too involved in the administration of their departments, and lose sight of the broader political objectives they seek. The more the SNP government focuses on administering Scotland the more it will be blamed for its mistakes and for the choices it makes, and this will take its toll on the SNP's popularity.

Alex Salmond however is a shrewd politician, and is alert to these dangers. His strategy appears to be to use every opportunity to raise issues where there are potential clashes between the jurisdiction claimed by the two Parliaments, allowing him to question the current terms of the devolution settlement. He has already achieved some successes. He has queried the agreement between Britain and Libya over prisoner release, on the grounds that if it covered al-Megrahi, who was jailed for the Lockerbie bombing, any such release would be a matter for the Scottish courts, and should have first been discussed with the Scottish authorities. He has raised the issue of Scottish fisheries, arguing that Scotland should take the lead in negotiations over fishing quotas in the EU, even though, like all matters of external relations, this is a reserved matter for the Westminster Parliament. He also wants Scotland to have a civil service independent of England, and for the revenues of Scottish oil and gas to come under the control of the Parliament.

On nuclear issues the SNP has strong support within the Parliament for opposing the renewal of Trident and for opposing the building of new nuclear power stations. In both cases the issues are reserved for the Westminster Parliament to decide, and a Labour administration in Holyrood would probably have taken similar stances. The difference is that the SNP can use both issues to point up the constraints of the devolution settlement, and the way that on important questions Scotland cannot settle issues in ways which it would prefer. On the question of nuclear power stations it is likely that Westminster will agree to Scotland putting most of its energies into increasing renewables rather than nuclear power, and there are some suggestions that this was already agreed with the previous Lib/Lab administration. But Alex Salmond will seek to claim it as a success for the SNP against Westminster.

This approach is also being applied to certain aspects of domestic policy in order to demonstrate that an SNP administration can make a difference (without increasing taxes). The Scottish Parliament had already made a number of decisions which diverged from those in England, but with a SNP government this acquires a new edge. One of the first actions of the new SNP Minister of Health was to reverse the decision to close Accident and Emergence Services at Ayr and Monklands hospital. The graduate endowment (£2000 paid by graduates after they graduate) has been abolished. The SNP Executive has also declared that it will cancel the plans for Edinburgh trams and an airport rail link, and is reviewing some of the contracts made with the private sector to provide public services.

THE FUTURE OF THE UNION
The political landscape after Tony Blair remains a confused one. Labour faces an effective opposition on two crucial fronts, a resurgent Conservative party in the South of England, and a resurgent SNP in Scotland. Both threaten Labour's majority at Westminster, but the tactics for dealing with the two challenges are very different. All the parties now have to decide both how they campaign in the areas where powers have been devolved and how they campaign in England. With no sign of any significant revival in their support in Scotland the Conservatives are concentrating on improving on the position they achieved in the 2005 election when they narrowly won the largest share of the vote in England.

The new territorial politics which devolution has produced will have a major impact on the next general election. If the Conservatives win that election and form a government they will face the dilemma of how to handle devolved administrations in Cardiff and Edinburgh. If Labour however maintains a majority after the next election, but only a slim one, and if the Conservatives are clearly the leading party in England, the temptation for the Conservative leadership will be to emphasise that they are the English party, and press English votes for English laws, or even the idea of an English Parliament. The problem with playing the English card for the Conservatives is that nothing is more likely to accelerate the dissolution of the Union. But as the prospect of a majority at Westminster recedes the Conservatives may well become more ready to try any expedient. Before 1914 the Conservatives became incensed that the Liberal government was relying on the votes of Irish Nationalists in the House of Commons to pass its legislation on Home Rule and were on the brink of precipitating a major constitutional crisis. The issues this time may not be as fundamental or as polarised, but the temptation to exploit the situation could still be strong.

The problem for Labour and the Liberal Democrats in Scotland is that they have to find a strategy to avoid the fate of the Scottish Conservatives in the 1980s, when they increasingly appeared as no more than an adjunct of the English Conservative party. At the same time they are Unionist parties, they have to find a Unionist message that can still work, while being sensitive to the new context in which the citizens of Wales and Scotland are increasingly looking to their local administrations rather than to Westminster for the delivery of public services.

The Nationalists do not have it all their own way either. They will also have to confront serious problems. Before the SNP can hold a referendum in Scotland they must first become the majority party in the Parliament, or at the very least find coalition partners prepared to support a referendum on independence. They are still a long way from either, and even further from winning more seats than Labour in the Westminster Parliament. Their strategy is to convince Scottish voters that they can be trusted with governing Scotland, pressing at the same time for more powers to be devolved to Scotland, until the electorate sees no difference between a Scottish government with full devolved powers and complete independence. They have proceeded cautiously, claiming that the union of the Crowns will remain even when the union of Parliaments is no more, and avoiding in their White paper on Scotland's future any discussion of citizenship. Many voters will not like the idea of having to give up their British citizenship. Instead the issue is presented as one of simply transferring powers between one government and another.

The SNP also has a problem with the EU. Its programme has always stressed that an independent Scotland would become a full member of the EU, and this would guarantee no change in terms of access to the UK and the rest of the single market. But a sizeable minority in the SNP favours the Norway solution for Scotland – outside the UK and outside the EU. For Ireland joining the EU was a popular and positive step. The Irish embraced a European identity partly as a means of escaping from the shadow of Britain, and becoming part of a much larger association. Scottish opinion however appears much more negative to the EU, and according to the main opinion polls, the Scottish public is as eurosceptic in terms of attitudes to the EU as their English neighbours. Flashpoints such as EU fisheries policy make Europe an increasingly difficult issue for the SNP. Many in Scotland will suspect that in any bargaining process within the EU, Scotland is more likely to protect its interests as part of the UK than on its own.

Disentangling Scotland from the UK will be far from easy. Some of the loyalties and symbols of Britishness go very deep. A government in Westminster prepared to make concessions to Scottish demands for more powers will make it hard for Scots ever to arrive at the point where a majority will want independence regardless of the consequences. If Scotland can acquire both devolved government and membership of the UK why change? This is why secessions from established democracies are so rare. The Bretons, the Catalonians, and the Quebecois, for example, have not yet managed it. Secessions, when they have occurred, as with Slovakia from Czechoslovakia in 1992, or Hungary from Austria in 1918, do so normally after the collapse of a dictatorship, a civil war, or a military defeat.

But the Union is fragile now, and the devolution settlement has yet to achieve real legitimacy. Much will depend on how the different parties respond, and how imaginative politically they prove to be. The SNP has outpointed its rivals so far. Labour, the Liberal Democrats and the Conservatives have been left floundering for a convincing narrative and policy for the Union. Labour resolutely refuses to admit the seriousness of the West Lothian question, when to most other observers it is clear that the position is not tenable in the long run. Some solution will have to be devised, probably involving more explicitly federal institutions, if the devolution settlement is to command legitimacy not just in Scotland and Wales but in England too. Labour politicians often seem blind to the weakness of the arguments they put forward to defend current arrangements. Their argument is simple – devolution might be contradictory but if no-one objects too much then it is fine. But since people are beginning to object and increasingly people in England are regarding the present arrangements as unfair, sooner or later that is going to matter politically. The longer the problem is ignored the more assistance it will give to those who want to end the Union, because the Union will come to be seen as something that primarily serves the interests of the political class, and in particular Labour, north and south of the border. That is a dangerous situation for any party to be in. Labour can avoid it, but it should recognise that the need for constitutional thinking did not stop with the passage of the Scotland and Wales Acts. It has only just begun.

NOTES

1. Gordon Brown, Speech in Edinburgh, 8.9.06.
2. Margaret Thatcher, Speech at a Dinner at the British Embassy, Washington, 20.2.85.
3. Tony Blair, Speech to the US Congress, 18.7.03.
4. Simon Heffer, 'If it's good enough for the Scots, it's good enough for the English', *The Daily Telegraph*, 29.11.06.
5. Michael Fry, 'Scotland Alone', *Prospect*, December 2006.

The sound of the suburbs
The shaping of Englishness and the socio-cultural landscape after New Labour

Rupa Huq

In many ways the essence of 'Englishness' is encapsulated in traditional understandings of what constitutes 'suburbia'. These twin concepts often evoke landscapes frozen in time. Yet twenty-first century multi-ethnic suburbia conjures up a range of issues relevant to contemporary English national identity and the respacing of urban Britain. Beyond the sprawling metropolis, the suburbs provide a rich diversity of experience. Suburbia is beyond the centre of the city, it is where the often silent majority live, work and play. The traditional view of suburban life comprising pensioners seeing out their days, nosey neighbours peering from behind net curtains, cars being cleaned on the weekend, and most of all a universal whiteness, is in desperate need up updating. Twentieth-century migration has given birth to the multi-ethnic twenty-first century suburb. Suburbia has been examined as a town planning or geographical subject, yet there is an urgent need to consider the suburbs as dynamic social and cultural spaces.

SUBURBIA IN FACT AND FICTION: POPULAR STEREOTYPES
The 13 July 2005 *Daily Mail* headline 'Suicide Bombers From Suburbia' was clearly designed to shock. The words were swiftly relayed all over the blogosphere and web[1] - the tale of young men who had betrayed their outward ordinary appearances with their extraordinary deeds:

> Normal people leading normal lives, good people from good families –
> one loved cricket, another was a young father. A third happily told his
> parents last week that he was off to London 'with his mates'. All three
> had a deep Islamic faith, but no one thought of them as radicals.

The *Mail*'s sentiments were clear. Unchanging certainties of who lives in suburbia are undergoing a process of fracture – a fundamental break from the norm. On the same day as this exposé, the *Mail* also reported how the BBC's own internal processes have highlighted the Corporation's failure to reflect contemporary Britain in its programme roster – 'BBC sitcoms too "safe, white and middle class"'.[2] At once these two stories highlight socio-cultural shifts on the periphery and their wider implications. The suburbs are just not what they used to be.

Suburbia has always been seen as something archetypically English. Yet, the contention now is that it also harbours a new enemy within. All of the features that we have comfortably associated with suburbia – stability, safety, respectability and whiteness – no longer epitomise the English suburb as they once did. Instead risk and danger lurk around suburban corners. No longer can we comfort ourselves with the notion that an Englishman's home is his castle, a retreat into a privatised world untouched by external forces. The suburbs, which have always been about all that is ordinary and mundane, are now a site of extraordinary happenings, calling into question received notions of Englishness in the face of growing diversity. After all, recent events have shown us that not only do suicide bombers live in the suburbs(Beeston, Leeds), but it is here also that playground stabbings take place (Edgware, Middlesex), police carry out dawn raids (Forest Gate, on the eastern edge of the London post-code map) and the far right thrive politically (the next-door town of Barking, Essex). This is all in contrast to the state of affairs that Andy Medhurst described as 'what one might call the *newslessness* of suburbia ... a cornerstone of the vision of tranquillity that sold the suburban dream'.[3] Formerly predictable urban-suburban dichotomies are undergoing twenty-first century upsets.

Suburbia has long been a much-maligned entity, constantly the object of derision from urban elites. You can detect a sneer for example in the tone of George Orwell's reference to 'The inner-outer suburbs. Always the same ... Just a prison with the cells all in a row. A line of semi-detached torture chambers'.[4] John Betjeman is similarly disparaging and famously railed against the development of the once-rural setting of Slough in Buckinghamshire in 1937, urging 'Come, friendly bombs, and fall on Slough/ It isn't fit for humans now/ There isn't grass to graze a cow/ Swarm over, death!'. Sociological literature in the field has tended to display traits of metropolitan elitist snobbery, with a disproportionate amount of attention focused on urban locales at the expense of suburban settlement. According to popular wisdom, the inner cities, by contrast, have an edginess that is missing from the cloying comfort-zone of suburbia. Suburbs are commonly conceived of as close-knit, with 'local' facilities, unlike cities, which let in people from outside.

In some of the writing on suburbia there is a sense that to dwell there is a matter of choice, whereas inner-city living is more of a constraint: 'Those who could afford to choose where they lived abandoned the city centres ... to philanthropists ... the working classes and urban poor', claims Iain Chambers. This is a description which concurs with that of Everett M. Rogers, and of suburban population diffusion: 'the outward flow of people who have choice and jobs, who leave behind depleted services, boarded up shops, half empty classrooms, derelict homes and spaces'. This suggests that inner-city dwelling is not a choice. And the notion of 'white flight' adds an ethnic dimension – the implication being that it is the minorities who are left behind in the inner cities. The term is American in origin and has been propounded by US sociologists such as William Frey: the increased availability of suburban housing after the second world war led to an outward movement by white people from the central city and an expansion of black people into previously white neighbourhoods. Writing in a UK context, in the aftermath of the 2001 northern riots, Arun Kundnani discusses the white flight phenomenon in the context of the notion that it was minorities there who were leading segregated lives; he argues that explanatory factors for this segregation also include the instinct for minorities to bond together for fear of racial attack, and discriminatory housing allocations policy by local authorities.[5] (William Frey has also pointed to the role of federal and state authorities in stoking segregation in an American context: 'evidence ... suggests that racially motivated movement patterns and discriminatory housing practices, when superimposed upon market forces ... served to exacerbate the selective mobility of whites to the suburbs'.[6])

Defining suburbia is problematic, as it often seems to be a result of a process of elimination. We know that the suburbs are not the country and not the city: there is a sense of us knowing what suburbia is in opposition to, rather than what it is. Suburbia is in many ways the territory of in-between. And the semi-private spaces of suburbs are derided for their supposed dreariness but at the same time aspired to for their merits – which are also their demerits. The inner city and the suburbs are always painted in opposition to one another, as a relationship of opposites.

SUBURBAN	URBAN
White	Ethnic mix
Quiet	Noise
Space	built-up environment
Aspiration/affluence	multiple deprivation, decay
Choice	Constraint
Uniformity	Difference
Homogeneity	Quirky
Conformist	Bohemian
Boredom	Excitement
Fuddy-duddy	Youth
Privatised space	Community

The broad thrust of public policy thinking in recent years has tended to treat the inner cities as a problem to be approached in problem-solving terms, through initiatives such as the Office of Deputy Prime Minister's Urban Task Force, or the 'Excellence-in-cities' programme. (The latter was defined as 'a multi-strand policy initiative of the Department for Education and Skills (DfES) that is aimed at driving up standards in deprived urban schools and radically improving the educational outcomes and life chances of young people in the most economically disadvantaged areas of England'.[7]) To date, the government has not unveiled a comparable 'excellence-in-suburbs' policy agenda – it seems that such a notion would not have much political currency given prevailing trends. In response to this, in September 2007, a suburban fightback was launched with the publication of a report, *Successful City-Suburbs*, from the Local Government Association, which claimed that outer-London boroughs were being starved of money, in favour of inner-city regeneration. According to Mike Freer, leader of Barnet Council in North London: 'Eighty per cent of people in the UK live in suburbs; we are the vast majority of the population. We need to stop suburbs declining. Some may say they are already in decline. This is our response to that challenge'. In the *Daily Mail* Richard Littlejohn also added his voice to the debate, with a characteristically dramatic call to arms in a contribution that contrasts the sensible suburbs with an insurgent inner city: 'Not content with screwing the south of England to subsidise his native Scots, Gordon Brown is now screwing the suburbs to pay for the burgeoning client state in the inner cities. Of course, the suburbs tend to vote Tory, which is why [he] hates them'.[8] (This is, of course, a typical Littlejohn over-generalisation, for his own effect and purpose. Many suburbs have voted

Labour since 1997; and constituencies such as Harrow and Croydon helped turn the seemingly forever-blue electoral map of 1980s London majority-red in the Blair years.)

Conversely, conventional wisdom suggests that the inner city, with its hustle and bustle, is left behind by those who are able to escape to the peace and quiet of suburban choice. When Brixton-raised John Major predicted that 'Fifty years on from now, Britain will still be the country of long shadows on county cricket grounds, warm beer, invincible green suburbs, dog lovers and old maids bicycling through the morning mist', he was roundly attacked by liberals for his cultural Canutism and white leanings.[9] Yet, if read simply as a celebration of the mundane, its sentiments fit with a prime minister who was caricatured as a grey individual and seemed to cultivate an image of ordinariness. The suburbs have always been seen as dull by opinion formers, but they have also been seen as desirable and sought after by the populace – as something to aspire to. Those in the inner cities are those who are left behind, perhaps in need of slum clearance. (Major's predecessor Lady Thatcher memorably remarked in 1987 that something should be done about 'those inner cities' – the losers under Thatcherism.)

Progressive outward diffusion of ethnic groupings from inner-city areas to suburban areas has been longstanding in both the UK and US. Stanley Waterman and Barry Kosmin conducted a study focused on Jewish residential patterns in the London boroughs of Hackney, Redbridge and Barnet – these last two being outer-London whilst Hackney is in the inner-city. Although they do not use the word 'ghetto', they are interested in 'high concentrations' of minorities in a small number of boroughs. Their conclusion is that the 'integration-segregation continuum' is a dynamic process.[10] Thus it is wrong to separate these two terms, and to automatically see strong minority neighbourhoods as simply self-segregating: common sense dictates that endangered social groups gather together. Thus the suggestion in 2001 by then home secretary David Blunkett, after the urban disturbances, of a problem of 'parallel lives' angered many. They had built up local communities that they were proud of, and had made secure, in the face of often violent racist attacks.

Meanwhile, over a decade ago, British geographer Ceri Peach made the observation that British Asian groups were facing the alternatives of following an Irish future (ghettoisation, lack of mobility) or Jewish future (suburbanisation).[11] He concluded that Bangladeshis seemed to be concentrated in inner-London areas but that Indians, in London, have a suburban population distribution. He also observed a 'notable outward residential shift' by the Caribbean born population between

1981 and 1991. As so frequently is the case, the routes people took often followed familiar transport and road links – for example from Paddington to Brent along London Underground's Metropolitan line, or from Brixton to Croydon, where overground railways and the A24 lead.

NEW REPRESENTATIONS OF SUBURBAN MINORITIES

Hanif Kureishi's *Bhudda of Suburbia*, published in 1990, is written about, in retrospect, as a groundbreaking work of fiction on English Asian identity. It mixed fiction with the author's background of being a youngster of English/Pakistani parentage in Bromley on the south London/Kent border. The novel's anti-hero and narrator Karim makes a declaration of his identity at the outset:

> Englishman I am (though not proud of it, from the South London suburbs and going somewhere. Perhaps it was the odd mixture of continents and blood, of here and there, of belonging and not, that makes me restless and easily bored. Or perhaps it was being brought up in the suburbs that did it.[12]

A decade on there is a new generation of black and Asian chroniclers of suburbia. Among this post-Hanif Kureishi generation is Zadie Smith, whose first novel *White Teeth* was set in Willesden, with a plot centring on Bangladeshi twin brothers, and Gautam Malkani, whose *Londonstani* is a fictional account of the ducking and diving of a gang of 'desi' mobile phone obsessed young men in Hounslow, west London. Malkani's central character and narrator Jas follows the youth cultural ideal of not 'selling out', which for him means neither adopting the lifestyle of the majority white population nor deserting his suburban surroundings.

> In't no desi needin to kiss the white man's butt these days, an you definitely don't need to actually act like a gora. Fuckin blanchod. din't matter what you called them. Coconuts, Bounty bars, Oreo biscuits or any other fuckin food that was white on the inside. Good desi boys who didn't ever cause no trouble. But how many a them'll still be here in Hounslow in ten years time, workin in Heathrow fuckin airport helping goras catch planes to places so they could turn their own skin brown?[13]

This new vein of contemporary postcolonial fiction emerged at the same time as the Asian Underground club-scene and the advent of series such as *Goodness Gracious Me*, written and performed by young Asians.

Following New Labour's cool Britannia rhetoric, which aimed to update traditional imagery of Britishness, it seemed that Asians had gone from invisibility to hyper-visibility. As Sukdev Sandhu remarks: 'Previously we had to make do with sitcoms such as *It Ain't Half Hot Mum* and *Mind Your Language*, in which Asians wore comical headgear and were the butts rather than the tellers of jokes… Now times have changed and everywhere one turns there's a new magazine, conference or clubnight dedicated to staging the antics of young Asians in Britain'.

Sarfraz Manzoor has made a similar point:

> If someone had told me fourteen years earlier, when I had been watching Indian films with my family on our rented video player, that there would be a time when Ashla Bhosle would feature in a number one hit single, I would have considered them insane. It was as insane as a group of British Asians becoming pop stars. As unlikely as the thought of being Asian might be considered as being cool, that white people might pay to watch a film about a Pakistani family growing up in the seventies or read a book about a Bangladeshi woman or laugh at a comedy sketch where the joke was on them and not the Asians performing the skit.[14]

A suburban sensibility can be discerned in much of this work. The weekly chatshow *The Kumars at Number 42*, starring Sanjeev Bhaskar and Meera Syal, both cast members of *Goodness Gracious Me*, is set around the exploits of an extended British-Indian family living in a mock Tudor house in suburban Wembley, north west London. If the suburbs have been previously characterised by their younger denizens as somewhere to escape from, there is now a vein of commentary in an almost 'Return of the Native' narrative. Sarfraz Manzoor has recently reinterpreted his own childhood in Luton in light of the fact that the 7/7 bombers came from the same place. In a defence of secular Islam and British values he writes: 'When I had been growing up the town had been something of a national joke, but recently it had been inextricably linked with Islamic radicalism'.[15] The Channel 4 documentary *The Hidden Jihad*, by second generation Asian journalist and DJ Imran Khan, showed Imran revisiting his childhood hometown of Peterborough to find, to his evident disbelief, that his male contemporaries had all turned away from clubbing and women to become devout Muslims. Writer Sukdev Sandu has similarly reminisced about his own boyhood in Gloucester:

> Asians who, like me, grew up in areas of England such as Horsham or Cheam or Gloucester, where brown faces were scarce, became increasingly embarrassed by our parents' accents, by their insistence that we

wear outdated polyester clothes and drench our hair in coconut oil
before going out. It was easy to forget the love that made them do this.

Sukdev Sandu and Sarfraz Manzoor share an underlying affection for
their first generation forebears, and give recognition to the sacrifices
that they made.

CHANGES IN SUBURBIA

Apart from this understandable nostalgia for the ways in which new
communities have been constructed there is also an interesting account
to be compiled of changes in suburban consumption. The old suburban
high streets have been affected by the growth of out-of-town shopping
and the advent of the retail park, linked closely to the coming of the car
economy. In 2005, when cut-price Swedish furniture store Ikea opened
a branch in the north London suburb of Edmonton, riots ensued in the
scramble to seek bargains. Five people were hospitalised and several
more injured. This is not behaviour traditionally associated with the
suburbs. And many suburbs are becoming identikit 'Tesco towns',
with multiple branches of the chain. Partly because of this there has
been a movement against retail giants like Tesco in recent years; for
example the New Economics Foundation think-tank has probed these
themes in their coining of the term 'clone town Britain'. They claim: 'In
place of real local shops has come a package of "identikit" chain stores
replicating on the nation's high streets. The individual character of
many towns is evaporating. Retail spaces once filled with independent
butchers, newsagents, tobacconists, pubs, book shops, greengrocers
and family owned general stores are filled with supermarket stores, fast
food chains and global fashion outlets'. Interestingly, ethnic commerce
has reinvigorated many suburban high streets, including Rusholme –
scene of Manchester's 'curry mile', often visited by coach trips from the
rest of the UK and sometimes even further afield.

A similar phenomenon in Green Street, in East Ham, London, has
been researched by Sean Carey and Nooruddin Ahmed, who vividly
describe its composition:

The number, concentration and sheer variety of south Asian shops (and
stalls in the Queen's Market) including beauty and hairdressing salons,
'high' and 'low' fashion outlets, jewellery, household and electrical,
furniture, telecoms, Internet cafes, money exchanges, music and DVD
outlets, opticians, pharmacies, photographers, printers, travel agents,
Indian and Pakistani sweet shops, grocers and food stores (including
several halal butchers and fishmongers), wedding and birthday party

specialists and Islamic book and clothing shops offering consumers a wide range of goods and services at highly competitive prices exceeds anything available in comparable shopping areas of Tower Hamlets or, indeed any other area of east London.[16]

Whilst the grocery shops of Southall, Wembley, Tooting, Brick Lane and Green Street evolved due to a demand for produce from 'back home' in locations that were relatively cheap but central, more recently local authorities have been actively encouraging clusters of ethnic commerce. The 1990s saw a Manchester City Council backed 'There's Only One Rusholme' campaign. More recently, the London Borough of Redbridge has been aiming for Ilford Lane to become another Green Street. The borough's Unitary Development Plan has earmarked sites, with subsidies to attract new businesses to this end. As with other developments discussed in this chapter, this sharply contradicts notions of the suburbs – in this case suburban shopping – as boring.

East London has tended to be viewed in an idealised manner as a 'parish pump' community. Willmott and Young, for example, refer to 'the kind of informal general "matiness" which characterises the old East End communities'. This conjures up the idea of jolly cockneys who triumph through adversity. As John Clarke as argued, from a sociological point of view the East End has been seen as the archetypal working class community. The idea of authenticity in East London has provided a context for David Downes's work on delinquency and that of Phil Cohen on skinheads. But this area too has been subject to massive change. Cohen's work is known for its much quoted perspective that skinhead activity is response to a disappearing way of life: skinheads were victims of the urban renewal and slum clearance that cut through their traditional communities, and saw the manifestation of aggressively working-class sartorial style as a compensatory solution. So this is an authenticity that is struggling to reproduce itself.

And many were keen to leave: for the traditional East End inhabitant, a move to suburbia was a definite step-up. A respondent in Peter Willmott and Michael Young's later study of the middle-class East London suburb of Woodford describes it as 'the place I've been looking for all my life – a nice country village within easy reach of London'. At the beginning of the book the authors flag a series of differences between Bethnal Green and Woodford, and one of the key ones is the split between public and private. In their words: 'In Bethnal Green people are vigorously at home in the streets, their public face much the same as their private. In Woodford people seem to be quieter and even more reserved in public'. As the authors stress, these are both East

London locations, but the former is inner-city and the latter suburban. There is an interplay between districts such as these in suburban drift, and suburbia has long been a site of diaspora location. (A more recent study, *The New East End*, is a tale of disenchantment, anger and resentment on the part of the remaining white working-class, with friction between established communities and new arrivals against a backdrop of an increasingly transient population.[17])

THE SOUND OF THE SUBURBS

In a pre-punk era George Melly observed: 'Despite his carefully grubby and poverty-stricken appearance, and painfully restricted vocabulary, the average young pop fan today is drawn in the main from a middle-class or suburban background and is educationally in one of the higher streams'.[18] There is a rich vein of English pop documenting the daily ordinariness of English suburbia, of which Morrissey and The Smiths are key protagonists. Earlier, in the 1960s, the Kinks and the Beatles proved erudite chroniclers, on tracks like *Autumn Almanac* and *Penny Lane*. And in the 1980s the Pet Shop Boys even had a hit single simply entitled *Suburbia*, the performance of which on tour in 1991 was accompanied by a slickly choreographed dance routine featuring women vacuuming.

Pop fans and performers have hailed from many different types of suburb, including working-class variants. For all its urban posturing, punk was an intrinsically suburban phenomenon. The South London 'Bromley contingent' were so-called because they were based on the South London/Kent border which had earlier spawned David Bowie. Billy Idol and Siouxsie Sioux were among members. Later Britpop also revelled in urban chic whilst the background of its practitioners revealed suburban roots. Jon Savage discusses the Sex Pistols' Wormholt estate in Acton, West London: 'Although it was only a mile away from Hammersmith, Wormholt, just over the road from White City, was quite different. It was a sprawling council estate that, despite the benefits of thirties town planning, was as much of a rabbit warren as the slums of Dickens's London had been a century before'.[19]

The Smiths were strongly associated with Manchester. Their cultural specificity helped to define this quintessentially English band – who are all sons of Irish immigrants. Their songs and album and singles covers are full of Mancunian landmarks – most famously the picture of Salford lads club on the inside gatefold sleeve of the Queen is Dead album. A current bearer of the UK suburban pop mantle are Hard-Fi of Staines, to the west of London's Heathrow airport. Their songs include the 2007 single *Suburban Knights*. The band's Richard

Archer has described Staines as a strength: 'The thing about Staines is it's insular ... but because it's insular it's helped us out. We were never like, "Oh the NME and all our mates in Camden are telling us that we have to make this kind of sound." So we just listened to the music that we loved ... soul, dub, hip-hop reggae house'.[20]

Transport has always been one of the defining features of suburban London, as seen in the coining of the concept of metroland in 1915 to describe the area to the north west of London in Middlesex, Hertfordshire and Buckinghamshire through which the Metropolitan Railway operated and served.[21] Transport and the stress of commuting feature in several pop songs that deal with suburbia. On the 1995 album *The Great Escape* Blur, from Colchester in Essex, paint a pen-portrait of poor Ernold Same that commiserates with him for his sad repetitive life of drudgery 'Ernold Same caught the same train/ At the same station/ Sat in the same seat/ With the same nasty stain/ Next to same old what's-his-name/ On his way to the same place/ With the same name/ To do the same thing/ Again and again and again'. In 1979 the Jam, from Surrey commuter town Woking, had evoked similar stereotypes with their pin-striped commuting character Smithers Jones; a regular on the 8am train to Waterloo: 'Sitting on the train, you're nearly there/ You're part of the production line/You're the same as him, you're like tinned-sardines/ Get out of the pack, before they peel you back.' Paul Weller later had a volume of collected lyrics published under the title *Suburban 100*. Transport has been key in the production of suburban youth cultures. Accounts of the punk Bromley contingent commonly describe how the British Rail line to London Bridge threw a lifeline to the nascent punks from deep south London suburbia. For the Clash meanwhile, over in west London, the A40 elevated section provided the same function by road: 'Up and down the Westway, in and out the lights/ What a great traffic system – it's so bright,' on the track *London's Burning*. The same road was later eulogised in Blur's *For Tomorrow*.

SITUATING SUBURBIA IN THE CULTURAL CARTOGRAPHY OF TWENTY-FIRST CENTURY BRITAIN

The twin currents of continuity and change have informed the unfolding of twentieth-century suburban history. The 'ethnicisation' of suburbia has contributed to its political reshaping, with changes to parts of Britain's electoral map that in the Thatcherite 1980s were always obstinately blue. Matthew Engels conveys the sense of change after the Blair landslide: 'Of course everyone still had a glow from the Great Day. They came from all the improbable ex-Tory constituencies of Middle

England and swapped stories about How They Did It, when they knew they would win and the expression on the defeated Tory MP's face when they found out too'.[22] Bill Schwarz describes this moment of victory in 1997 as a fundamental 'break-up of the Conservative nation'. He argues: 'The old Tory vision of the Union had, in the 1990s, come to mean little more than the politics of a contracting England ... Electorally, the conservative nation resembled nothing so much as the geographic cluster of subscribers to *Country Life*'.[23] Ten years later the landscape has changed once again. Labour remains in power, but the next general election looks more competitive than any post-1997. The 'ethnicisation' of suburbia brings with it other challenges. Following the rise in the BNP vote in Barking and Dagenham in outer east London, the respected pressure group Operation Black Vote has called the borough 'the racist capital of the UK'.[24] This dubious distinction was an epithet earlier applied to Burnley in Lancashire, when in 2001 a number of BNP councillors were elected there.

When I interviewed Dagenham Labour MP Jon Cruddas in 2007 he enthused about his constituency:

> I think what is extraordinary about Dagenham is the way it's dealing with extraordinary forces rather than the way it isn't ... If you had these patterns of demographic change in the middle of Surrey ... you would have a political earthquake. They wouldn't deal with it. Actually what is extraordinary in Dagenham is the ability of the community to deal with all the changes ... There's not violence, there's no riots. It's safe, stable, quiet, honest, so I think the BNP will go and what I think will be left, with hindsight, is the extraordinary ability of the community to accept and adapt to these changes. I tell you, if it was a rich middle-class community in the middle of Surrey. it wouldn't be such an orderly series of changes – the golf club would be on fire ... I don't know demographically any community that's changed as quickly as this historically ... this is unprecedented and these are sort of epiphenomenal things. I've been the MP since 2001 and the demographic change in that time is absolutely extraordinary.

In Burnley the perceived newcomers were Pakistanis although British citizens. In Dagenham it is black Africans, their arrival driven by the relatively low cost of housing in the area. British Asians following a pattern of suburban drift have been joined more recently by Somalis and Eastern Europeans. The London suburban trajectory of British Asians from Tower Hamlets to Redbridge is following the Jewish communities' earlier passage from the inner to outer city.[25]

These complexities of suburbia have made an impact on representations of English identity that contrast markedly with Blair and Brown's simplistic fixation with 'Middle England' – which, as Schwarz points out, is always presented as unproblematic and unchallenged. Urban relations are dynamic, never static: they are shifting landscapes both culturally and socially. Doreen Massey has commented: 'If it is now recognized that people have multiple identities then the same point can be made in relation to places. Moreover, such multiple identities can be a source of richness, or a source of conflict, or both.'[26] Multiculturalism has led to a respacing of urban Britain, and a redrawing of the suburban map. This does not apply literally to its boundaries, but can be understood in terms of mapping its socio-cultural characteristics, and considerations of what 'Englishness' means today. The English Suburb of the twenty-first century is as much about urban jungle as it is about village green. We ignore this at our national peril.

NOTES

1. See eg http://comment.independent.co.uk/commentators/article299194.ece
   www.csmonitor.com/2005/0714/p06s02-woeu.html;
   http://abcnews.go.com/WNT/Investigation/story?id=936882&page=1;
   www.theage.com.au/news/war-on-terror/london-bombing-suspects-named/2005/07/13/1120934271528.html?oneclick=true
   http://www.spiked-online.com/index.php?/site/article/851/
   http://news.bbc.co.uk/1/hi/uk/4677727.stm
2. 'BBC sitcoms too "safe, white and middle class"', *Daily Mail* 13.7.05; also 'Governors say comedy output is still too white, middle-class and cosy', *Guardian* 13.7.05.
3. A. Medhurst, 'Negotiating the Gnome Zone: Versions of Suburbia in British Popular Culture', in R. Silverstone ed, *Visions of Suburbia*, Routledge 1997. www.irr.org.uk/2001/october/ak000003.html.
4. G. Orwell, *Coming up for Air*, Penguin 1937.
5. A. Kundnani, 'From Oldham to Bradford: the violence of the violated', www.irr.org.uk/2001/october/ak000003.html.
6. W Frey, 'Central City White Flight: Racial and Nonracial Causes', in *American Sociological Review*, 44, 1977, pp425–448.
7. www.nfer.ac.uk/research-areas/excellence-in-cities/.
8. R. Littlejohn, 'Sending Out an SOS … Save Our Suburbs', *Sun*, 7.9.07.
9. www.number10.gov.uk/output/page125.aspp.
10. S. Waterman and B. Kosmin, 'Residential Patterns and Processes: A Study of Jews in Three London Boroughs', in *Transactions of the Institute of British Geographers*: New Series 13(3), 1988, pp79-95.
11. C. Peach, 'Does Britain have ghettos?', *Transactions of the Institute of*

British Geographers 21(1), 1995, pp216-35.

12. H. Kureishi, *The Bhudda of Suburbia*, Faber and Faber 1990, p3.

13. G. Malkani, *Londonstani*, Harper Perennial 2006, p23.

14. S. Manzoor, *Greetings From Bury Park: Race, religion and rock'n'roll*, Bloomsbury 2007, pp257-8.

15. Ibid, p262.

16. S. Carey, and N. Ahmed, 'Bridging the Gap: The London Olympics 2012 and South Asian-owned Businesses in Brick Lane and Green Street', 2006, www.youngfoundation.org.uk/publications/reports/bridging_the_gap.

17. G. Dench, K. Gavron, and M. Young, *The New East End: Kinship, Race and Conflict*, Profile books 1996.

18. G. Melly, *Revolt into Style: the pop arts in the 50s and 60s*, OUP 1970.

19. J. Savage, *England's Dreaming: Sex Pistols and Punk Rock*, Faber and Faber 1991, p72.

20. E. Caesar, 'Hard-Fi: The Staines Massive', *Independent*, 22.7.05.

21. www.museumoflondon.org.uk/English/Collections/OnlineResources/X20L/Themes/1/1184/.

22. M Engel, 'Hallelujah Chorus Sings Leader's Praises', *Guardian*, 4.11.97.

23. B. Schwarz, 'The Break-up of the Conservative Nation', *Soundings* 7 1997, at http://amielandmelburn.org/articles/break-up.htm.

24. OBV at www.obv.org.uk/index.php?option=com_content&task=view&id=344&Itemid=127.

25. See also K. Brodkin, *How Jews Became White Folks and What That Says About Race in America*, Rutgers University Press 1998.

26. D. Massey, 'Power, Geometry and a Progressive Sense of Place', in J. Bird, *Mapping the Futures: Local Cultures, Global Change*, Routledge 1993, p65.

All white on the right

Graham Macklin

Any discussion of Englishness and Britishness has to address the influence of a far right which actively promotes an explicitly racialised vision of national identity. However, even amongst the far right, visions of race and nation are subjects of debate. There is surprisingly little consensus on the extremist fringe, where various visions of race, nation and identity remain highly contested subjects. What does unite the disparate far right and populist parties, however, is a politics heavily determined by a version of a white England under threat from unwelcome cultural and, specifically, racial change.

THE BNP'S CHANGING STANCE

Foremost amongst the parties occupying this space is the British National Party (BNP). The BNP was founded in 1982 following the disintegration of the National Front into warring factions in the wake of its abysmal showing in the 1979 general election. The BNP's founder, John Tyndall, ruled the party as a personal fiefdom, achieving little beyond keeping the forces of British fascism together through the wilderness years of the 1980s and 1990s. Ousted in 1999 by Nick Griffin, the BNP subsequently underwent a concerted 'modernisation' programme, similar to those embarked upon by its Continental counterparts two decades previously, aimed at convincing both new party members and voters that it had shed its neo-Nazism and was now a respectable and electable political force.

This process received a huge boost through the unhappy conjunction of external events in 2001. The most serious race riots in Oldham, Burnley and Bradford for fifty years, al-Qaida's attacks on America on 9/11 and a rising tide of hostility towards immigrants from the tabloid press, which increasingly linked risks to national security with a hysteria about both Islam and asylum-seekers. These factors, and the consequent overarching politicisation of race relations policies, has gifted the BNP the ideal climate in which to re-launch itself. The party has escaped from the Hitlerite ghetto from whence it had come to become a broader based racial nationalist party, though its leadership cadres have been careful to retain the purity of their ideological core.[1]

Shortly after becoming leader Griffin took two major steps towards achieving this end. Firstly, to Tyndall's abject horror, he sought to expunge open expressions of anti-semitism and Holocaust denial from party debates and publications. A difficult feat to accomplish, as Griffin himself was convicted of inciting racial hatred in 1998, largely on account of articles he had written denying the Holocaust as a hoax.

Secondly, and equally importantly, Griffin successfully faced down the party's own Clause 4 type moment by ending the BNP's commitment to compulsory repatriation. After all, the image of black, Asian or Jewish neighbours being herded into trucks and carted off in the middle of the night left a bad taste in the mouth even with those who clamoured for tighter immigration controls.

On 11 March 2000 the BNP held a general members meeting in Milton Keynes to overhaul the party constitution. In its statement of principles the BNP defined itself as 'a party of British Nationalism, committed to the principle of national sovereignty in all British affairs'.[2] As such the BNP is determined to remove Britain from the European Union at the first opportunity. It is also a unionist party committed to maintaining the unity and integrity of the British Isles, which places it in diametric opposition to, and indeed competition with, civic-nationalist parties such as the Scottish National Party and Plaid Cymru. Such a stance also places the BNP on an ideological collision course with English independence parties, including the English Democrats.

Although the BNP denies it is a racist party, according to section 2 (2) of its constitution, membership is reserved for those of the 'indigenous Caucasian', who belong to one of several ethnic 'folk' communities, which means bluntly only those who are white.[3] The BNP rationalises this position by claiming that it is not racist but simply protecting 'diversity' from those who would see all racial characteristics dissolved in the 'rootless coffee-coloured consumerism' of multiculturalism, a political reality loathed by the BNP.[4]

The BNP portrays Britain's white majority as a victimised and embattled demographic minority, a once proud people cowed into submission by its twin foes – political correctness and the race relations industry. It rails against what it describes as anti-white racism, which supposedly casts the British as strangers in their own land. The indigenous British, argues the BNP, are losing out to undeserving immigrants and asylum seekers who are 'sponging off' the benefit system, and putting pressure on public services, housing and employment, not to mention out-breeding host communities. All of which threatens to extinguish the fragile flame of white society, a process aided and abetted by Westminster politicians controlled by a vast conspiratorial network of global capitalists aiming at the creation of a homogenous one-world government.

For the BNP nation and identity are indivisible. The party's core ideal is that a nation's history is defined by race, and in particular the white race. This point is made simply in the BNP constitution, which states that British nationality is reserved for those of white ethnicity – those whom it defines as the indigenous peoples of Britain. It is this 'single brotherhood of peoples'[5] which the BNP pledges to defend. The BNP is alone in British electoral politics in committing itself to a strictly racial interpretation of who is and who is not a part of the nation, which would thus facilitate 'the preservation of the national and ethnic character of the British people'. The BNP is 'wholly opposed to any form of racial integration between British and non-European peoples'. Of course the BNP actively discourages racially mixed marriages. Richard Barnbrook, the BNP London Mayoral candidate, believes that the children of such unions 'are washing out the identity of this country's indigenous people' – which is ironic, given his own widely publicised relationship with a BNP member who has a mixed race daughter.[6]

Opposed to 'non-white' immigration, the BNP believes in a revolutionary vision of racial restoration that would see the 'overwhelmingly white makeup of the British population' restored to the primacy it held prior to the British Nationality Act (1948). The party's 2005 general election manifesto expressed its commitment to the construction of a racially-based state, whereby 'all economic and social structures, institutions and legislation must be built or developed around the fundamentals of ensuring the freedom and security of our people and maintain our unique cultural and ethnic identity'. Although Griffin has dropped the party's commitment to compulsory repatriation as the principal means through which Britain shall return to the way 'it has traditionally been', the manifesto promised, the BNP will 'stop all new immigration except for exceptional cases', whilst also offering 'generous grants to those of foreign descent resident here who wish to leave permanently'.[7]

Quite aside from the un-stated economic consequences of this scheme, it also completely fails to address the presence of second or third generation ethnic communities who, having been born in England, would have nowhere else to leave to. The BNP is similarly vague on what fate would face those who decline 'generous' repatriation grants. It does, however, explain that the policy would involve deporting the several million immigrants which it defines as illegal, foreign-born criminals, and those asylum seekers who do not qualify to stay here because they 'passed safe countries on their way to Britain' (which, given Britain is an island, presumably means every single asylum seeker). The BNP would also conduct a review of 'all recent grants of residence or citizenship to ensure they are still appropriate'.[8] There is no indication as to how far back this review would go. However, given the public BNP ambition to revert Britain to what it conjures up as a racially homogeneous state before the 1948 arrival of Afro-Caribbean migrants, we can only assume that such a review would extend to reappraising nearly all the citizenship grants dispensed over the last sixty years. Whether this review would also extend to dependents is not made clear. Leading BNP ideologues, including Arthur Kemp, have drawn a number of lessons from the fall of South African apartheid; most notably this has meant recognising that only the complete separation of races will ensure the preservation of the white race.[9] For the BNP there is no room for self-segregation into ethnic homelands in Britain. Instead immigration is a zero sum game, all or nothing, and preferably nothing.

Glimpses of how the BNP intend to facilitate such exclusion are already visible in council chambers across the country where the BNP has representation. In December 2006 BNP councillors in Barking and Dagenham tried to impose a ban on the wearing of the Burqa and the niqab in public 'in the interests of public safety', whilst also tabling a proposal to ban Halal meat for Muslim schoolchildren in the borough. This would in effect mean Muslim children could no longer enjoy a school meal alongside their classmates. Forcing these kids to bring a packed lunch would facilitate the sort of socially engineered racial separation the BNP welcomes, a division which would ultimately be reflected in the local community.[10] Other BNP councillors in Stoke on Trent have specifically targeted funding proposals for ethnic community initiatives, which, if successful, would deprive them of access to social services, interpretation agencies and charities. The BNP website meanwhile attacks the provision of AIDS services for immigrants on the grounds that they have not contributed to them financially – a move that could only damage public health.[11]

These largely unremarked upon developments are a logical conclusion of the BNP's politics of exclusion and its insistence that national identity is determined by racial origin, combined with culture, language and historical experience. It is claimed by the BNP that this recalibration of racism is such that it is not racism at all: instead, a spurious common-sense politics is invoked. Yet their entire thesis is underpinned by a widely discredited racial science, updated to include findings on genetics and DNA, that allegedly support the claim that blacks and Asians are genetically inferior. Former BNP press officer Dr Stuart Russell regularly stated that Blacks were less intelligent than whites; he believed that 'black kids are going to grow up dysfunctional … and are probably going to mug you … To put it crudely, there's no black Mozart, no black Dickens'. Confronted with a recording of his speech by *Sky News* Russell admitted: 'If I thought I was going to be recorded … I would not have used such intemperate language, but let's be honest about it, the facts are there'.[12]

The BNP's racial nationalist ideology has not remained static in other areas. The recent influx of Eastern European migrants creates a problem for the party, since these migrants are white. This has led the BNP to re-conceptualise its stance on race and identity. Shifting, at an ideological level at least, from racial nationalism to ethno-nationalism, has enabled the party to discriminate against white Eastern European migrant labourers by arguing for 'genetic diversity' even amongst whites. Whilst such ideological about-turns allow the BNP to oppose white immigration, BNP legal officer Lee Barnes has assured members that this still allows the BNP to retain its commitment to the '14 words' that remain a 'strategic goal' for the BNP.[13] The '14 words' – 'we must secure the existence of our people and a future for white children' – were first coined by the US white supremacist terrorist David Lane. Barnes's justification, however, only served to confuse and anger hard-core fascists.[14] Griffin, on the other hand, in his 'modernising' guise, was keen to distance the BNP from what he describes as the neo-Nazi '14 words' cultists'.[15] This was a curious denunciation given Barnes's high standing in the party.

It is, however, Muslim communities that have born the brunt of BNP racism in recent years, through its campaign against Islam, which, one party leaflet proclaimed, stands for 'Intolerance, Slaughter, Looting, Arson and Molestation of women'.[16] Although the BNP claims that it does not hold all Muslims responsible for the actions of a few, this claim does not withstand serious scrutiny. The party advocates banning Muslims from holding certain forms of employment and indeed advocates banning 'all Muslims' from flying.[17] The BNP has even gone so far as to suggest that one way to deter Islamist militants would be to bury their corpses with pork.[18]

This vilification of Islam is contrasted with the positive beliefs that Nick Griffin claims the party stands for, summed up in the BNP party slogan 'Freedom, Security, Identity and Democracy'. Here too the party has changed its language, talking up the 'threat' to British culture from immigration as being a 'religious' and 'cultural' threat rather than an overtly 'racial' threat. Thus, for example, the party newspaper *Voice of Freedom* recently ran a picture of a group of Muslims praying with a church spire in the background under the headline 'Change Beyond Belief'.[19] Griffin is also firmly wedded to the thesis propounded by neo-Conservatives in the US that Britain is facing not only a Clash of Civilisations but also a malign conspiracy which threatens, through the 'dhimmitude' of Western leaders, to turn Europe into 'Eurabia'.[20]

This appeal to one version of our Christian heritage and identity is now the core of the BNP message that the traditional British way of life is under violent threat from another, more strident, faith. In an effort to channel religious antipathy into its overarching anti-Islamic campaign, the BNP has founded a religious front-group, the Christian Council of Britain. The name itself betrays a mocking mimicry of the Muslim Council of Britain.[21] Its allegedly Christian message is ironic, given that even a cursory glance at the on-line catalogue of the BNP merchandising arm reveals the commitment of the party's inner core to the ideals of, or belief in, the merits of a pre-Christian Anglo-Saxon paganism! This confused vision of the nation is further reflected in the cultural symbolism of the BNP, which combines modern symbols such as the Union Jack with many pre-Christian ones, in particular Celtic crosses and Runes.

The tone of the language used by the BNP in its discussion of Islam has become increasingly militant. This landed Griffin in court twice in 2006 for derogatory remarks about Islam, though he was acquitted on both occasions. The BNP website enjoins readers to join the 'resistance', whilst Griffin himself regularly talks about the coming racial 'civil war', a conflict that Richard Barnbrook recently stated to be 'inevitable'. Such language deliberately raises the temperature and tone of the debate on race and immigration, and the logical outcome of such rhetoric was to be seen in the jailing, for two and a half years, of BNP member Robert Cottage, who pleaded guilty to stockpiling chemicals and weapons in preparation for precisely the sort of 'civil war' that party publications constantly talk about.[22]

As a nationalist party, the BNP advocates the complete withdrawal of Britain from the European Union and the restoration of national sovereignty, which for the BNP means 'the right to make our own laws, our own international trade agreements and our own economic policy, and control our own borders'. Equally importantly for the BNP, withdrawal from the European Union 'would remove the right of all the recent wave of East European cheap labour immigrants to work here'.[23]

BNP/UKIP RIVALRY

It is certainly arguable that the anti-EU and anti-immigrant United Kingdom Independence Party (UKIP), founded in 1993, can be defined as a right-wing nationalist party, however much UKIP might resent the description. Unlike the BNP, however, UKIP is completely committed to parliamentary democracy; indeed its entire rationale is founded on its supposed defence. UKIP is certainly therefore not a fascist party, even if others depict its membership as 'little Englanders' or 'BNP in blazers'.[24] Nevertheless the BNP and UKIP are locked in the same battle for voters increasingly disowned by the Conservative Party and unrepresented by the Labour Party. UKIP leader Nigel Farage admits that his party functions as a safety valve – something the BNP regularly accuse it of – allowing voters to 'express their anxieties about immigration, but without having to vote for a party that is violent and racist'.[25]

It would be no exaggeration to state that UKIP represents a significant impediment to further BNP progress in its vote. Support for UKIP deprived the BNP of representation on both the European Parliament and the Greater London Authority in 2004. The election saw UKIP surge ahead of the BNP with 16.8 per cent of the vote, gaining twelve MEPs to add to the three it had gained in 1999. It also gained two seats on the Greater London Assembly. Demoralised, within the space of a year BNP membership plummeted from 7,916 to 6,008.

In 2008, however, it was the BNP who were in a far better position; UKIP appeared to be on the decline, lurching from crisis to crisis.[26] During 2007 UKIP suffered several high profile defections, an investigation by the Electoral Commission that led to the forfeiture of a £367,697 donation (though this was eventually regained following a high court battle), and revelations that MEP Tom Wise was being investigated for fraud, and that UKIP donor David Abbott had also funded the BNP. In large measure these problems are a reflection of UKIP's struggle to maintain momentum outside of the European electoral cycle. The BNP regularly trounces UKIP in local elections, but Griffin has now set his sights on winning Euro-Elections. He sees the funds that accrue from securing MEPs as crucial to the party's future strategic development. Thus he explicitly rules out any chance of an electoral pact with UKIP, instead pledging to destroy it.[27]

Conservative Party leader David Cameron memorably branded UKIP as a coterie of 'fruitcakes, loonies and closet racists', a characterisation roundly rejected by Farage, who demanded but did not receive an apology.[28] It is certainly true to say that there is a cross-fertilisation between the members and voters of the BNP and UKIP. Polling data indicates that those who expressed a 'liking' for UKIP are also more likely to express support for the BNP. Evidence of this cross-support was visible in the 2004 London Mayoral election, when one fifth of UKIP voters gave their second preference vote to the BNP, whilst one half of BNP voters gave their second preference to UKIP. Further research reveals the existence of a right voting block in London, consisting of the BNP, UKIP and traditional Conservative supporters.[29]

In attempting to convert antipathy towards asylum and immigration into populist political currency, UKIP's anti-immigration stance was, admits one leading member, 'perhaps uncomfortably close to the Front National in France of Jean-Marie Le Pen' – though the party insisted it was a question of 'space not race'.[30] For the BNP this represents everything that is wrong with UKIP. Asked to expound on the difference between the two parties, the former BNP Group Support Officer Tony Lecomber observed that: 'UKIP accept fucking anyone. At the end of the day it's a racial thing. We're the BNP, we are who we are because of race. We don't want blacks here.'[31]

This then is the crux of the difference between the two parties. UKIP stands for civic rather than racial nationalism. Estranged UKIP founder Alan Sked believed the party to be 'a nation-ist, not a nation-alist party'.[32] For Griffin such a characterisation is the antithesis of his own definition of nationalism because on this definition, 'any Congolese refugee who picks up enough of Shakespeare's tongue not only to ask for asylum and benefits but also to pledge loyalty to England or Scotland is miraculously turned into an Englishman or a Scot'.[33] BNP national officer Mark Collett makes the point in a less prosaic manner: 'Just because a dog is brought up in a stable doesn't make him a horse.'[34]

Immigration represents an increasingly central plank of UKIP strategy, though one coupled with its opposition to the EU. Determined to break the mould and dispel its image as a one policy party, its leadership has announced a proposal for a five year freeze on immigration, a policy angrily dismissed by the BNP as a gimmick designed to steal its support.

UKIP can clearly see the gains to be had from being identified with the immigration issue. With the Conservative Party and the Labour Party both squabbling over the centre ground of British politics, and the BNP still beyond the pale for many voters, UKIP believes it can successfully reinvent itself as a populist party to the right of the

Conservatives, marginalising the BNP in the process. UKIP also support the creation of an English Parliament for English MPs. This offers a direct challenge to the BNP concept of 'British' nationalism. Politically, however, the group at the forefront of this burgeoning 'English lobby' is the English Democrats Party (EDP), founded in 1997 by solicitor Robin Tilbrook, and stating that it is 'not left, not right, just English!'. The EDP maybe a small party, but opinion polls indicate that its basic premise has a large reservoir of potential support. An ICM poll for the Campaign for an English Parliament (CEP) organisation in April 2007 found 67 per cent of respondents favoured the establishment of an English Parliament.[35]

THE BNP AND OTHER NATIONALIST PARTIES

Ironically, despite casting itself as a 'British' nationalist party the BNP have found few takers for their message outside their English heartlands in outer East London, the Midlands and parts of Yorkshire and Lancashire. The BNP has traditionally fared badly in Scotland, where it has had to compete with the Scottish National Party (SNP), who the BNP describe as 'false flag' nationalists existing solely to break up the 300-year-old union. In the May 2007 Scottish Parliamentary elections the BNP polled a mere 1.2 per cent of the popular vote. Although the BNP claims an active membership in both Edinburgh and Glasgow, it struggled to find enough activists to stand in these elections and was forced to import at least fourteen of the thirty-two candidates from South of the border.[36] The future for the BNP in Scotland is hardly brighter, following a series of resignations and sackings in December 2007 that has virtually destroyed the few Scottish branches of the party.

Despite pledging its wholehearted support to the Ulster Loyalist community, the BNP, which in the past has courted paramilitary groups including the Ulster Defence Association (UDA), has made negligible progress in the six counties. Whilst groups such as the UDA have been happy to indulge individual far right activists, viewing them as a potential source for guns and drugs, Loyalist paramilitary groups regard the BNP as an organisation with the same deep-seated suspicion they have for all those involved in mainland politics.

It is a different story in Wales, however. In the May 2007 Welsh Assembly elections the BNP polled 4.3 per cent of the vote, a marked improvement on 2003 when it struggled to achieve 0.3 per cent. In the North Wales constituency the BNP missed out on an Assembly seat by just 2,580 votes. And in Wrexham, where the BNP campaigned hard against Polish migrant labourers, it polled 9.4 per cent of the vote. The

BNP also polled strongly in Alyn and Deeside and Clwyd South, where it gained more than 7 per cent of the vote.[37]

BNP ideologues see that despite their core commitment to the union there is now room for the BNP to exploit and indeed fuel a sense of English chauvinism for its own ends, wrapping the party in the St George flag. BNP Deputy Treasurer David Hannam has argued that unless the BNP wants to become 'outdated' it needs to ride this wave of support of English nationalism. The shift appears entirely opportunistic. In 2006 the BNP AGM passed a motion committing the party to support for an English parliament on the premise that this would strengthen the Union: 'an English parliament for a stronger Britain'.[38] Hannam wrote: 'crucially, our literature is going to have to be more English friendly ... and we are going to have to incorporate our pro-English parliament stance at grassroots level, otherwise we will be pipped at the post by another false-flag party'. Arguing that prefixes such as Black- and Asian-British make Britishness synonymous with the multicultural Britain he is so opposed to, Hannam claims that Englishness is now the only 'refuge for the racially aware voter'.[39] For Hannam: 'English equals white, other ethnicities, born here or not, are explicitly excluded from the nation'. This represents a racial nationalism no longer wedded to Britishness, raising the spectre of devolution, which, for many BNP members, remains an anathema. John Bean, editor of the BNP Magazine *Identity*, did not accept Hannam's argument that independence was ' inevitable'. Others viewed advocating the abandonment of 'British' nationalism as equally spurious, since they believed it to be broad enough to embrace all white-British ethnic identities without contradiction or conflict.

Such a change of policy would leave the BNP in a quandary. But the BNP baulks at the idea of being supplanted by an English nationalist party, let alone one that does not hold to its exclusively racialised definition of Englishness. The EDP views immigration in similar terms to the BNP, as a threat to 'English cultural unity and social cohesion', and proposes a range of measures to restrict immigration. But unlike the BNP, the EDP does accept the reality of multicultural society. The EDP believes that all ethnic groups should be free to promote their own culture and identity, whilst stating that, 'the culture of England should be that of the indigenous English'. Crucially, the EDP defines Englishness not in terms of race but in terms of civic identity. To be English, argue the EDP, is to 'share a sense of communal history, language and culture ... a sense of belonging'. The 'people of England' are defined in purely civic terms as 'all those UK citizens who live in England ... all those UK citizens who are on the electoral roll of an

English constituency ... [and] therefore includes the people of many nations, all of whom share a common UK citizenship'. Much to the disgust of the BNP this has led the EDP to field Asian candidates in elections.[40]

Arguments over race, nation and identity on the far right and populist fringe of British politics are much more complex than their opponents often imagine. These conflicting views, however unpalatable, represent genuine ideological divisions, which for many are insurmountable. Disunity is more prevalent than unity, even within the same party. Indeed at times the BNP is far from being an ideologically cohesive or consistent party. There is not much comfort to be had from this, however. These divisions mask the fact that such views on race, immigration and nationhood have a stronger resonance within contemporary society than Liberals and Leftists may care to admit. The shift of all three Westminster political parties to the soft centre of British politics has ensured that large spaces remain unrepresented. On the far right it is the BNP which is making the greatest headway in exploiting this crisis of representation. It feeds off genuine feelings of powerlessness, disillusionment and disenfranchisement, which should not be lightly dismissed. The BNP filter these trials and tribulations through the prism of race and immigration, its solitary solution to its ultimate aim of a racially purified nation. They are unlikely to succeed at a national level, but their politics of division and exclusion are ignored at the peril of those who value inclusion and diversity. The English left has historically chosen not to engage in any deep and meaningful way with the mainstay of right-wing politics, the notion of identity framed by nation. However, if a positive, progressive politics is to triumph over a backward-looking racially based vision of English nationhood and identity it is precisely these issues with which the left will have to grapple. To do so it will need to articulate a meaningful understanding of community and belonging, identity and nation, that is divorced from the definition the BNP provides.

NOTES

1. Nigel Copsey, *Contemporary British Fascism: The British National Party and the Quest for Legitimacy*, Palgrave 2004.
2. *Constitution of the British National Party* (eighth edition 2004), p2.
3. The BNP constitution defines those eligible to join the party as having to be from one of the following white communities: 'i) The Anglo-Saxon Folk Community; ii) The Celtic Scottish Folk Community; iii) The Scots-Northern Irish Folk Community; iv) The Celtic Welsh Folk Community; v) The Celtic Irish Folk Community; vi) The Celtic Cornish Folk

Community; vii) The Anglo-Saxon Norse Folk Community; viii The Celtic-Norse Folk Community; ix) The Anglo-Saxon-Norse Folk Community; x) The Anglo-Saxon-Indigenous European Folk Community; xi) Members of these ethnic groups who reside either within or outside Europe but ethnically derive from them.'

4. *Rebuilding British Democracy* (2005 BNP general election manifesto), p20.
5. *Constitution of the British National Party* (eighth edition 2004), p3.
6. *Guardian*, 20.12.07.
7. *Rebuilding British Democracy* (2005 BNP general election manifesto), p53.
8. http://www.londonbnp.org.uk/manifesto.html [Accessed 3 January 2007].
9. http://www.stormfront.org/forum/showthread.php/majuba-declaration-boer-nation-born-300815p9.html [Accessed 3 January 2007].
10. *Barking and Dagenham Post*, 18.12.06.
11. http://news.bbc.co.uk/1/world/europe/Jersey/6347185.stm [Accessed 6 December 2007].
12. *The Sunday Times*, 30.04.06.
13. http://www.bnp.org.uk/columnists/brimstone2.php?leeId=67 [Accessed 6 December 2007]. Note whilst completing the editing of this article the BNP revamped their website rendering many of the BNP website links cited inoperable. However, they can still be found on the Internet and so the original references have been left in place.
14. http://www.stormfront.org/forum/showthread.php/racial-ethno-nation-alism-248740.html [Accessed 6 December 2007].
15. http://www.bnp.org.uk/?p=389 [Accessed 3 January 2008].
16. *The Truth about Islam* (BNP leaflet).
17. http://www.bnp.org.uk/news_detail.php?newsId=1078 [Accessed 6 December 2007].
18. http//www.bnp.org.uk/news_detail.php?newsId=990 [Accessed 27 June 2006].
19. *Voice of Freedom*, no. 74, 2006.
20. http://www.bnp.org.uk/columnists/chairman2.php?ngId=29 [Accessed 16 February 2006]
21. http://www.christiancouncil.org.uk/ [Accessed 6 December 2007].
22. *Guardian*, 1.08.07.
23. http://www.londonbnp.org.uk/manifesto.html [Accessed 3 January 2007].
24. *Observer*, 30.05.04.
25. *The Times*, 19.08.04.
26. To state that the BNP are in the ascendant requires some qualification. This is in regards to its position vis-à-vis UKIP. The 2007 local elections saw the overall proportion of the BNP vote shrink from 19.2% across 356 wards in 2006 to 14.6% across 742 wards in 2007.

27. *Identity*, no. 79, June 2007.

28. http://news.bbc.co.uk/1/hi/uk_politics/4875026.stm [Accessed 3 January 2007].

29. Joseph Rowntree Reform Trust, *The Far Right in London: A Challenge for Local Democracy*, JRRT 2005, pp13-14.

30. Peter Gardner, *Hard Pounding: The Story of the UK Independence Party*, June Press 2006, pp193-194.

31. *Evening Standard*, 6.10.04. Lecomber was expelled for 'making a serious error in judgement' in trying to solicit the murder of a Cabinet minister in 2006. His exile was brief, however, and he is now back working on behalf of the BNP in Redbridge, East London, *Searchlight*, no. 390, December 2007. The 2006 BNP accounts now list him as 'nominating officer'.

32. Mark Daniel, *Cranks and Gadflies: The Story of UKIP*, Timewell Press 2005, p174.

33. *Identity*, no. 66, May 2006.

34. *Guardian*, 1.5.02.

35. http://www.thecep.org.uk/OmEnglishParliament.pdf [Accessed 6 December 2007].

36. *The Scotsman*, 8.4.07.

37. *Searchlight*, no. 383, June 2007.

38. http://www.bnp.org.uk/?p=54 [Accessed 3 January 2008].

39. *Identity*, no. 83, October 2007.

40. http://www.englishdemocrats.org.uk/

Labouring for England

Stephen Brasher

In early 2007 Gordon Brown and Douglas Alexander published a Fabian pamphlet putting the case for a continuation of the Union to defend progressive values. A *Guardian* editorial suggested that: 'There is a sense that he [Brown] sees the union ... as a defence against a less generous and more reactionary English identity'.[1] But might there be less honourable motivations? *The Guardian* certainly seemed to think so: 'Sceptics might easily point out that Brown and Alexander seem to become fonder of the union the more its continuation becomes essential to their careers'.[2] These observations share the widespread belief that Labour's support, and its general election victories in particular, owe much more to its strength in Scotland and Wales than in England. There is a presumption that Labour could not win a general election for any future English Parliament. Labour wants the union because England is Tory. But appearances can be misleading. In the general election of 1906 Labour's candidates managed only 5.3 per cent of the vote in the English constituencies. Yet less than forty years later, in its landslide victory of 1945, the Labour percentage in English constituencies exceeded the Tory percentage, and the same was true in the general elections of 1950, 1951, 1964, 1966, Oct 1974, 1997 and 2001. In the 2005 general election the Labour share of the English constituencies' vote was only 0.25 per cent behind the Conservatives. This is a much better showing than many people might imagine. The Tories are perhaps not as dominant in England as is often supposed. So is there a Labour England? And if so, could it survive and even thrive without Scotland and Wales? To make a proper decision about this we need to examine the evolution of Labour England; how it began, and how it and the political landscape has changed over the past century and more.

The original vision of Labour England conjures up the green and pleasant land of William Blake's visionary *Jerusalem*, and a longing to escape the dark satanic mills. Or the soundtrack might be provided by choirs singing Edward Carpenter's socialist hymn *England Arise*:

'England Arise! The long night is over, Faint in the East behold the dawn appear. Out of your evil dream of toil and sorrow, Arise O England for the day is here.' Before Labour existed as a party represented in Parliament, William Morris advanced ideas of how England could be saved by socialism from rampant Victorian capitalism. His 1890 novel *News from Nowhere* envisaged England as a sparsely populated rural idyll and, as the leading character is told, with nothing 'which you, a native of another planet, would call a government'.[3] Morris's near contemporary Robert Blatchford was a soldier turned journalist whose *Clarion* newspaper was probably responsible for introducing more people to socialism than any other English publication in the nineteenth century. In his famous work *Merrie England* he addresses his remarks to a fictional cotton spinner, John Smith from Oldham, an epitome of what he saw as the working man of the time: 'I think also that you will agree with me on three points; Firstly, that Oldham is not a nice place to live in. Secondly that the factory is not a nice place to work in, thirdly that you don't get as good a living as you desire.'[4] A few pages later he re-iterates his point with an interesting geographical comparison. 'As a practical man, would you of your own choice convert a healthy and beautiful country like Surrey into an unhealthy and hideous country like Wigan or Cradley?'.[5] Blatchford seems keen to get rid of potential Labour strongholds. As Keith Laybourn states, 'Up to the 1890s socialism was in the business of "making socialists" and it did not matter to which socialist organization an individual belonged'.[6] By implication, it did not matter too much where they were either. The whole of England would be won over.

The Labour Representation Committee was founded in 1900. Blatchford's Clarion Socialists, together with localised campaigning by the SDF, ILP and trade union branches, gradually gave way to a more national profile. From the beginning the nascent Labour Party was identified with Scotland, Wales and the industrial areas of England. The first county councils to fall under its control were Durham, Glamorgan and Monmouth in 1919, all heavily influenced by the mining industries in these areas. And until the 1945 elections these were still Labour's only county councils (with the significant exception of the Labour control of the London County Council.) The electoral landscape of the interwar period looks a very strange place to us today. Parliamentary seats were often unopposed, both at general elections and by elections. Seats were often lost by the party that held them, generally the Liberals, because they failed to put up a candidate. Tacit or open electoral pacts between parties were commonplace. Nowadays, we expect political parties to contest every seat, however hopeless, at both general and by- elections. Labour did not actually manage this until 1950, and the Liberals did not do so between the end of the First World War and 1983.

It is a commonplace assertion that the interwar Liberal collapse led directly to the party's replacement by Labour. George Dangerfield's much revered work *The Strange Death of Liberal England*, first published in 1935, states the case dramatically: 'Fires long smouldering in the English spirit suddenly flared up, so that by the end of 1913 Liberal England was reduced to ashes. From these ashes, a new England seems to have emerged'.[7] But was this new England a Labour England? Dangerfield paid little attention to electoral politics, and in general terms gives the impression that the House of Lords played more of a part in dethroning the Liberals than the Labour Party. It is important to establish if he was correct. Did one party simply replace the other? The Liberals had been a national party, as likely to win seats in rural Devon as the East End of London. 'Only in a few great urban areas, London, Birmingham and Merseyside did the Conservatives stand to lose more from Labour competition.'[8] The assumption is that one 'progressive' party would replace another, and that the Tory vote would be barely touched. But a closer look at the evidence produces a more complex picture.

Labour did not seriously break through in these 'Tory' areas until 1945, but it would be wrong to assume that they had not been trying to make progress. In particular, Labour developed an anxiety about winning rural seats. As Ross McKibbin explains: 'Attending such beliefs was the sentimental feeling that the rural seats ought to be won – that it was the party's mission to liberate them from the feudal burdens under which they were supposed to languish'.[9] Indeed, the role of the National Union of Agricultural Workers (NUAW) has come to take on an almost mythical importance in Labour Party history, especially in Norfolk where Liberal defector Charles Noel Buxton delivered North Norfolk to Labour as early as 1922. Two presidents of the union, Edwin Gooch and Bert Hazell, were to represent the same seat until 1970. But, as a new study points out: 'The usual assumption was that a railwayman would be first choice to organize a rural party ... the rail unions had members scattered in virtually every constituency'.[10] The National Union of Railwaymen (NUR) made significant contributions to Labour's fighting fund for the countryside in the interwar years, but with precious little to show for it. Labour had a target list, but as Claire Griffiths writes in her conclusion: 'Of the eighteen seats which could be considered rural, according to the criteria used in this study ... most of the eighteen were, in practise, mining seats'.[11] In other words, the rural seats that Labour hoped to win in reality had dual influences in their electoral politics. By and large the Labour agricultural vote could not really manage without the railway vote or the mining vote.

SOCIAL AND POLITICAL CHANGE

Another on Labour's list of 'rural' seats might offer us a better clue about where a larger Labour England was to emerge from. Though nobody who lives in Mitcham and Morden today would consider it in any way rural, it was as a Surrey 'county' seat (still part of Surrey county council, and not a borough in its own right) that it qualified when Chuter Ede made a sensational by election gain in 1923 – in a seat Labour had not previously contested. Of Labour's triumph Herbert Morrison said: 'the new school of Labour politicians is a scientific school. It knows that noisy tub thumping does not make up for a careful organisation'.[12] A further famous by election ten years later, in 1933, reinforces the point. At the time Labour's gain in East Fulham was put down by many to the strength of pacifist feeling among an electorate keen to stop re-armament and a move to war; but, as Martin Ceadel argues, John Wilmot, the Labour candidate, may have been helped by Tory attempts to discredit him for his involvement with a local shareholders Provident Association: 'since the association was known to protect the small investor against fraudulent company promoters it was a source of political strength – not least among middle class voters – for Wilmot, who made his career in banking and later in business'.[13]

The inference is clear. Labour were making, or hoping to make, progress among 'ordinary' middle-class voters in 'ordinary' areas. Herbert Morrison was still making the point a decade later. Recalling his switch from Hackney South to Lewisham East at the 1945 general election, he talked of his preoccupation 'with a longstanding inferiority complex among my colleagues about Labour's chances in what they called respectable suburban areas': 'I felt this attitude was at least twenty five years behind the times and I was ready to put my theory to the test in my own political life'.[14] Labour had failed by only 402 votes in Lewisham East in 1929 and the debacle of 1931 had probably depressed its vote for a generation. But Morrison, the arch calculator, could see the ground shifting. Other constituencies, such as Brixton and Hackney North, were first-time Labour gains at the 1945 election, and the picture is similarly nuanced elsewhere. When Jack Diamond lost his Manchester Blackley seat to the Tories in 1955 he went to Gloucester in search of a better Labour prospect. When Roy Hattersley fought and won Birmingham Sparkbrook in 1964 he was contesting a genuine marginal, which he gained by just over a thousand votes.

Social change has had other effects in the decades since the second world war. Sparkbrook again became marginal at the 2005 election – not to the Tories, who polled under 10 per cent, but to the anti-war Respect Party, who polled 27.5 per cent from a standing start, in a constituency that had the highest proportion of Muslims (48.8 per cent) of anywhere in Great Britain. Here the ethnic minority vote helped the left, but race is frequently deployed to win votes for the right. Race and immigration has had a contradictory effect on voting patterns. Labour's 1945 election triumph saw little if any discussion of race, outside of the issue of Indian independence, but by 1964 this had changed. Nicholas Deakin's *Colour and The British Electorate*, published in 1964, contained case studies of six constituencies where voting was likely to be affected by race: Sparkbrook, Brixton, Bradford, Southall, Smethwick and Deptford. Labour held five of these seats in the 1964 general election of that year. The sole exception was Smethwick, infamously lost to the Tory Peter Griffiths, notorious for his racist campaign that included the slogan: 'If you want a nigger for a neighbour, vote Labour'. Smethwick was regained in the 1966 general election, however, and over forty years later Labour still holds all of these seats, though the English political landscape has changed considerably. In his conclusion Deakin stated Labour's dilemma succinctly: 'For the Labour party, whose emotional commitments are the brotherhood of working men and more recently, the commonwealth ideal, the tension between these ideals and the hostility felt by a section of its supporters is strong and will probably increase.'[15] The intervention of Enoch Powell considerably increased this discomfort. As Taylor and Johnston point out, 'Powell's popularity was demonstrable in that whereas the national swing to Conservative in 1970 was 4.7 percentage points, in Wolverhampton the swing … was 9.1 and 8.7 percentage points.'[16] They also hypothesise that Labour's better than average performance in West Midlands seats in the 1974 elections was due to Powell's anti-EEC instruction to vote Labour.

Today Labour is, arguably, managing to successfully negotiate previously contrary shifts in votes. It has won three successive general election victories, including many English suburban and rural seats won for the first time, while still holding eighteen of the twenty seats with the highest proportion of Black and Asian voters. Triangulation might have been expected to be more difficult than that. It is often said that Labour's commitment to multiculturalism has cost it votes in so called 'white flight' areas such as Aldridge Brownhills or Bromsgrove in the West Midlands – seats held up until the 1970s but never since. Yet is arguable that it has gained just as much ground amongst ethnic minority voters, particularly in previously marginal urban areas where the Tories have been almost eliminated. Labour would hope that increasing diversity in an independent England would work in its favour.

Labour might also have hoped for fertile ground in the social experiment that was the new towns movement. The first, Stevenage, was started under the Attlee government in 1948 and, until it boasted a seat of its own, helped Labour to win first Hitchin (1945 and then 1964-74) and then Hertford until 1979. Stevenage remains Labour's only reasonably sure bet in Hertfordshire at both council and general election levels. But otherwise the political inheritance is more mixed. The growth of Telford helped Labour to maintain its hold on the Wrekin seat as mining in Shropshire declined, and it now forms a safe seat of its own. But Peterborough, famous for marginal contests in both pre and post war elections has stayed just that – marginal, and leaning to the Tories in all but Labour landslide years. Elsewhere, the extensive relocations of working-class populations, coupled with the large-scale building of public housing, has similarly either reinforced existing voting patterns (Warrington, Washington, Corby, Runcorn) or created marginal status (Hemel Hempstead, Welwyn Hatfield, Milton Keynes and – most famously of all – Basildon). Only in Bracknell has Labour never posed a serious parliamentary threat. It seems that new town status helped Labour to become competitive in these previously rural areas, but not dominant.

It was the Conservative hegemony of 1979-1997 that did the most damage to the concept of a Labour England. Four successive election defeats led many to believe that Labour could never win another election – even with Labour's enduring electoral strength in Scotland and Wales. In looking at the decline of Labour's share of the vote, although the advent of Mrs Thatcher is usually pinpointed as signalling its beginning, it is important to go back to Labour's unexpected defeat in 1970. In 1970 seats such as Falmouth and Camborne (Labour since the Second World War) and Dartford (sometimes Labour even before the second world war), were lost. And although some seats were temporarily regained in the 1974 elections, the spectre of electoral defeat was already evident with the loss of these previously solid Labour constituencies. In John Mortimer's *Paradise Postponed*, the character Leslie Titmuss is ridiculed by his Labour-voting contemporaries when in the 1950s he joins the Young Conservatives.[17] Two decades later he becomes the local MP, in a seat apparently modelled on Faversham. Labour lost Faversham in 1970 and has never regained it. After the

1992 election Giles Radice wrote the Fabian Society pamphlet *Southern Discomfort*, declaring that 'Taken as a whole the South East (excluding London) has become one huge Tory safe seat.'[18] After the 1997 general election this picture of Tory dominance in England was challenged, but even in 2006 John Denham MP wrote, in another Fabian Society pamphlet on the same theme, *Southern Discomfort Revisited*: 'In the recent past we seem to have slipped into old habits ... Some people think that the South is inherently hostile territory for Labour; a place where we can only hope for strongholds, and a few toeholds. They fear that Labour could only win here at the expense of losing our soul'.[19] It can hardly be denied that there are a large number of seats that Labour can never hope to win in the South. Postwar Surrey has seen only one non-Tory MP, and then only for four years (LibDem MP Sue Doughty in Guildford, 2001-5). And in Cambridgeshire, which has gained more parliamentary seats than anywhere else in the postwar period, only Cambridge itself is likely not to be Conservative. But the problem can be overstated. Labour currently hold five seats in Sussex, where they had previously only ever held one before, and that for only four years (Brighton Kemptown 1966-1970). And Robert Tressell, author of the most important work of English socialism *The Ragged Trousered Philanthropists*, whose 'Mugsborough' is of course Hastings, would be astonished that the place where 'they were never able to form a branch of their (socialist) society'[20] now has a thrice elected Labour MP, the first non-Tory there for over a hundred years. (He would probably be quite chuffed to find out that there is also a local council ward named after him.) Stanley Baldwin would be equally amazed that his beloved Harrow school is now in a constituency represented by a Labour MP, Gareth Thomas, MP for Harrow West, who, though a beneficiary of the 1997 landslide, may well continue in the Commons, thanks to favourable boundary changes.

THE DEATH OF TORY ENGLAND?

Perhaps the most astonished of all would be George Dangerfield: to find that anyone ever had cause to write a book called *The Strange Death of Tory England*. Its author, Geoffrey Wheatcroft, makes an interesting counterpoint to the usual portrayal of Labour as a 'northern' party, when he asserts that after the 1997 election 'the Tories had become an English party'. Or indeed, as he argued, they were a regional party of Southern England, 'unhappily similar to the Bavarian Christian Social Union or the Northern League in Italy'.[21] Wheatcroft surely has a case. The Tories are now just another political party, having to compete in places they had always previously taken for granted. Cornwall has had no Tory MPs since 1997, and Labour held on to all its eight seats in Kent in 2005, despite being written off in the county for most of the previous thirty-five years.

Dangerfield would also be astonished to find out that the Labour mining seat has been joined by the Labour seaside seat. Previously Tory Blackpool now has two Labour MPs, and is joined by Morecambe, both Brighton seats, Hastings, Margate, Weymouth, and Scarborough (until 2005).[22] Plus of course, Hove. As Brian Cathcart memorably recalled in his book of the 1997 landslide, 'Hove. Hold on. Hove? *Hove?*... If the Tories can't hold that he [Jeremy Paxman] observed, something really seismic must be going on'.[23]

Hove was a seat that the Liberals failed to win even in their series of by-election triumphs in the early 1970s, and Labour's three consecutive victories there in general elections from 1997 to 2005 might seem to indicate to outside observers that Liberal England had not revived. But the Liberal Democrats now have the highest total of MPs for the third party since 1931, and they have expanded far beyond the Celtic fringe that was supposed to be their final redoubt. In 2001 Chesterfield was the Liberals' first gain from Labour at a general election since the second world war, and subsequent by elections and general election gains in 2005 have re-enforced the point. Few would dispute that a large part of the switch in votes was as a result of the Iraq war – forming a curious reverse echo of Labour's emergence as the main opposition party after the first world war, when sections of the Liberal Party at all levels left for Labour over their discomfort with the first world war. This Liberal Democrat advance seems to threaten Labour from the centre left, but it is important to remember that the vast majority of their MPs hold what were previously long-term Tory seats, even most of those it won from Labour in 2005. In the early postwar period Labour's percentage vote was helped by Liberal decline. But sixty years on it is arguable that it is being helped by Liberal Democrat revival. And it is not just a third party that impacts on Tory and Labour England. Even under the first-past-the-post system, the Green Party, BNP, Respect and others are now targeting their support, to try to impact at a parliamentary level in a way not previously seen in British politics.

Electoral change is like geological change. It is easy to draw conclusions from recent spectacular events, but it is also necessary to look at trends on a longer time scale. Boundary alterations, social change and Britain's electoral system all conspire to make it easy to draw interesting but erroneous conclusions from electoral statistics. Labour

England was a long time in the making, yet it looks as if it could survive any future break-up of Britain. But it would be unlikely to be able to govern without help. The survival of Labour England could well depend on, and lead to, the birth of Coalition England. It is difficult to imagine that any purely English election would be fought on anything other than some sort of PR system, and this would have huge implications for Labour England. Although it would have lost its many Welsh and Scottish MPs, Labour would be in a key position to form a progressive coalition with the Liberal Democrats and any Green MPs that might well also be elected. In the slightly longer term, Labour could hope to pick up support in some areas where its vote has been suppressed by the current electoral system, while conceding some ground in its heartlands. It is also clear that it would be well-nigh impossible for the Tories to have an overall majority in any English parliament. Labour was never quite as dominant as it seemed at its times of triumph, nor quite as diminished in its eras of defeats, especially during the Thatcher years. It has survived and won by changing and adapting as English society has changed and adapted. It is perfectly possible that at some point in the future Labour's accommodation with Englishness will take shape without the constitutional presence of Scotland (and less likely, Wales). It is an accommodation, therefore, that will prepare Labour rather well for such a shock to the system.

NOTES

1. Editorial, *The Guardian*, 9.4.07.
2. Ibid.
3. William Morris, *News from Nowhere*, Reeves and Turner 1891, p88.
4. Robert Blatchford, *Merrie England*, Clarion Press 1894, p14.
5. Ibid, p22.
6. Keith Laybourn, *Rise of Socialism in Britain*, Sutton Publishing 1997, p50.
7. George Dangerfield, *The Strange Death of Liberal England*, Paladin, reprint 1988, p14.
8. Ross McKibbin, *The Evolution of the Labour Party 1910-1924*, OUP (pbk edition) 1991, p48.
9. Ibid, p151.
10. Claire V.J. Griffiths, *Labour and the Countryside – the politics of Rural Britain 1918-1939*, OUP 2007, p153.
11. Ibid, p323.
12. Norman Howard, *A New Dawn – the general election of 1945*, Politicos 2007, p130.
13. Martin Ceadel, 'Interpreting East Fulham', in Chris Cook, *By-elections in British Politics*, Macmillan 1973, p124.

14. Howard, op. cit., p130.
15. Nicholas Deakin (ed), *Colour and the British Electorate 1964*, Pall Mall Press 1964, p166.
16. P.J. Taylor and R.J. Johnston, *Geography of Elections*, Penguin 1979, p296.
17. John Mortimer, *Paradise Postponed*, Viking 1985.
18. Giles Radice, *Southern Discomfort*, Fabian Society 1992, p1.
19. John Denham MP, *Southern Discomfort Revisited*, Fabian Lecture 2006.
20. Robert Tressell, *The Ragged Trousered Philanthropists*, unabridged version, Lawrence and Wishart 1955, p430.
21. Geoffrey Wheatcroft, *Strange Death of Tory England*, Allen Lane 2005, p233.
22. Robert Waller and Byron Criddle, *Almanac of British Politics*, 8th edition, Routledge 2007.
23. Brian Cathcart, *Were you still up for Portillo?*, Penguin 1997, p72.

New traditions for an old country

Billy Bragg

In recent years the English Question has moved from the outer fringes of political debate into the chamber of the Westminster parliament itself. While devolution has brought power closer to home for the peoples of Scotland, Wales and Northern Ireland, the English have been left to wonder how they might benefit from a little devolution of their own.

Yet where to start? Would an English parliament be able to sustain politics that were distinctive enough from Westminster to deliver the kind of benefits that Scotland has enjoyed in terms of health care and education? For the Scots, devolution was a simple enough proposition. Westminster's powers ended at the border. England, however, has no such border with which to distinguish itself from the British parliament based in its own capital city. Where does Britain end and England begin?

Since my book, *The Progressive Patriot* was published in 2006, I've taken part in numerous debates about the politics of national identity.[1] Time and again, I've encountered the inability of the English to be able to differentiate clearly between their own country and the British state. It's not merely the annoying habit of saying British when we mean English and vice versa – a subconscious tic that even I am prey to. There is a genuine paucity of English signifiers for us to call upon when engaging with our neighbours.

The Irish, Welsh and Scots recognise each other with nicknames that have roots in their distinct national identities. 'Paddy' is derived not from the English 'Patrick' but from the Gaelic 'Padraig'. 'Taffy' comes from the English perception of the Welsh pronunciation of 'Dafydd', while 'Jock', related to Jacob, may be associated with anti-English Jacobite sympathies. Of course these are all blokes' names, which tells us something about how the representation of national identity – like many representations – is male-dominated. And this name-calling can also be abusive, racist even, though, to be fair, more often than not they are the stuff of affectionate banter and self-identification. For example, look at how many Irish and Scots drinking holes are known as 'Paddy's Pub' or 'Jock's Bar'.

Yet what name do we have for the generic English? The Scots have a word for us, *Sassenach* – and there are equivalents in Welsh and Irish – which translates as 'Saxon', but that is a descriptive term rather than a nickname and comes loaded with negative connotations. 'Tommy' is a name used for the English soldier but you never hear that used in a civilian sense. 'Pommie', 'Limey' or 'Rosbif' don't really fit the bill as they are not derived from genuine first names. 'John Smith' might be thought of as an archetypal English name, but our neighbours don't need the addition of a surname to signify their nationality, and of course it's very close to 'John Bull', the name given to the archetypal Briton. Why has no familiar nickname for the English developed over the three hundred years of the British union? It's something of a historical anomaly.

Do such trivialities really matter? I believe they do if we hope to find a way to differentiate between our English and British identities. Behind the mateyness mostly inherent in the concepts of 'Paddy', 'Taffy' and 'Jock', our fellow Britons are able to appreciate their own national cultures without feeling obliged to first shake off the trappings of Britishness.

Another example of England's lack of a sense of self is the issue of national costume. Everyone is familiar with the Scotsman's kilt and most of us have seen pictures of Welsh women wearing their traditional black hats and embroidered shawls. The Irish can signify all manner of things by simply 'wearing the green'.

However, England fans looking to express their patriotism are reduced to dressing as St George, who, incidentally, wouldn't have qualified to play for our country as he was born in the Lebanon. Desperate for something to signify her nationality, the organisers of the Miss World contest used to send out Miss England dressed as a Beefeater. Even Ken Bailey, the England mascot-man who paraded with the national team in the 1960s, 1970s and 1980s wore a Union Jack waistcoat – check out his Subbuteo figure if you don't believe me.

Without a familiar nickname, national costume, not even a national anthem with which to define ourselves within the British state, we have instead to look for other cultural markers that the English identify with.

Anyone who watches TV will be aware of the popularity of bodice-ripping costume dramas such as *Pride and Prejudice*. This has always been a factor of English culture, but over the past decade they have made a significant contribution to the way we see ourselves. Whereas

Big Brother shows us the worst aspects of our society, costume dramas show us the virtue of respectability and good manners, values that the English at their best have traditionally sought to uphold.

Authors such as the Bronte Sisters, Mrs Gaskell and John Major's favourite novelist, Anthony Trollope were all born during the Regency Period that provides the backdrop to their most popular works. Although strictly referring to the period 1811-1820, when George III was deemed unfit to rule and his son the Prince Regent ruled in his place, the term is popularly used to denote the early years of the nineteenth century before Queen Victoria came to the throne. Jane Austen's novels, which with their gentle humour define the genre, were all published between 1811 and 1817.

The Regency period was also a time of great social change. On the world stage, Napoleon was finally defeated in 1815, allowing Britain to begin consolidating its overseas empire. Domestically, the advent of the railways in the 1830s had begun to transform England from a horse-drawn society into one in which the pace of change thundered along, leaving little time for the social niceties that Austen had worked into her plot lines. No sooner was it over than the English began to look back on the Regency Period with nostalgia.

The greatest of the Victorian novelists, Charles Dickens, made his reputation with a book that looked back to a time within the memory of most of his audience, lovingly painting a portrait of a happier, simpler existence. *The Pickwick Papers* was set in the 1820s and tells the story of a group of friends, based in London, who travel around England in search of nothing in particular. In its leading character, Mr Pickwick, Dickens gave us perhaps the most likely candidate for an archetypal English figure.

Middle-aged, balding, stout of girth and red of cheek, Samuel Pickwick is usually depicted in tailcoat tights and gaiters, cherubic face adorned with circular spectacles, topped off with a short-crowned top hat. At heart a generous old soul, Pickwick's naivety gets him into all sorts of unfortunate misunderstandings, which, though often calamitous, never seem to dampen his spirits. Over the past few decades, West End and TV versions of darker Dickens classics such as *Nicolas Nickleby* and *Bleak House* have seen *The Pickwick Papers* fall from popular taste, yet the character of Pickwick retains a strong hold on the English imagination.

The Scots have a word, 'tartanry', which alludes to the kitschier elements of Highland culture, which often obscure the real nature of contemporary Scottishness, suggesting that nothing can truly be Scottish unless it is draped in tartan. In England, this attachment to kitsch manifests itself in a faux-antiquity that harks back to the simpler, gentler, pre-industrialised world of *The Pickwick Papers*. Ye Olde Shoppe signs; fox-hunting prints in suburban pubs; businesses that refer to themselves as 'purveyors'; villages designed by Prince Charles. All represent a subtle shorthand that seeks to provide a comforting sense of middle-class superiority, but this sentimental attachment to the Regency style is nothing less than a pervasive Pickwickery that seeks to stifle any hint of originality in English taste.

Our strong yet subliminal identification with this period of our history creates difficulties when we seek to define where Britishness ends and Englishness begins. Although the Scots and the Welsh identities have their roots in the Regency Period – the clan tartans were invented by Sir Walter Scott in 1822 and Welsh aristocrat Lady Llanover designed the 'traditional' women's garb for the Eisteddfod of 1834 – both were subsequently taken up as symbols of nationalist movements in opposition to the British state.

The English Regency, however, merges seamlessly into the classical Britishness of the Victorian period, once again blurring the line between English and British. Is it any wonder therefore that the English slip unconsciously between these two identities? Should that necessarily be a problem? Aren't we both English and British at the same time? Well, yes, but we're also both British and European, and we don't seem to have the same trouble there in distinguishing which is which.

In the past, such distinctions might have been academic. The English dealt with the question of our national identity by not dealing with it – some argue that being vague about who we are is our defining characteristic. Yet soon we may have to give the issue our full attention. While England, Scotland, Wales and Ireland have each existed in some form or another for over a thousand years, Great Britain is a relatively recent construct and one whose existence has been marked by periodic change.

The first British state was only founded in the eighteenth century, consisting of England, Wales and Scotland. In the nineteenth century, Ireland was added. During the twentieth century, the Irish became independent, leaving only Northern Ireland within the Union. The twenty-first century will doubtless witness a continuation of this trend of change, particularly if the benefits of devolution lead seamlessly towards independence.

There is no point in hoping that, just so long as the English continue to sing *God Save the Queen as* our national anthem, the English Question might go away. Momentum is already building up behind the break-up of Britain and, for once, the English, the majority nation, are not driving the process forwards. Most of the impetus is coming from the Scottish National Party, who have used their narrow victory in the 2007 Scottish Parliament elections to put independence back on the agenda. Clever use of their budgeting powers has allowed the SNP administration to offer better social services to their citizens, making the case for greater devolution.

In normal times, such talk north of the border would be countered by the Conservatives, traditionally a staunch unionist party. But these are not normal times. The Conservatives have only one MP in Scotland and are a minority party in the Scottish Parliament. However, the electoral arithmetic at the last election gave them a small majority among the English seats at Westminster. Unable to resist the temptation, the Tories have begun demanding that, as English MPs can no longer vote on domestic Scottish issues – that power has been devolved to Edinburgh – then Scottish MPs should no longer be allowed to vote on domestic English issues. The fact that the Prime Minister Gordon Brown represents a Scottish constituency only adds to the Tories' sense of mischief.

Sections of the London-based 'national' media have followed this lead by drawing attention to what they perceive as lavish public spending in Scotland, pointing out that the better standards of social services that the Scots enjoy are subsidised by English taxpayers. Never mind that the whole point of the devolution settlement was to allow the Scots and Welsh to set their own priorities. By stoking up English anger, the Tories and their media allies risk playing into the hands of the SNP.

For there can be no going back from devolution. Voters don't like being disenfranchised. Margaret Thatcher may have abolished Ken Livingstone's GLC in 1986, but he had the last laugh when the Greater London Assembly was created in its eventual place and Ken was resoundingly elected London Mayor. If the Tories want to overturn the Union's status quo, the most likely outcome will be more powers devolved to Edinburgh, which in turn will enhance the SNP's argument for full independence. We risk being drawn into a constitutional crisis by a political party determined to exploit the cracks in the British union for its own ends, seemingly unconcerned by the possibility that the whole thing might break up.

While some may welcome such developments, the fact that the English question has yet to mobilise the political imagination of the English people may be indicative of a deeper malaise. The Union has served the English well, putting us in a dominant position in the British state, allowing the English to hold on to any lingering imperial pretensions. While the Scots confidently seek out their own relationship with the European Union, being British is a comfort blanket with which the English hide a sense of insecurity.

Our continuing reluctance to drop *God Save the Queen* in favour of an English national anthem is fast becoming an embarrassment. Despite our passion for the England teams that line up on the pitch, we belt out a national anthem that doesn't belong uniquely to us. Are we England fans or Britain fans when England play Scotland? To even ask the question reveals the confusion at stake, and perhaps a residual unwillingness, discomfort even, with being merely English?

This cultural cringe is fed by current manifestations of English nationalist sentiment. These tend to take the form of resentment; towards the Scots, for their alleged profligacy with our money; towards the EU, whose federalist plotting apparently requires that Britain be broken up into digestible regions; and towards the politicians who must all be mad for cooking up and collaborating with such a crazy idea as devolution in the first place. While the debate is controlled by Little Englanders, we have no hope of engaging with the vast majority of the fair-minded English who would like a little more devolved power for their nation

Traditional depictions of Englishness may also be a contributing factor. If, every time we go looking for a contemporary English identity we are offered nothing more than the banalities of Pickwickery, there is little chance of us forging a forward-looking sense of who we are, one which allows us to confidently sit down with our neighbours and make devolution work for us all.

At such times nicknames, costumes and anthems take on a much greater significance. For if we hope to overcome the confusion then we need a debate not just about what it means to be English in the twenty-first century, but how best to communicate the styles and ideas that we believe define us in the modern world.

We've already begun this process with the flag of St George. Twenty years ago, the only place you were likely to see this age-old symbol of Englishness was flying from the tower of an Anglican church or in the hands of the far right. Since then it's been dusted down and shorn of its bigotry by people looking for some meaningful way to portray their sense of national identity. The challenge we face is to find other signifiers that make the sense of pride we feel in being English accessible to all our fellow citizens.

NOTE

1. Billy Bragg, *The Progressive Patriot: A Search for Belonging*, Bantam Press, London 2006.

Is it 'cos I is English?

The contradictions of an early twenty-first century national identity

Richard Weight

'**B**eing English is a bit like breathing. I only think about it when someone tries to stop me doing it.' So said a caller to a BBC Five Live discussion I was involved in recently. His comment captures two aspects of English national identity: the traditional belief that Englishness is such a natural state of being there's no need to crow about it in the way that immodest foreigners do about their nationality. And the contemporary view that English national consciousness has grown in the last decade because the English are being actively prevented from expressing who they are.[1]

Who exactly has their hand on the windpipe of fifty million people? Some argue that a Scottish political elite is running Britain, helping to ensure that the Treasury's generous fiscal subsidy to the Scots is maintained and – symbolically – replacing Edward Elgar with Adam Smith on the £20 Bank of England note.[2] All this echoes the Scotophobia of the late eighteenth century in which people questioned the Union on the grounds that Scots had taken over the British state through chambers of commerce, having failed to do so on the battlefield. How justified is contemporary English anxiety?

The Scottish National Party fostered and exploited anti-Englishness from when it was founded in 1934, but it has now begun publicly to celebrate Englishness and the bonds that our countries share. In a St George's Day article for *The Times*, former SNP Leader John Swinney wrote: 'Moving on from Britain has never meant breaking the social ties that we share. From Sean Connery to *Coronation Street*, from Robert Louis Stevenson to Shakespeare, common cultural experiences are shared by all residents of this island.'[3] This policy has been a pragmatic attempt to reassure moderate Scots that independence would not mean the Balkanisation of Britain, while also encouraging the growth of English nationalism in order to put pressure on the Unionist establishment at Westminster.

The reality is that anti-Englishness is still rife north of the border and continues to underpin Scottish identity. One study by the University of Glasgow found that among immigrants in Scotland who have experienced ethnic jokes 'very often', 74 per cent of English respondents believed that the Scots were 'generally Anglophobic', while only 37 per cent of Pakistanis believed that such jokes showed the Scots to be 'generally racist'.[4] The SNP's articulation of civic, as opposed to ethnic, nationalism has been so successful that Asian Scots (the country's largest ethnic minority) now vote for the SNP more than any other political party, despite continuing to suffer prejudice on the same scale as that experienced by minorities in England.[5] That's because Scottish nationalists have convinced them that what they share with white Scots is a history of being colonised by the English. This audacious re-writing of Scottish history, in which England's former imperial partner presents itself as a fellow victim of rapacious Anglo-Saxons, may be disingenuous, but it has done what the English have so far failed to do – create what political scientists are now calling 'multicultural nationalism'.

RIVERS OF CRUD [6]

Englishness has also come to rest on victim-hood, a feeling that all nationalist movements depend upon to mobilise support. But England's sense of oppression is not yet accompanied by self-confidence or political vision, which north of the border put the SNP in power for the first time in 2007. English anxiety about Caledonian influence in southern affairs is compounded by jealousy of the fact that the Scots and Welsh have a clear sense of who they are and are free to articulate that identity, not least through the Scottish Parliament and Welsh Assembly they voted for in the devolution referendums of 1997. On the 2001 census, the options for white people in England and Wales were 'British', 'Irish' and 'Other', while in Scotland a Scottish option was included. This seemed to confirm that the white English had become a non-people.[7]

The English identity crisis is closely bound up with the politics of race. Those who feel that their English nationality is being denied usually point to 'political correctness gone mad', by which they mean that ethnic minorities are indulged at the expense of the majority.[8] The result, they feel, is that tolerance – that great English virtue – is abused, thus calling into question the efficacy of multiculturalism, rather than the willingness of the English to live up to their principles. Apocryphal stories abound of taxi drivers being banned from flying the George flag during football tournaments.[9] The educational underachievement and anti-social behaviour of working-class children have even been blamed on the confusion about what Englishness is. One youth worker in Birmingham told *The Times*: 'Black kids are proud to be black, Asian kids are proud to be Indian or Pakistani. There's not a lot of cultural identity for white Anglo-Saxon males'.[10] The belief in 'tolerance abuse' has intensified with the rise of Islamic extremism, and the fact that most of the men convicted for terrorist offences in the UK have been English-born, or raised here, whereas in the US most have been foreign nationals.[11]

Attitudes to race and religion exemplify the way that ignorance about the origins and nature of modern England, far more than political correctness, is hampering the development of a modern English identity. England, which defined itself for 400 years as a Protestant nation is now one of the world's most secular societies, with 69 per cent of the population never attending a religious service, up from 26 per cent in 1964. Charles Darwin graces the Bank of England's £10 note and nobody minds (imagine what would happen in the US if he appeared on the dollar bill).[12] The white majority place religion seventh out of ten in their list of priorities, compared to second for Asians and third for the predominantly Christian Afro-Caribbean population.[13] Whites are consequently less likely to practice whatever faith they have, and the Church of England has acknowledged that in some inner cities black immigrants and their descendents are keeping open many churches that would otherwise have to close.[14] Yet Christianity is tacitly defended as part of a white national heritage that's being destroyed by immigration. This was apparent in some of the reaction to the Archbishop of Canterbury's clumsy suggestion that aspects of sharia law might be introduced to Britain. It was also apparent when British Airways legally stopped an employee from displaying a crucifix on her uniform. The *Daily Express* opined that 'Britain is a Christian country ... and the British people are very angry at continuing assaults on their heritage and culture' by 'politically correct busybodies'.[15]

The English sense of victim-hood mines a deep seam of Powellism in the nation's psyche, according to which the working classes have been betrayed, forced against their will and without consultation to live in an alien and dangerous multi-racial environment, which its middle-class architects can physically avoid because of their greater wealth. Ostensibly liberal commentators have recently been burning this fossil fuel again, with one of the most noxious clouds being pumped into the atmosphere by Michael Collins. In his 'biography of the white working class', *The Likes of Us*, he imagines a golden age of working-class monoculture unsullied by immigration. 'White flight' to the suburbs he sees as an almost biblical exodus forced upon the Cockney 'salt of the

earth' by the criminal reality of life lived with black people since the
1950s. His folk devils are 'middle-class liberal journalists', whose accusations of racism from the comfort of their 'lofts and lattes' are really
motivated by snobbery.[16] Ubiquitous use of the term 'chav', and in
America 'white trash', does show that class hatred is still rife. But to
blame the black English, even indirectly, for the 'decline' of white
working-class culture is absurd, because that culture, like every other
in these Isles, was never pure. And the way it changed in the second
half of the twentieth century had much to do with consumerism and
the influence of America, which is ironic, because that's something
Collins's Cockney heroes share with the black working classes they
supposedly fear so much.[17]

Throughout Europe since the eighteenth century 'rootless'
cosmopolitan intelligentsias have been blamed for frustrating nationalism. George Orwell's criticisms of the English left were certainly
necessary in the 1930s and resonated again in the 1980s. 'England is
perhaps the only great country whose intellectuals are ashamed of their
own nationality', he famously wrote in *The Lion and the Unicorn*.[18]
That's less true now though, and if there remains a gut feeling of
English nationalism as 'awful, horrible, leave it to the yobs', it's as
likely to come from the right.[19] For example, Simon Heffer's study of
Englishness, which bravely advocated the end of Union, concluded
that the 'civilised and educated classes' were best fitted to lead the
breakaway rather than 'the spiky-haired louts with red and white faces'
who follow the national football team.[20]

G.K. Chesterton's 1907 poem *The Secret People* is often quoted as
the cry of a majority denied a voice in their own country: 'Smile at us,
pay us, pass us; but do not quite forget/ For we are the people of
England who have not spoken yet'. The cultural critic Patrick Wright
nails the poem's appeal: 'It is a semi-instinctive theory of encroachment
that allows even the most well-placed man in the world to imagine
himself a member of an endangered aboriginal minority: a freedom
fighter striking out against "alien" values and the infernal workings of a
usurping state'.[21] The secret people are not actually very secret. They
can be heard daily on radio phone-ins, in bars and restaurants, on public
transport and, yes, in taxis, bemoaning the fact that they are forbidden
from being English. The question is: are they being listened to?

BRITS WHA HAE!

English nationalists are heard loud and clear by politicians and policy
makers; they're just not being given the answers they want.
Conservative leaders since Margaret Thatcher have whipped up British

nationalism by encouraging discontent with immigration, Europe and devolution. But their instinctive unionism has stopped them properly addressing 'the English question', while the essentially Victorian, imperial vision of Britain on which their unionism is based precludes any imaginative reform of Britishness.[22] In contrast, Labour leaders since Neil Kinnock have engaged with historical debates about national identity. As well as delivering devolution to Scotland and Wales, the Blair and Brown governments have confronted traditional left-wing distaste for patriotism and made a concerted attempt to nurture post-imperial Britishness. When mooting the idea of a 'British Day' comparable to America's 4th of July, Gordon Brown declared: 'We in our party should feel pride in a British patriotism and patriotic purpose founded on liberty for all, responsibility by all, and fairness to all'.[23]

Attempts to articulate a radical Englishness have been less frequent because the Labour Party has its own electoral interests in maintaining the Union and discouraging any initiatives that might further the cause of separation. Former Home Secretary David Blunkett is one of the few who has argued that a radical Englishness could be made to serve the reform of Britishness. Speaking to the Institute for Public Policy Research in 2005 he said:

> We can build a new sense of English identity, finding its place among the plural identities of the United Kingdom and supporting a wider Britishness. Englishness can be experienced, asserted and celebrated in the fabric of existence as a community: in our habits, casts of mind, the culture that we daily create and re-create. We can find it in our traditions of fairness and civic duty and in our spirit of imagination and invention. In this way we can overcome bigotry, insularity and hostility.[24]

Fine words, but as yet nothing practical has been done to build an English national identity that's fit for purpose. There is no English national anthem so we still have to put up with singing *God Save the Queen* (of the 32 countries that took part in football's 2006 World Cup, England was the only one not to have its own anthem). There is still no St. George's Day Public Holiday, despite the fact that it is also Shakespeare's birthday (and as St George came, like Morris Dancing, from the Middle East, the holiday would also symbolise England's historic diversity).[25]

There has also been no resolution of the constitutional imbalance left by devolution, since New Labour's flirtation with regional assemblies failed to excite voters. The workings of government may not vex the English people as much as symbols of nationhood do, and in any case a Bill of Rights for all Britons would do more to foster citizenship than the creation of an English parliament or a reduction in the voting rights of Scottish MPs.[26] But the constitution surely does matter, and the most pragmatic reformers should remember that allowing people, in Evelyn Waugh's phrase, to 'put out more flags', will not necessarily stop the demand for a more political expression of their nationality. After a vigorous campaign, in 1960 the Welsh were finally given the right to fly their national flag in public, having previously had to ask permission from the Crown to do so (it's still absent from the Union Jack, one reason why that flag lacks legitimacy). A people thought to be unconcerned with political devolution and placated by the fluttering of a red dragon went on to support the creation of a Welsh Assembly.

More people in England currently favour the creation of an English parliament than they do membership of the Euro.[27] As well as underlining discontent with New Labour's constitutional settlement, that's a reflection of the Euroscepticism of the English, compared to their more cannily open-minded Scottish and Welsh neighbours, for whom membership of the EU is somewhere between a welcome check on English power and an alternative to the UK. English xenophobia won't be tempered without concrete acceptance of England's uniqueness. But, instead, the New Labour project seeks to foster a more civic Britishness. So, for example, Lord Goldsmith (appointed to head the Government's 'citizenship review') suggested that *God Save the Queen* 'is outdated and needs a rewrite' with words that are 'more inclusive'.[28] The reconfiguring of Britishness, including a re-write of the national anthem, remains a necessary project that all progressive Britons should support. But to be successful it must be accompanied by recognition of the distinctiveness of the four nations that comprise the UK, including the English elephant that stands, blowing its trumpet, in the smart open-plan living room that's been designed for its cuter co-habitants. The need to act is becoming more urgent, for when the Conservatives eventually return to power there will be fewer opportunities to address English discontent progressively.

Both liberal and conservative unionists talk a great deal about the need to instil 'British values', while debating which histories have shaped and demonstrated those values. Whether they prefer the Chartists or Churchill, each side agrees that among the things we cherish are 'liberty', 'duty', 'tolerance' and 'fair play'.[29] The search for British values has spilled over into debates about what constitutes Englishness. That's a good thing if we are to avoid returning to an exclusively ethnic definition of Englishness based on bloodlines rather than culture lines. So what should be in our patriotic primer for the

twenty-first century? Given how many people still think multicultural England began in the 1950s, it's vital that more realise, for
example, that fish and chips are as much a product of immigration
(invented with the help of continental Jewish refugees in the nineteenth
century) as that cliché of diversity Chicken Tikka Masala.[30] The
language we speak should also be historically amplified. Next time
you're gazumped in the housing market or you eat some nosh, remember that those terms are originally Yiddish, many more of which are
found in the Oxford English Dictionary (founded by a Scot), alongside
those words of Asian, African and Caribbean origin that so vex today's
guardians of the morals of English youth.

It's also important that we include modern pop culture in our story
of England, however embarrassing some find its association with sex
and drugs, and however compromised it is by corporate commerce.
While the Beatles are second only to Shakespeare on most people's list
of what makes them proud to be English, there's still a Puritanism on
the left, as well as the right, that regards pop culture as an improper
source of pride. That Puritanism condemned 'Cool Britannia' to the
dustbin of spin when in fact Blair was saying something important
about the need to broaden the parameters of patriotism. When the Sex
Pistols reformed for their thirtieth anniversary concerts at Brixton
Academy in 2007, this was not only four men exploiting nostalgia to
sort out their pensions but also fans sharing in a collective enjoyment
of critical patriotism every bit as authentic as support for England's
underachieving football team. With St George Cross flags as well as
Union Jacks adorning drum kits and speakers, the band took to the
stage with Vera Lynn's *There'll Always Be An England* playing on the
PA, cheered on by fans ranging in age from 10 to 60, who sang together
with equal gusto when the Pistols performed their own *God Save the
Queen*.

There is still no future in England's dreaming and the proper exca-
vation of our English history has to do more than deliver up 'values'
like so many golden torcs at an Anglo-Saxon burial site.[31] Otherwise it
risks becoming too moralistic and that deadens any expression of love
for one's country.[32] We must avoid essentialist views of national character and remind ourselves that whatever values we hold dear are not
peculiar to us. Being ever ready to distinguish history from myth and
legend, we must also acknowledge that values are not the same as
virtues. We've certainly had some finest hours (for example the abolition of slavery, the bicentenary of which was celebrated in 2007 much
more enthusiastically than the tri-centenary of the UK in the same
year). But, as Gordon Brown reminds us, 'the past is also strewn with

examples of how we failed to live up to our ideals' (like the profiting from slavery in the first place). Together with our Scottish neighbours, we need to confront those failures more than we have previously.[33] So, taking all this into account, what could England's future look like? In his impressive study of English identity, Krishan Kumar concludes: 'English nationalism, that enigmatic and elusive thing, so long conspicuous by its absence, might newborn show what a truly civic nationalism can look like.'[34]

MONGREL GLORY

Perhaps the time has come to stop running scared of ethnic nationalism in our pursuit of civic ideals that all can salute, for one may actually serve the other. England is not only one of the most diverse countries in the world; it is also one of the most hybrid. Our ethnic culture is not as simple as population statistics suggest (90 per cent white), for culture cannot be easily carved up in the way that boxes on a census form can be ticked. Nor is it a lifestyle option.[35] Culture is inherently eclectic, something we shape, experience and consume under countless influences, only a few of which we are aware of at any given time. That's even truer today than it was 300 years ago when Daniel Defoe famously wrote 'A True Born Englishman's a contradiction! In speech, an irony! In fact, a fiction!'[36]

A poll taken after the 2004 Olympic games found that double gold medal winner Kelly Holmes was as much a source of pride as the Queen, a vote confirmed by the rapturous reception she was given by the predominantly white citizens of her home town of Hildenborough in Kent, on her victory-parade return from the Games.[37] That scene illustrated more than just tolerance and 'fairness', which in the poll mentioned earlier came third as the 'British' quality most people valued (after 'defiance of Nazi Germany' and 'people's right to say what they think').[38] A mixed race woman, Holmes is a testament, like Zadie Smith, Lewis Hamilton and many others, to English hybridity.

Mixed relationships are more prevalent and accepted in England than in most western countries (since polling began on the subject in 1958, the number of people disapproving of intermarriage has fallen from 71 per cent of the population to 15 per cent today).[39] The number of mixed couples has more than doubled in the last twenty years, as a consequence of which mixed race people are now the third largest ethnic group in the UK and the fastest growing one. How many of us if we really knew our history would discover that we too are 'mixed' in some way? Modest estimates put the figure at 10 per cent of the population, but the true figure would probably be much higher were

everyone to have a DNA test.[40] It's not a straightforward barometer of
progress, not least because some minorities are more likely to intermarry than others.[41] But it does indicate that multiculturalism, far from
being the artificial imposition of modern social engineers bent on
destroying ancient customs, is in fact the attribute of a country volun-
tarily becoming more heterogeneous.

Some minorities still prefer to shelter under the umbrella of
Britishness, because it relates to the passport that usually legitimises
their passage and presence. But as Mark Perryman has consistently
pointed out, support for the England football team testifies (almost as
much as the team itself) to the increasingly multi-racial identification
with England, since fans of all colours have reclaimed the George flag
from the Union Jack since the 1996 European Championships.[42] With
respect to Monty Panesar, no wonder Norman Tebbit holds to the
cricket test rather than the football test. Gary Younge of the *Guardian*
is well qualified to discern the racial difference between England and
Scotland. He was born in England to West Indian parents and grew up
during the 1980s in Stevenage, Hertfordshire, before attending university in Edinburgh:

> It is now no longer possible, or desirable, to forestall the inevitable – it
> is time to find an accommodation between blackness and Englishness.
> Paradoxically, such a task might be easier here than in any other parts of
> the United Kingdom. The Scots and the Welsh still think of themselves
> as primarily white nations where black people happen to live ... The
> English no longer have that self-image; the apparently seamless link
> between Englishness and whiteness has long since been broken. Even
> though nobody would question that England is, and most likely always
> will be, predominantly white, it ... is almost impossible to imagine it
> without black and Asian people. From pop to politics the black experi-
> ence is now intimately interwoven into the fabric of English daily life in
> a way that is not so obviously the case in Scotland or Wales.[43]

Is the black experience really so interwoven in our daily life? After all,
as Younge acknowledges, it's 'primarily concentrated in urban areas',
with regions like the south west of England having similar minority
population levels to Scotland and Wales.[44]

Writing as someone who has strong rural as well as urban family
roots, I don't want to see an Englishness in which the flat, austere
beauty of Norfolk fields are erased from the national imagination. But
I am under no illusion that those fields mystically represent the 'real'
England, elsewhere lost to industrialisation and immigration. For

starters, much of Norfolk's intensively farmed land was reclaimed from the sea by Dutch engineers in the seventeenth century, land which is now worked by other foreigners from Eastern Europe because most locals don't want to.[45] Throughout England, the number of migrant workers in rural areas has more than trebled since 2003, while young English men and women continue to leave for better opportunities in the city.[46] Thanks to a media that's almost as globalised as our economy, it's difficult for people who remain in the countryside to ignore the urban England that 80 per cent of the nation inhabits, even if they never go to the Indian restaurant or Chinese takeaway that can be found in most village high streets. Country and city, though still very different, have more in common with each other than either care to admit. So why pretend that diversity is some metropolitan conspiracy foisted upon a long-suffering yeomanry, or, conversely, that every Caucasian in a thatched cottage is a member of the BNP?

This is not a happy land. Immigration is higher up the list of voters' concerns than it has been since the 1970s, and attacks on ethnic minorities have risen sharply in recent years.[47] And let's face it: 'hybridity' is not going to enter our political lexicon in the way that Churchill's 'Finest Hour' did. Nor is it going to be the rallying cry for a new Englishness. It smacks too much of the liberal elite, that amorphous yet powerful body of men and women who are periodically blamed for England's identity crisis. 'Hybridity' belongs to an intellectual argot of ambiguity; it's the language of uncertainty, which for those in search of certainty is at best unsettling and at worst frightening. But whatever reassuring words or phrases the English settle on to describe how hybrid they are, it is this central feature of our nation which we must embrace as the foundation of our national identity in the coming century.

For, it is the depth of our hybridity that makes the English so different. Different from the Scots and Welsh, because ethnic and national minorities make up a smaller proportion of those countries (only 1 per cent compared to 15 in England); different from the rest of Europe, because in most continental countries there is a smaller number and range of ethnic/national minorities (they form an average of 8 per cent of the population of EU members).[48] There is also greater hostility towards minorities on the Continent, manifest in ruthless assimilationist government policy, and a failure to monitor discrimination effectively.[49] The Paris riots of 2006 were a result of that; so too was the Spanish racial abuse of black England footballers in 2004 and of racing driver Lewis Hamilton in 2008.

We are also different from the United States because, although

America is more diverse than England and proud of it, America is not as integrated.[50] True, minorities are more likely to salute the Stars and Stripes because in the American Dream they have an aspirational, mobilising ideal that's less freighted with class than anything Britain offers. And despite current anxiety about the Latinisation of the US as a result of the Mexican influx, immigration remains central to the creation story of modern America whereas it continues to be seen as a marginal aberration here.[51] Our Ellis Island is the Channel Tunnel, our Statue of Liberty an electrified fence and a barking Alsatian.

However, as Americans themselves admit, less racial mixing occurs in their private and public spheres than in England. Because a smaller proportion of the US population live in inner cities, and because of the more ghettoized geography of urban, suburban and rural America (a hangover from enforced segregation), Americans are less likely to go to school with, reside near, socialise with, date or marry people of different ethnic backgrounds.[52] That difference is reflected in American advertising and TV programmes, where the races are seen to work together but little else.[53] It's an Alamo of the mind as well as the body, since few Americans, whatever their ethnicity, question the self-segregation that pervades their society.[54] Of the world's largest nations only Brazil outdoes us in the scope of its genetic make-up, but away from the football field it too is economically more stratified along racial lines than England (at least we can beat the Brazilians off the pitch if not yet on it).

Hybridity, then, is what makes England special, something with which we can define ourselves *and* something of which we can be proud without being complacent. It's not a form of cultural relativism because the ingredients of our hybridity and the culture it produces are unique to us. It links our rural and urban lives. It links us to Europe, to America and indeed to most of the world. It links us to the past, as a pre-colonial then colonial nation, and to our future as a post-colonial one. If these sweeping panoramas are not your cup of tea, remember that in myriad ways hybridity is present in our daily lives – often, like our DNA, without us even knowing it (not least that cup of milky sweet tea, product of our links with China, India and the Caribbean). It's not an aberration, still less a betrayal. It's who we've always been. There is, as Billy Bragg has observed, a hyphen in Anglo-Saxon. It's a term that fails to capture the variety of early English culture, which contained French and Islamic influences.[55] But in any case, if being a 'people of the hyphen' was good enough for Germanic tribes over a millennia ago, it's surely good enough for us now, unless of course you believe that skin colour remains the defining criterion of Englishness. If you do, you're the real minority, for polls taken since the turn of this century show that around 80 per cent of the population think you do not have to be white in order to be English.[56]

On the first of July 1963 the Beatles released *She Loves You*, composed under the influence of American rhythm 'n blues and English music hall song. A month earlier in the *Spectator* Colin MacInnes, author of *England, Half English* and the first herald of British youth culture, begged his readers to embrace what he called their 'mongrel glory'. MacInnes knew what he was talking about. On his mother's side he was a relative of Rudyard Kipling and of the Conservative Prime Minister Stanley Baldwin, both celebrants of Englishness in the imperial age. With Scottish origins on his father's side, he was brought up in Australia. As an adult, he was an habitué of Soho, an area of London that's been home to immigrants since Mozart and Casanova lived there. Of recent arrivals from the West Indies and West Africa who formed part of his social circle, MacInnes wrote:

> Whatever their origins of place and race, they are now Britons in every sense that we are. The alternative is a continuing, nagging misery and pretence: the fatal weakness of not seeing what our country is. History is unkind to pretension that is not sustained by power … The choice is to be terrified and be; or cling to safe hatreds, and destroy ourselves as no bomb ever will.[57]

The English can solve the identity crisis that currently afflicts them without living MacInnes's extraordinary life.

Therapy will not come through creating an English parliament or a St George's Day Bank Holiday, nor even by winning the World Cup again; and the English patient certainly won't be cured by 'clinging to safe hatreds' – blaming others for their malaise, whether it's the Scots and Welsh or foreign immigrants and their descendants. Therapy will come through that cliché of the American self-help book: 'learn to love yourself'. The English must embrace what they've become since the Second World War and what they've always to some extent been: one of the world's most richly diverse nations; neurotically insular yet adventurous and culturally porous when it suits them. When the English find the courage to celebrate their mongrel glory; when they realise that the only people stopping them from being English is themselves; then, and only then, will they start to breathe easily once more.

NOTES

1. The number of people living in England who describe their national identity as British fell from 63% in 1992 to 48% in 2007, while those who

describe themselves as English rose from 31% to 40%. See National Centre for Social Research, *Perspectives on a Changing Society: British Social Attitudes 23rd Report*, 24.1.07.

2. For concern about the replacement of Elgar by Smith see *Daily* Express, 2 April 2006. For a typical expression of general Scotophobia see Geoffrey Wheatcroft, 'Hammered by the Scots', *Guardian*, 23.6.03, in which he characterized the Blair era as 'an influx across the border [of] Scotch carpetbaggers' while back home 'Edinburgh is giddily spendthrift with English money'.

3. *The Times*, 23.4.02.

4. Asifa Hussein and William Miller, *Multicultural Nationalism: Islamophobia, Anglophobia, and Devolution*, Oxford 2006, p95.

5. Ibid., pp164-5. At the 2003 Scottish Parliament elections, 47% of Pakistani Scots voted for the SNP, compared to 28% for Labour. As Hussein and Miller argue, even allowing for Muslim opposition to the Iraq war, 'it is almost inconceivable that *any* English National Party, however moderate, could win twice as much support from Blacks and Asians as from the average voter in England'.

6. I owe this phrase to Mike Phillips' brilliant critique of Michael Collins work in the *Guardian*, 24.7.04.

7. The fact that the white Welsh were also not offered such an option seems not to have mattered to English critics.

8. Simon Heffer, for example, writes 'It is a self-evident truth that if multi-culturalism is actively encouraged it must be at the expense of the indigenous culture in all its forms. At a time when a nation is re-establishing itself, that could be destabilizing and harmful', *Nor Shall My Sword: The Reinvention of England* (1999), pp42-43. What is self-evident is that this is a wilful re-writing of English history as audacious as that of the Scots with whom Heffer has lost patience. For at what moment did the 'indigenous culture' cease to be shaped by other cultures and become pure in the first place?

9. See for example, 'Cabbies refuse order to remove England flags from taxis', *The Times*, 30.5.02. The order in this case came from Portsmouth City Council because taxi drivers had broken by-laws. At every football tournament since the 1998 World Cup, stories such as this have appeared in the media, with council officials usually portrayed as politically correct apparatchiks determined to frustrate English patriotism.

10. Penny Wark, 'Lost White Boys', *The Times*, 15.11. 07. Such anecdotal evidence does not explain why the most underachieving social group, boys of Caribbean descent, reputedly have a stronger cultural identity than their white counterparts.

11. *The Times*, 16.6.07.

12. National Centre for Social Research, *Perspectives on a Changing Society: British Social Attitudes 23rd Report*, 24.1.07.
13. *Independent*, 18.8.04.
14. *Church Times*, 22.9.06. Non-whites make up 17% of English churchgoers (double their proportion of the national population) and in major cities the figure rises considerably, up to 58% of churchgoers in London. Meanwhile, in rural England, church attendances have fallen by a third since 1989.
15. *Daily Express*, 24.11.06.
16. Michael Collins, *The Likes of Us: A Biography of the White Working Class*, Granta 2004, p262.
17. Kate Gavron and Rushanara Ali, in 'The Angry East End', *Prospect*, March 2006, rightly argue that housing policy since the 1960s, in which need is assessed on absolute grounds rather than local affinity, has sometimes disadvantaged the indigenous population. But this is something that has also benefited the Irish and currently benefits Eastern Europeans so it is not an issue of colour as some argue.
18. George Orwell, *The Lion and the Unicorn: Socialism and the English Genius*, Penguin, 2nd Ed., 1982, pp63-5.
19. 'Britain Rediscovered', *Prospect*, April 2005. These words belong to the journalist and author Neal Ascherson and were part of a roundtable discussion that included Gordon Brown, Linda Colley Tariq Modood and Billy Bragg.
20. Simon Heffer, *Nor Shall My Sword: The Reinvention of England* (1999), p133.
21. Patrick Wright, 'Last Orders', *Guardian*, 9.4.05.
22. The Conservative think tank AGORA is an exception, organizing cross-party symposia since 2004 on the future of national identity in Britain.
23. *Guardian*, 14.1.06. Brown was addressing the Fabian Society. See also *Fabian Review*, '"Who Do We Want To Be" The Britishness Issue', Volume 117, No.4, Winter 2005.
24. Rt. Hon. David Blunkett MP, *A New England: An English identity within Britain*, Speech to the Institute for Public Policy Research (ippr), 14.3.05, p11. See also Blunkett's speech to the Social Market Foundation on 26.6.02, in which he urged the English to reclaim the George Cross from the far right, 'Fly the flag against racism', *Guardian*, 27.6.02.
25. For more on the North African origins of Morris dancing, see Adam Lively, *Masks: Blackness, Race and the Imagination*, Vintage 1999, pp15-16.
26. The devolution Acts of 1999 brought the size of Scottish constituencies in line with those of England. This took effect in the 2005 election, as a result of which the number of MPs sitting for Scottish constituencies in the UK parliament was reduced from 72 to 59.

27. An ICM poll commissioned by the Campaign for an English Parliament in April 2007 found 67% in favour. This compares to only 23% in favour of the Euro, according to the last ICM poll on the subject in 2004.

28. *Daily Mail*, 4.12.07.

29. See for example, Rt. Hon. Gordon Brown MP, British Council annual lecture, 7.7.04.

30. Fish and chips were voted one of 20 'Icons of England' in a poll of 350,000 people conducted by the Department for Culture, Media and Sport in 2006.

31. For the debate on this, see 'In search of British values', *Prospect*, October 2007.

32. Bikhu Parekh, 'New Englands', *Times Literary Supplement*, 2.2.07, makes this point well: 'Shared values', he writes, 'are not enough to hold a society together. The Scottish National Party shares British values, but seeks Scottish independence'. Equally, Parekh continues, 'One's son may not share one's values, indeed one may be hostile to his way of life, but one does not therefore disown him or love him less. Patriotism has a similar thrust, and we fail to understand its psychological basis if we take too moralistic a view of it.'

33. Rt. Hon. Gordon Brown MP, British Council annual lecture, 7.7.04.

34. Krishan Kumar, *The Making of English National Identity*, Cambridge 2003, p273.

35. Paul Gilroy, *After Empire: Melancholia or convivial culture?*, Routledge 2004, p167.

36. Cited in Jeremy Paxman, *The English: A Portrait of a People*, Penguin 1999, p58. Paxman concludes, 'Defoe was right. The English are a mongrel race, and it has taken the development of communities living in England that are visibly different to demonstrate the point', op. cit., p59.

37. Anthony King, 'What does it mean to be British?' *Daily Telegraph*, 27.7.05.

38. Ibid. When asked 'What defines Britain? 54% said a 'sense of fairness', 59% said defiance of Nazi Germany and 61% 'the right to say what you think'.

39. Barbara Tizard and Anne Phoenix, *Black, White or Mixed Race? Race and Racism in the lives of young people of mixed parentage*, Routledge, 2nd Ed., 2002, pp36-7. For other useful statistics see Yasmin Alibhai-Brown, *Mixed Feelings: The Complex Lives of Mixed-Race Britons*, Women's Press 2001, pp74-85.

40. Official estimates in 2001 put the mixed-race population at 677,000, 14.6% of the minority population and 1.2% of the total population, compared to 350,000 (11% of minorities and 0.6% of the total) in 1997. See *National Statistics* 2001.

41. Afro-Caribbean Britons are the most likely to intermarry and Asian Britons are the least likely, religion being one factor in that disparity. See 'Inter-ethnic Marriage', *National Statistics* 2001.

42. Mark Perryman, *Ingerland Expects: Football, National Identity and World Cup 2002*, ippr 2002. See also Jonathan Glancey, 'By George!', *The Guardian*, 20.6.02.

43. Gary Younge, 'On race and Englishness', in Selina Chen and Tony Wright (eds.), *The English Question*, Fabian Society 2000, pp112-113.

44. Ibid., p114.

45. Approximately 80,000 Eastern Europeans are currently working in East Anglia. One difference between town and country in this respect is that the level of xenophobic abuse immigrants suffer is more common and ferocious in rural areas. See Patrick Barkham, 'On the margins', *Guardian*, 26.9.07.

46. *Daily Telegraph*, 17.7.07. The reported rise of 209% does not include illegal immigrants, so it is a conservative estimate. According to a Commission for Rural Communities report, in some rural districts the increase has been even higher. Eight districts saw sixfold rises in the period 2003-6 while in Herefordshire it was tenfold. Despite this, there are 400,000 less people aged 16-24 in the countryside than there were 20 years ago, one reason why the average age of the city dweller is 38 compared to 44 in the country.

47. The Ministry of Justice reported 41,000 attacks on people because of their race or religion in the year 2005-6, a 12 per cent rise on the previous year. *Independent*, 30.10.07.

48. See the 'Report on Racism and Xenophobia in Member States of the EU' by the European Union Agency for Fundamental Rights, EUAFR, August 2007.

49. The 2007 *Report on Racism and Xenophobia in Member States of the EU* concluded that Britain was the only country that had an effective system for monitoring hate crime.

50. The last census for each country showed that in 2001 7.9% of the British population described themselves as being from an ethnic minority, compared to 24.9% of the US population in 2000.

51. See Jonathan Freedland, *Bring Home the Revolution: How Britain Can Live the American Dream*, 4th Estate 1998, p157: 'For them immigration is a promise. To us it is a threat', he writes.

52. A similar proportion of the English and American people live in rural areas (approximately 20% according to the last census for each country). But twice as many Americans live in suburbs as the British. Moreover, according to one survey, only 5-10% of Americans live in integrated communities, defined as those with a non-white population of more than

10 per cent (deemed by estate agents to be the tipping point at which 'white flight' is set in motion). See Lola Adesioye, 'Separate Reality', *Guardian*, 21.1.08.

53. Blacks and whites in America are more likely to watch different entertainment shows than Britons; advertisers follow suit, targeting different ethnicities in separate commercials. See Freedland, op. cit, pp136-7.

54. The numbers of white Americans who approve of interracial marriage rose from 4% in 1958, when polls were first taken, to 61% in 1997, while the number of blacks approving rose from 58% (when first polled in 1972) to 77% in 1997. But the number of people who disapprove is still more than double that of the UK. See Renee C. Romano, *Race Mixing: Black-White Marriage in Postwar America*, Harvard 2003, pp2-3. Overall, the number of mixed marriages as a proportion of all unions is similar in each country, around 2 per cent according to the last census. The key difference is that in America marriage between black and white is rare – making only 0.6% of the total in 2000, while in Britain it is the most common form of mixed marriage. Also, official figures do not account for the number of non-marital mixed relationships, thought to be much higher in the UK than in the US.

55. Billy Bragg, *The Progressive Patriot*, Bantam 2006, p55.

56. See for example *Guardian*, 27.6.02.

57. *The Spectator*, June 1963, reprinted in MacInnes, *Out of the Way: Later Essays* (1979) p100.

Where's the white in the Union Jack?

Race, identity and the sporting multicultural

Ben Carrington

The movement from colonisation to post-colonial times does not imply that the problems of colonialism have been resolved, or replaced by some conflict-free era. Rather, the 'post-colonial' marks the passage from one historical power-configuration or conjuncture to another. Problems of dependency, underdevelopment and marginalisation, typical of the 'high' colonial period, persist into the post-colonial. However, these relations are resumed in a new configuration. Once they were articulated as unequal relations of power and exploitation between colonised and colonising societies. Now they are restaged and displaced as struggles between indigenous social forces, as internal contradictions and sources of destabilisation within the decolonised society, or between them and the wider global system.

Stuart Hall, *The Multicultural Question*[1]

I believe and hope to prove that cricket and football were the greatest cultural influences in nineteenth-century Britain, leaving far behind Tennyson's poems, Beardsley's drawings and concerts of the Philharmonic Society. These filled space in print but not in minds.

C.L.R. James, *Beyond a Boundary*[2]

Scene 1: **12.46 pm, Wednesday 6 July 2005**
In a tense room in a downtown Singapore hotel, filled with celebrities, politicians, royalty and the world's expectant media, a 15-year-old sailor cadet from the Singaporean Navy slowly carries a silk pillow embossed with five interlocking rings towards Jacques Rogge, the President of the International Olympic Committee (IOC). Lying delicately on top of the pillow is a large white envelope. For the first time

109

in days, the hall is in silence. Rogge clumsily opens the envelope, pauses momentarily, and says: 'The International Olympic Committee has the honour of announcing that the games of the 30th Olympiad in 2012 are awarded to the city of ... London'. Cries of jubilation ring out; camera bulbs flash, David Beckham embraces London's Mayor Ken Livingstone, UK government officials and politicians are seen joyously dancing, and groups of young children shriek 'We won, we won!' in front of the assembled international television crews. Simultaneously, 6,750 miles away in London's Trafalgar Square, thousands of people break into cheering and singing as news of the announcement is relayed via huge screens. Balloons are released and ticker-tape falls, seemingly, across the whole of London. The nation rejoices. At this very same moment three young men from Leeds and another from Aylesbury, are making their final plans for their one-way trip to London the following day.

Scene 2: 8:50am, Thursday 7 July 2005
Hundreds of feet below street level, rush-hour commuters are packed into London's over-crowded and poorly air-conditioned underground system. Most are reading the early morning newspapers, all with 'special souvenir editions' proudly proclaiming the previous day's successful Olympics announcement. The headlines are unequivocal: 'One Sweet Word: London' states the *Guardian*; 'Britain's Golden Day' announces the *Independent*. Londoners are enjoying their collective role in this local and national achievement. Moments later, above ground, reports begin to appear of a 'power surge' on the tubes. Confusion arises as 24-hour television news channels begin to show pictures of stations being closed as police and other emergency services frantically arrive in increasing numbers. Earlier reports of a 'power surge' are questioned and news emerges of a number of possible explosions. An hour after the initial incidents on the tube, a bomb explodes on a bus in Tavistock Square, central London, killing 13 people and injuring scores of others. It soon becomes clear that London has been subjected to a wave of linked bombings. Three separate explosions on the underground are reported. In the end over 700 people are injured, many seriously, and 56 people are dead, including the four suspected bombers.

A number of urgent questions arise from the above juxtaposition: what, if anything, connects these two seemingly unrelated events, beyond their tragic and temporal association with the city of London? Further, how can an activity as seemingly trivial as sport have a place within any serious discussion concerning politics, war, terrorism, and the nature of democracy itself? In a moment of historical cruelty that bordered on pathos, the newsstands of 7 July 2005 were filled with the previous day's images of smiling Londoners, joyful to the point of tears, celebrating what was, in the words of Ken Livingstone, 'one of the best days London has ever had'. Amongst the discarded morning papers full of headlines of London pride, severed, bloodied and disfigured human bodies were now dying. Whilst at first glance the two events seem only to be joined by the fate of circumstance, a dominant theme connects the two. This theme speaks to a broader tension that has been central to political discourse in Britain, and indeed much of Europe and elsewhere, for at least the past two decades, namely the question of 'multiculturalism'.

The initial commentary as to why London had beaten the other cities (including Paris, Madrid, New York and Moscow) to host the 2012 Olympic summer games focused on the decision to include 30 'inner city' children from London's East End amongst the 100 representatives each city was allowed in the voting hall. Instead of the slick film produced for Paris by the renowned film maker Luc Besson, the London bid chose to focus on London's racial and ethnic diversity. It was the ordinary, everyday, lived multiculturalism of contemporary London, its cosmopolitan openness if you will, that was seen to have swayed the IOC voting members. The immediate news coverage thus praised London's (and Britain's) successful multiculturalism and the role that sport in particular had played in producing both social cohesion and community integration whilst respecting cultural and ethnic diversity. As the leader in the *Independent* newspaper put it:

> The final video presentation to IOC delegates yesterday made great play of the city's ethnic diversity. This was a masterstroke. London is a true world city, with inhabitants from every nation on Earth and citizens from a huge number of backgrounds. It is hard to think of a city more firmly in the tradition of the Olympic movement, which seeks to bring together all nations under the common banner of sporting excellence.[3]

However, in the days and weeks following the attacks of 7/7 a counter discourse concerning diversity and difference began to emerge as an apparent attempt to make sense of the atrocity. Once it became clear that the four bombers were in fact British and these were 'home grown' terrorists, the public debate shifted to examining the role of multiculturalism itself in 'fanning the flames' of terrorism. Many right-wing, as well as some liberal, commentators suggested that multiculturalism had 'gone too far' in promoting separate, segregated communities. Rather than assimilating into British values and mores, 'ethnic communities' had been allowed, if not actively encouraged, to celebrate their difference. According to such arguments, this had led to a break down in the normative order, a lack of respect on the part of ethnic minorities towards the institutions of 'Britishness', and the spread of extremism and radical Islamism among many. For some conservative pundits London (and by extension Britain as a whole) was now *Londonistan*,[4] a seething, amoral place where relativism and political correctness prevented honest discussion about the 'fifth column' infiltration of 'Islamofascists' into the very heart of the nation. Thus, in the space of 24 hours, 'multiculturalism' had shifted from a signifier that embodied all that was great and strong about Britain, to become all that was wrong and weak with contemporary British society. Further, the embrace of multiculturalism was so dangerous, we were told, that it could, if left unchecked, result in the end of British liberal democracy itself.

In the midst of these discussions sport was once again invoked as a cultural practice that could help to guide the nation through the tumultuous events of 7/7. It emerged that one of the suicide bombers, Shazad Tanweer, was an avid cricket player and had studied for a sport science degree at university. Newspaper headlines drew upon this apparent contradiction about a man whom they described as the 'cricket-loving suicide bomber'. The implicit and somewhat simplistic suggestion seemed to be, how could someone who loved a sport as quintessentially English as cricket, and whose father owned a fish and chip shop, commit such a (non-British) heinous act? Sport's supposed integrative function was asserted once again when Trevor Phillips, then Chair of the Commission for Racial Equality, wrote in *The Observer* that the Olympics should act as a catalyst for social cohesion, not just for the city of London, nor even the country, but for the entire world; arguing that the 'unity in diversity that won us the Games and that saw us through last week's dreadful carnage will be at the heart of the 2012 Games':

> By the time London is finished, everyone on Earth should want to know how we created the diverse, integrated society we have. The 2012 Olympic flame will illuminate some wonderful sport. But it should also light the path ahead for the future of our common humanity.[5]

At the core of this argument are a number of unexamined and often contradictory assumptions concerning the role of sport within society. Sport is seen to be a largely unimportant cultural activity, relegated to the realm of voluntary leisure and disconnected from real politics. Yet, at the same time, it is accorded great powers to produce both national social cohesion and community integration. It is seen to be irrelevant to the major concerns of world politics and international relations, and yet somehow capable of preventing young men from engaging in acts of political violence as a response to global events. What is lacking in this thinking is any attempt to theorise the nature of sport itself as a contested social activity, to historicise these relationships, and to provide a sociological account of sport's role within a deeply racialised, class-bound and gendered post-colonial society such as Britain.

BACK IN THE DAY

Football can perhaps be used as a paradigmatic case study through which to chart the movement throughout the late nineteenth and twentieth century of black subjectivity in Britain – from a situation where the lesser 'negro' breeds first became marginal 'coloured people' and then 'black', and finally and more complexly 'black British', with the variants, soon after, of black English, Welsh, Scottish and – in a somewhat more fraught context – black Irish, towards what might now be tentatively called a black European identity.[6]

Black athletes have played professional football in England since the late nineteenth century. The Ghanaian born Arthur Wharton is often credited with being the first black player to turn professional in 1889, and black footballers played intermittently for various clubs in Britain throughout the early and mid twentieth century. Viv Anderson's debut for the men's England national team in 1978 can be seen to mark a pivotal moment when the far right chant of 'There Ain't No Black in the Union Jack' began to lose its populist hold. In 1995, Paul Ince became the first black player to captain the men's England team, and now an England team *without* black players is barely imaginable. These symbolic shifts should not be dismissed as 'merely cultural' as they have had profound political effects in reshaping the imagined national community of millions and what it means to be both English and British. As Stuart Hall notes:

> Take sport in Britain. Nothing is closer to the heart of the average Englishman – as opposed to the fields where classically blacks have been outstanding, such as cricket or boxing – than the heartland of soccer. There isn't an occasion when you can pick up a decent Sunday paper, with its photos of Saturday's matches, and not see black faces. Are blacks in the boardrooms of the clubs? Of course not. Are they relatively powerless in the institutions which organise the game? Of course. The

question is whether they have any currency, any visibility in the culture of sport where the nation's myths and meanings are fabricated. The answer must be 'yes', and to say this is to note the significant degree to which the culture has turned in the past fifteen or so years.[7]

But this culture did not change easily. The black presence in the 'national game' was resisted, often violently, by the main footballing gatekeepers, be they the fans, coaches, managers, or sometimes other players themselves. Throughout the period from the 1970s to the mid 1990s in particular, questions of race, nationalism and belonging continued to powerfully collide within the arena of sport. The terrace chant of 'two world wars and one world cup', as Paul Gilroy suggests, served to highlight 'the bewildering effects of England's post-colonial melancholia'.[8] For many, serious sport, to paraphrase Orwell, has nothing to do with promoting inter-racial understanding, inter-national solidarities and cultural exchange, but is xenophobic racism without the cross burning.

We should remember, too, that it was in *1995*, and not 1895, that *Wisden Cricket Monthly* could in all seriousness, and under the guise of trying to stimulate a 'national debate' on race, nationality and sport,[9] print an article by a renowned right-wing crackpot, Robert Henderson, under the title 'Is it in the blood?'.[10] The article alleged that black English cricketers playing for England against the West Indies, or South Asians playing against India and Pakistan for that matter, did not try as hard as their 'unequivocally English', that is to say white, counterparts. This was because black cricketers suffered from post-colonial revenge fantasies against 'the Empire', meaning that such players subconsciously wanted England to lose and thus played poorly. Henderson subsequently argued that English national teams should ideally be all white but if we had to have a few, in his words, 'negroes' then team managers should enforce racial quotas that limited the number of blacks to no more than two or three players in any one team.[11] This made Norman Tebbit's 1990 'cricket test' for supporters – his suggestion that Asian and black people had to support England in cricket Test matches or else they were disloyal subjects – seem positively progressive, in as much as Tebbit at least allowed for complete inclusion into the national imaginary for the former colonial subjects, albeit one predicated on complete cultural emasculation. Black athletes playing in the national colours become, for Henderson and other right-wing scribes, ethno-national interlopers, 'spoiling' the pristine veneer of the imagined and always lilywhite national body politic.

Yet despite the protestations of the likes of Henderson and the racist culture that was widely embedded within football, we have seen important transformations in the national game. These include an officially backed anti-racist campaign since the early 1990s , 'Kick it Out', and a spectacular growth in the numbers of black as well as foreign-born players at the top clubs, with the result that black players have come to embody both local pride and the national spirit in a way almost unthinkable a decade ago. We have seen England teams with more black players than white and the very recent, slow but gradual emergence of black England supporters actively following the team at 'home and abroad'.[12] This represents an important shift that has dramatically undermined common-sense racisms about black people's questionable status as rightful citizens. This post Macpherson-era politics has meant that questions of 'institutional racism' that previously could not be spoken, let alone debated, are now a part of the national discussion, albeit a discussion that remains fraught with ambiguities and silences.

THERE AIN'T NO BROWN IN THE UNION JACK: ASIAN AS THE NEW BLACK

Largely absent from the above narrative of gradual inclusion and belonging in the national game are South Asian players and communities; and this is significant, not least because in demographic terms they constitute a bigger proportion of the British population than those of black African and black Caribbean descent. It is also important to note that recent discussions concerning the limits of multiculturalism have occurred during a period when the term 'Black' as a political signifier, which previously included South Asian *and* black cultural identities, has largely collapsed.

For a long while South Asians were held up as the model minority, in sharp contradiction to blacks. South Asians were seen to be hard-working, industrious, traditional, family-orientated and religious. True, they may have had the *wrong* religion, being seen largely as either Sikh, Hindu or Muslim (understanding the differences seemed to matter little), but at least they had, so the argument went, a strong value system and a set of traditional beliefs that was helping to integrate them into mainstream British society, unlike the lawless, troublesome and inherently dysfunctional black families and their 'picaninny' offspring. In the same year that Henderson was penning his diatribe against black cricketers' supposed lack of will to win for the mother country, Paul Johnson was arguing in *The Spectator* that Britain should use the money gained by allowing rich Hong Kong multi-millionaires, fearful of the impending 'hand over' to China, to 'buy' their British citizenship, to fund a scheme for the repatriation of blacks. Freehold land could be bought in Africa, the Caribbean or even Brazil for this purpose. This part-time spiritual adviser to Tony Blair argued that this was now a necessary task, as 'the cultural gap between blacks and the other races of western democracy is too great to make assimilation likely'.[13] In contrast, South Asians' supposed reverence for tradition and conservative communal structures had made them model colonial subjects and inherently suited to eventual assimilation.

The past few years have seen a dramatic reversal of this narrative. It is now South Asian communities in general and South Asian (male) youth in particular who have become, in sociologist Stanley Cohen's terms, the new twenty-first century 'folk devils' around which a 'moral panic' can be generated. Whereas in the 1970s, the dominant icon of public danger was that of the black male mugger, intertwined in the 1980s with that of the inner-city black rioter, the 1990s witnessed a more ambivalent set of images and discourses – especially after the brutal murder, subsequent failed trials and finally the public inquest into the death of Stephen Lawrence, which arguably marked the most important shift in racial discourse in Britain during the second half of the twentieth century.[14] For the first time the brutal murder of a black teenager and the failure of the police to prosecute his seemingly known killers was seen to be a *national* and not merely a *black community* tragedy. If the 1990s can be seen to mark a moment of tentative inclusion for black communities in Britain, the moment when 'there ain't no black in the Union Jack' stops having any purchase, the same period signals the beginnings of a new racialised subject of exclusion. The Asian Muslim – a deliberate and powerful conflation of race, ethnicity and religion – becomes the new Other, against which British liberal democracy must stand. The urban disturbances that took place in the summer of 2001 in places such as Oldham and Bradford, and the rise of Islamophobia after the terrorist attacks that took place later that year in the USA, provide the local and global context for the New Racial Times.

The effects of the bombings on 7 July 2005 and the subsequent terrorist attacks in Britain (attempted and actual) have only served to accelerate and deepen these racialised representations: the dreadlocked black youth engaged in pitched battles with the police is now neatly displaced by the veiled and/or scarfed Muslim menace, made all the more sinister as this Other is now seen to be an enemy within. The notion that this terrorism is somehow both new and foreign to the UK is of course ludicrous. As Gary Younge notes, 'the emergence of "home-grown bombers" is mentioned as though this is a new development, when in fact we have been growing our own bombers for years. We have a whole evening dedicated to burning one – it's called Guy Fawkes night'.[15] The Asian Other that was previously understood to be docile, subservient, even weak, yet potentially assimilate-able, and – but for tone of skin and spice of food – almost one of us, has now turned.

In this context, the 'gains' of the late 1990s now seem perilously fragile and incredibly provisional. South Asians are now expected to 'prove' their loyalty to the rest of the nation, so-called liberal commentators now openly discuss whether or not we have had too much immigration, and whether some minority groups and their lifestyles aren't, after all, incompatible with the British way of life. And leading writers engage in public 'thought experiments' about how far 'we' can go in inflicting some pain and misery – deportations, strip searches and worse – back upon 'the Muslim community'.

WHERE DID ALL THE MULTICULTURALISTS GO?

Just over a decade after Norman Tebbit attempted a return to the political stage in the aftermath of the 1997 General Election by arguing that multiculturalism was a 'divisive force', and was widely condemned by Conservatives as much as by liberals, such views concerning the inherent incompatibility of multiculturalism with national unity have now emerged as mainstream positions. Multiculturalism is increasingly cited today as the prime generator of national destabilization. This reminds us of Stuart Hall's pertinent observation that multiculturalism in Britain was never genuinely embraced as an unequivocal good by the political elites (despite tokenistic and opportunistic statements). Rather, Britain experienced what he describes as a 'multicultural drift'. By the end of the 1970s, it found itself, almost without looking and planning, a changed place; it was stuck in the middle of a multiculturalist situation from which there was no return, and which it came, reluctantly, to accept. This helps us to understand the current 'retreat from multiculturalism' – *there never was a sincere investment in the idea that went beyond a strategic, rhetorical embrace.*[16]

We might suggest then that state multiculturalism lasted about three years in Britain. It can be dated, approximately, from May 1997, when Tony Blair and New Labour came to power, to the autumn of 2000, when the Parekh Report into The Future of Multiethnic Britain was published and denounced. After the 1997 Labour victory, the warm beer accompanied by old maids cycling across villages searching for Holy Communion lost out to the bright new cosmopolitan world of a racially inclusive and forward-looking 'young Britain'. Tebbit's 1997 claim that multiculturalism was a divisive force – 'one cannot uphold two sets of ethics or be loyal to two nations, any more than a man can have two masters' – was immediately labelled by his fellow Conservatives as anachronistic and out of place in the new party.[17] Tebbit, and other monoculturalists, were now officially dinosaurs, out-of-date political beasts from a by-gone age. New Tory leader William Hague vowed that just as Britain had changed so too would the Conservative Party. The Conservatives would henceforth be welcoming to all, offer 'patriotism without prejudice' and become a 'multiracial party'. A decade on from this vision (and after a further two defeats in which the party repeatedly failed to reinvent itself), Hague's fantasy Conservative Party re-emerged in the 2007 conference speech of David Cameron. Cameron name-checked his friend William Hague as a positive motivating force for change within the party, and attacked *Labour* for their overtly hyper-nationalist and subtly racist politicking. He condemned Gordon Brown's call for 'British jobs for British workers!' as unfeasible, if not illegal under current EU laws:

> Boy has this guy [Brown] got a plan. It's to appeal to that 4% of people in marginal seats. With a dog whistle on immigration there and a word about crime here, wrap yourself up in the flag and talk about Britishness enough times and maybe just maybe you can convince enough people that you are on their side. Well I say, God we've got to be better than that.[18]

As Cameron brought his speech to a close he implored the assembled delegates to change themselves and the nation by repeatedly using the refrain of 'we can get it if we really want it'.

The speech ended with perhaps *the* postmodern spectacle of twenty-first century British politics, as the blue-rinse set gave Cameron the obligatory standing ovation, shaking their greying booties and 'dancing' to Jimmy Cliff's reggae classic *You Can Get it if You Really Want it*, as it thundered out from the Bournemouth PA system.

But by the time of this latest implausible multicultural moment, multiculturalism had already been dead for years. Multiculturalism can only be embraced within mainstream political discourse when it is linked to a denial of racism's existence. This is a belief in ethnic difference without mentioning inequality, racial diversity without discussing discrimination; in short, an acceptance – 'tolerance' – of a bit of the Other, but one deliberately shorn of history as to how we ended up where we are. When the Parekh report was published in October 2000, its 'radical' idea was that Britishness should be re-imagined as a post-national 'community of communities'. The report modestly suggested that:

> Britishness, as much as Englishness, has systematic, largely unspoken, racial connotations. Whiteness nowhere features as an explicit condition of being British, but it is widely understood that Englishness, and therefore by extension Britishness, is racially coded. 'There ain't no black in the Union Jack,' it has been said. Race is deeply entwined with political culture and with the idea of nation, and underpinned by a distinctly British kind of reticence – to take race and racism seriously, or even to talk about them at all, is bad form, something not done in polite company...Unless these deep-rooted antagonisms to racial and cultural difference can be defeated in practice, as well as symbolically written out of the national story, the idea of a multicultural post-nation remains an empty promise.[19]

The report thus offered an opportunity to link discussions of race with nation, and to provide a genuinely different narrative of what Britishness was and could be. It was the, hardly disputable, assertion that Britishness had 'racial connotations', that put the right-wing press into apoplexy. On the day *before* the report's publication, and in a deliberate attempt to undermine its recommendations, the *Daily Telegraph* launched a front page assault, with the screaming headline: 'Straw Wants to Rewrite Our History: British is a Racist Word, says Report' (10.10.00).[20] Deliberately conflating *racial connotations* with *racist*, the *Telegraph's* misreporting set the news agenda for how the report would be covered. Members of the Commission, including Parekh himself and Stuart Hall, were predictably lambasted as failed old Marxists ('sub Marxist gibberish' as the *Daily Telegraph* put it), from provincial universities, and the report was presented as an attack on Britain herself. At the launch of the Report, and no doubt to the bemusement of the commissioners, then Home Secretary Jack Straw rejected the Commission's position on national identity, stating: 'I don't accept the argument of those on the narrow nationalist right, nor on the part of the left that Britain, as a cohesive whole is dead ... I'm proud to be British and I'm proud of what I believe to be the best of British values'.[21] The newspapers duly reported: '"Proud to be British" Straw raps race report' (*Times*, 12.10.00); 'Labour in retreat on race' (*Daily Mail*, 12.10.00); 'Race report angers "proud Briton" Straw' (*Daily Express*, 12.10.00). As McLaughlin and Neal note, 'New Labour had successfully distanced itself publicly from the [Parekh] Commission and report. In so doing, the New Labour government also signalled its willingness to lay down the terms on which future debates about Britishness would take place'.[22]

After Macpherson, 'institutional racism' might be seen to exist within 'institutions' in Britain but somehow not within the social structures of Britain itself. Thus, via a clever ideological manoeuvre, everyone could be in favour of multiculturalism-lite, but not if it actually challenged forms of white supremacy or acknowledged the history and effects of colonialism. It became at that moment an empty signifier without an actual referent, invoked to signify tolerance but without ever stating tolerance of what. The modest but significant Parekh report was killed, politically, by New Labour and the right-wing press. And with it any genuinely radical, transformative form of official, state multiculturalism.

This is the terrain on which liberals such as David Goodhart, editor of *Prospect* magazine, are able to present the so-called progressive dilemma, namely how to reconcile multiculturalism (diversity) and claims for equality (solidarity), encapsulated in the loaded question: Is Britain too diverse?[23] Goodhart argues that diversity itself undermines the collective forms of solidarity that are at the heart of the social democratic contract and the welfare state. 'Non-white' immigration is seen as a threat, as indigenous communities begin to wonder why their taxes should be wasted on the differently coloured and undeserving newcomers with whom they have few, if any, social or cultural connections. The answer to this question is to re-emphasise a progressive nationalism that is based on establishing British values that the newcomers have to learn if they are to be accepted, and that the indigenous can feel proud of.

Of course, this position rests on a number of cultural myths and historical falsehoods concerning the unchanging, stable and homogeneous society that supposedly existed in Britain up until the 1950s, when the black and brown folks are first seen to arrive. This fantastical reconstruction of a settled people negates the previous (pre-1948) waves of migration, as well as the internal class, regional, ethnic and linguistic cleavages that had to be violently suppressed in order to make England, and Britain. It also relies on a form of historical amnesia that refuses to account for and to engage with British imperialism and colonialism. The argument conflates questions of (English) nationality and identity with those related to the (British) state and citizenship. The profound political error that 'liberals' like David Goodhart make is to assume that solidarity can only be forged from racial or ethnic sameness. Rather, it is the recognition of shared social location and material interests, an ethical position of political identification and consciousness, that was, is and will be the basis for any progressive politics. Solidarity has nothing to do with the level of shared melanin in various peoples' skin. The precise sociological mechanisms for producing social solidarity are far more complex than Goodhart allows. Indeed, as Ray Pahl points out, it is 'the differences – or perhaps even the conflicts – that paradoxically produce solidarities and social glue'.[24]

This failure of political imagination allows some liberals to invoke the downtrodden 'white working class' as a single coherent subject which is besieged from 'above' by the terrors of capital and from 'below' by the waves of uncontrolled migration. This argument rests on a move to recast all dark skinned national subjects back into the category of the 'immigrant', thus allowing a series of binaries to be created from which the discussion, necessarily, turns to questions concerning integration (read assimilation), calls for the promotion of dominant British values, concerns about 'their' (in)compatibility with 'our' way of life, and the necessity, (according to Anthony Giddens) to get 'tough' on immigration. Thus all white people, regardless of their actual ancestry, become 'indigenous Britons' while the rest of us coloured folks, regardless of our complex and mixed genealogies become 'settled minorities'. Quite how long is required to make the move from 'settled' to 'indigenous' is never spelled out. Though we know, of course, that lurking behind such distinctions is the implicit criteria that only whites can ever be unequivocally English/British, no matter – as Enoch Powell once reminded us – what our passports might say. As Gilroy notes:

> *Prospect* has spearheaded the adaptation and updating of well-worn themes drawn from the Powell lexicon. Immigration is always an invasion, and the inevitably following race war is a culturally-based conflict born from a fundamental, pre-political incompatibility. The only vague novelty here lay in the folding of these ancient motifs into a nominally 'left' discourse.[25]

It isn't so much that we (the ex-colonial subjects) are here because you (the colonial masters) were there, but rather that you only became you *because* you were there. This is what Michael Hardt and Antonio Negri point to when they argue that only through opposition to the colonised subject does 'the metropolitan subject really become itself': 'The gilded monuments not only of European cities but also of modern European thought itself are founded on the intimate dialectal struggle with its Others'.[26] The foundational categories of Enlightenment thought – those of liberalism, secularism, universalism,

liberty and so on – not only came into being in the context of colonialism; they were themselves produced as a way of creating the very
notion of European whiteness that had to be demarcated from its abject
other, the 'non-European' black African. These are the white mythologies, as Derrida puts it, central to the creation of a 'racialised
modernity' and of 'the West' itself.[27]

Goodhart states that it is a 'fallacy' that colonialism was really all
that bad and can be blamed for all of today's ills, that all civilizations
have engaged in slavery and conquest at some point and that, besides,
we shouldn't evaluate the errors of the past (if indeed they were errors)
by today's moral standards – 'we should be careful not to judge the past
by the standards of the present'. This is an attempt to draw an absolute
break between the colonial past and the contemporary present,
through which the very 'idea of Europe' and of Britishness in particular is 'cleansed' of its racial entanglements. Thus 'the past' of the
Enlightenment is central to how we are to understand what modern
day Europe really is (secular, liberal, tolerant, etc), yet we shouldn't go
on about how 'the past' of colonialism matters today. Yet, as Stuart
Hall points out:

> … post-Enlightenment, liberal, rational, humanist universalism of west-
> ern culture looks, not less historically significant but less *universal* by
> the minute. Many great ideas – liberty, equality, autonomy, democracy –
> have been honed within the liberal tradition. However, it is now clear
> that liberalism is not the 'culture that is beyond cultures' but the culture
> that won: that particularism which successfully universalized and hege-
> monized itself across the globe … There have been theoretical critiques
> of the 'dark' side of the Enlightenment project before, but it is 'the
> multicultural question' which has most effectively blown its contempo-
> rary cover.[28]

Goodhart has no theory or account of racism – to provide one would
problematise his central argument and force him to consider the
continuance of colonial racism into the present – and no understanding
of how difference and hybridity can produce new forms of solidarity
rather than simply weakening the old.[29] More salient than the veracity
and intention of the assertions themselves is the fact that Goodhart's
arguments received such extensive coverage within the mainstream
liberal media. The arguments seemed to chime with an emerging political consensus reflecting the desire for a reassertion and promotion of
stronger British values as a way to shore up the fragility of our fractured and traumatised national body politic.[30]

ENGLISH MULTICULTURAL SPORTING FUTURES

To return to the question of the sporting multicultural; if Stuart Hall is right about the centrality of football in narrating the myths and meanings of the nation, then the lack of South Asian professional football players becomes a public marker that is seen to confirm *their* inherent difference from the rest of *us*. Black supporters and players can be issued with what Les Back and his co-authors call 'passports to inclusion' into contemporary footballing cultures;[31] but this is often at the expense of South Asians (although of course, such passports can be revoked and downgraded from citizenship to merely permanent residency at a moment's notice).

If we look beyond the world of football we can perhaps see a different performance of Englishness. The rise to public attention and even hero worship among England's sporting publics of Mudhsuden Singh Panesar and Lewis Carl Hamilton is worth considering for the 'fleeting, prefigurative glimpses of a different nation'[32] that they offer. Since his International Test debut against India in March 2006, where his first and symbolic Test wicket was that of Sachin Tendulkhar, 'Monty' Panesar has captured the imagination of cricketing fans like few South Asian players before him. He is often referred to in journalistic profiles as a 'cult figure', and is widely seen as the best England spin bowler for a generation or more. One hundred and ten years after K. S. Ranjitsinhji was given the same award, Panesar was selected as one of the five Wisden Cricketers of the Year in 2007. His exuberant celebrations at the fall of a wicket, together with his proudly worn beard and *patka*, has led to him being dubbed, among other nicknames, the 'Sikh of Tweak'.

Similarly Lewis Hamilton has re-written the record books in Formula One. Missing out on winning the driver's championship by a single point, while consistently out-driving his two-time world champion teammate Fernando Alonso, was an unimaginable outcome of his first season, when the expectation was the odd podium finish at best and a year spent gaining experience. His impact is such that he is credited with saving Formula One, at least in Britain, after the retirement of Michael Schumacher, and the possibility that the sport – despite the best efforts of Alonso and Kimi Raikkonen – would fade from public view and with this lose much needed sponsorship money. As Richard Williams put it, 'Single-handedly he has restored public interest in a sport that had sunk up to the axles in its own cynicism'. [33] Profiles and commentators have marvelled at Hamilton's steadfast concentration and focus and his willingness not just to learn but to excel. As Damon Hill enthused, 'He's come into F1 and dealt with everything that has been thrown at him with no problem at all. He seems to be completely at home. It's as if F1 is simply the next stage in his career, a logical progression – but he's acting like there's another stage beyond F1. I've never seen anything like it'.[34] Hamilton ended his rookie year as a national sporting figure by being voted as runner up in the 2007 BBC Sports Personality of the Year, and being awarded both *GQ* magazine's Sportsman of the Year and *F1 Racing* magazine's Man of the Year.

What is striking about both men is that they do not speak to the traditional ways in which British Asian and black athletes have classically been understood. They come from the sprawling suburbs – Panesar from Luton, Hamilton from Stevenage – and not the inner cities so beloved of the tabloid rags-to-riches, out of the ghetto, sporting narratives. Both are softly spoken. Panesar, a Loughborough University graduate, sometimes exhibiting awkwardness at journalists' predictable questions. Hamilton, a model of understatement and professional respect for his rivals, is variously described as 'likeable and humble'.[35] Both eschew the type of 'in-your-face' masculine bravado often associated with boxers and track athletes. Theirs is not the 'immigrant' story of the likes of John Barnes, Linford Christie and others who came to England early in their life and made it their home, but struggled with what W.E.B. Du Bois referred to as the war between being black and being a New World Citizen. For Panesar and Hamilton their Englishness is simply an unremarkable, uncontestable given. So, although they are 'mould-breaking', in as much as Panesar is the first Sikh to have played for England and Hamilton the first black Formula One driver to compete at the highest level, they are also establishing new paradigms about what it means to be English. There is, at this historical conjuncture, no script for reading the political significance of a black English Formula One driver or a devout Sikh leading England's bowling attack.

Of course both athletes, despite their current high public standing, are still framed in problematic ways. There are constant discussions about Panesar's physicality – 'oh, hasn't he got big hands?' – and the fake beards and imitation head scarves now worn at cricket grounds have an uneasy resonance that plays on (and sometimes ignores) the line between jovial hero worship and sporting admiration and white mimicry and caricature of the racialised other. An interview in *The Sunday Times* included the following: 'Take me as you find me, he [Panesar] seems to say – unruly beard, big goggly eyes, unsynchronised limbs and all. And the public has done just that. Fans love nothing more than the sportsman who blends wholehearted effort with a dash of clumsiness. He's Eddie the Eagle, Eric the Eel and court-jester-made-good all rolled into one'.[36] No wonder Panesar doesn't give much away in interviews. An accomplished, dedicated and thoughtful international cricketer is reduced to a cartoon-like comedic object of ridicule, whose apparent purpose is to entertain ol' massa in the field.

And no doubt a part of the fascination with 'young Lewis' derives from the sheer novelty of a *black man* in Formula One, a sport that is almost blinding by its near absolute whiteness. Of course, despite the best managed-efforts of McLaren and Ron Dennis to 'play down' the 'race stuff' and discourage journalists from asking Hamilton questions about his colour, it remains a constitutive part of the many narratives about Hamilton that talk in metonymic terms about him being a 'breath of fresh air', 'irresistibly different' and 'new and exciting'. Race seems to be both present and absent with Hamilton. As Younge notes, one response underneath a YouTube posting of Hamilton's driving exploits 'suggested that his driving proficiency came from "all that practice he's had nicking cars"': 'At other times the references are more oblique. He has been compared to Tiger Woods, Theo Walcott and Amir Khan – but rarely Nigel Mansell, James Hunt or David Beckham'.[37] At least Hamilton drives a silver Mercedes and not a black BMW – it's nice for some of the old stereotypes to at least be updated, if not broken, from time-to-time.

In a strange way there is an almost desperate yearning for these two gifted young men to become the faces of multicultural England. The *Wisden* cricketer of the year profile described Panesar as 'an instant multicultural icon, a figure proclaiming a success for racial integration in fraught 21st-century Britain'. The *Sunday Times* similarly noted that the 'public warmth' for Panesar could be explained in part as 'his presence ... makes the England cricket team more multicultural. People want their team to look like this'.[38] In this moment Panesar becomes the anti-Shazad Tanweer, reassuring 'us' of the redemptive, integrative function that sport – and cricket especially – is supposed to have in making the natives into Englishmen, even if they still refuse to drink the warm beer after the match. And we are also reassured that we really are a fair and welcoming nation. This is the type of multicultural arrangement that we can all settle on. Though cautious in their public pronouncements, and in Panesar's case often conservative in outlook, both athletes motion towards the type of convivial multiculturalism that Gilroy suggests has become a part of the everyday lived multicul-ture – as opposed to the formal, political and policy debates over official multiculturalism. As Panesar himself has said, 'If me playing for England does something to show that our society is multicultural, then that's good. I think it does show how Britain is a multicultural society, that there aren't any differences and we are all one as a country. That's good for Britain and good for the people of this country'.[39]

Hamilton too, in the few times he has been allowed to speak more freely, has talked of this role models being his father, Nelson Mandela and Martin Luther King, and his musical tastes ranging from Bob Marley and Marvin Gaye to Nas. He has appeared on MTV Base, and hung out with Pharell Williams when he competed at Indianapolis. Thus, unlike Frank Bruno, Hamilton doesn't need to hide his blackness or wait until he has won the world championship before he can come out of the 'racial closet'. For Hamilton there is no closet. As he puts it, 'Being black is not a negative. It's a positive, if anything, because I'm different. In the future it can open doors to different cultures and that is what motor sport is trying to do anyway. It will show that not only white people can do it, but also black people, Indians, Japanese and Chinese. It will be good to mean something'.[40]

This is a 'soft multiculturalism' that is sellable. It hasn't been lost on the advisers of both young men that a dash of colour that isn't too dark – light-skinned suburban black rather than inner-city ebony, conservative Sikh rather than outspoken radical Muslim – is hugely marketable. As Panesar's then agent David Ligertwood told *The Sunday Times*, 'He's a lot more in demand now. He's been popular all summer [2006], but that has turned into commercial interest ... There's an X-factor with Monty. He's not just another player. He stands out as a character. Everybody can see he's a good bloke and a fun guy, but a serious cricketer, and they warm to that. He also embraces his Asian background. People may have been looking at guys in the street with beards and feeling negative about them. Monty makes them feel good'.[41] Likewise, Hamilton's earnings have rocketed from his purported first year salary of £250,000 to what is now expected to be an earnings capability in the tens of millions *per year*, with media speculation that his final career earnings could be worth $1 billion. As one consultancy and PR guru put it in unabashed terms, 'Hamilton's ethnic background gives him a "value add" in terms of marketability. In the US, the African-American market accounts for $561bn ... boosted by stars such as Tiger Woods and the Williams sisters, but over here brands are only just beginning to catch on to the spending power of our ethnic communities ... Black icons are seen as trendsetters in terms of market value. Stars like Lewis Hamilton are worth their weight in gold'.[42] In a glossy advertisement in the 2007 special issue of *Esquire* magazine's 'The Big Black Book: The style manual for successful men', Hamilton is photographed gazing out of the window of a Bombardier Learjet, dressed immaculately in a tailored suit, the sunlight gently caressing his motionless frame. His poised, confident and beautifully young face does not look out of place in this private jet. Not even Ian Wright at the height of his media wave and fame could have been used to shift a few Learjets.[43]

ST GEORGE'S LAST STAND

Identity, as Stuart Hall suggests, is 'a structured representation that only achieves its positive through the narrow eye of the negative. It has to go through the eye of the needle of the other before it can reconstruct itself'.[44] As regards to what we should label as English ethnicity, the Other has changed to such an extent that it has become a part of the subject. There is no outside racial Other to Englishness any more. The centre itself has been reconfigured from within. Multiculturalism, read as the 'return of the repressed',[45] erases once and for all any notion of a retreat back into the myths of free born Englishmen. That historical moment has passed. There was never, literally speaking, much white in the Union Flag anyway, so the scramble to the St George's Cross is, for some, white England's last stand for purified racial homogeneity. But for these English ultra-nationalists, yearning for simpler symbolic representations, instead of a team of heroic white lions they find a classic left-arm spin bowler from Luton, by way of the Punjab, and a hero to the petrol heads made in Stevenage by way of Grenada. Though often disavowed by the floods of recent populist books on 'the English question', it is precisely this 'new' hybridity of Englishness that has *always* been its defining characteristic. Stuart Hall's words from the early 1990s have proved prescient when he suggested that it 'was only by dint of excluding or absorbing all the differences that constituted Englishness, the multitude of different regions, peoples, classes, genders that composed the people gathered together in the Act of the Union, that Englishness could stand together for everybody in the British isles. It was always negotiated against difference ... And that is something which we are only now beginning to see the true nature of, when we are beginning to come to the end of it'.[46]

The New England is the Old England. Once we recognise this, the debates themselves become increasingly sterile and anachronistic. The protagonists still fight out the political battles of ethnic versus civil nationalism, progressive versus traditional, forward-looking against backward-looking, as if it either matters or has an effect. The ritualistic debate that has occurred every two years for the past decade – depending on the England men's team qualifying for a World Cup or European Championship – over whether or not a progressive English nationalism can be achieved in the domain of football spectatorship is symptomatic of this. So before and/or during each tournament Mark Perryman and/or Billy Bragg writes a cautious but optimistic piece in defence of the New England and 'soft patriotism' in the *Guardian* and/or *Independent*, followed by a reply from Mike Marqusee and/or Joseph Harker condemning the naiveté of said argument, pointing instead to the continuing existence of anti-brown and black racism within much of English fan culture. *Both sides are of course right.* The growth in broader based support for the England national team reflects the post Euro-1996 changes in football fan culture, which accelerated after the 2002 World Cup.[47] A team of Rio Ferdinands, Ashley Coles and David Beckhams is profoundly different to one full of Stuart Pearces, Terry Butchers and Gazzas; the former reflects an urban, comfortable multiraciality and even metrosexuality that allows for a degree of South Asian and black identification with the national team that simply did not exist a decade ago. *And yet* the same 'traditional' fans' (albeit a subset) singing of 'I'd rather be a Paki than a Turk' is such a convoluted 'progressive' step of identification with the Other that it barely registers at all. Three steps forward, two and a half steps back.

The arguments over Englishness and sporting fandom are not without merit. They speak to the continuing, unfolding story of Englishness and its splintering into multiple narratives. They speak to the recognition that sport continues to hold a centrally important space in the nationalist imaginary, despite what the cultural elites would wish. But we need to recognise the debate itself as constitutive of a way of contesting and refusing Englishness that is, well, very English. Thus public discussions about sport and multiculturalism are always, ultimately about broader questions of belonging, identity and identification – both to the nation and to wider transnational forms. The sociological question to be addressed in this context concerns who is allowed to represent the nation and under what conditions of inclusion/exclusion. This causes us to think about both the possibilities for, *and limitations of*, using sport and particular athletes as cultural reference points for identity formation. Due to the resolutely priapic fabric of Britain's professional sporting cultures, for example, such national icons remain overwhelming male, despite the best efforts of individual stars such as Paula Radcliffe, Denise Lewis and Kelly Holmes. While Britain fails to produce outstanding sportswomen outside of track and field, and while women's team sports remain marginal (if they exist at all) to the mass media, national sporting icons will likely remain a largely male affair. This should strike a cautionary note for those who are optimists about the claims to be made concerning the sporting politics of representation: currently only men's teams are deemed worthy of truly symbolising the nation.

2012 AND THE SPORTING MULTICULTURAL

A critical and global analysis of the role of popular culture, and sport in particular, in helping us to live, work and play with and through difference, in an age still marked by the historical scars of Empire and racial exclusion, is a necessary and urgent task. It is one that needs to avoid uncritically over-inflating the importance of sport in general, as well as particular (usually male) athletes as if they are simple 'role models' for an entire nation. But we similarly and simultaneously need to understand and map the continued importance that sporting spectacles play in giving shape to what it means to be a national subject (however partial that subject is) when national sovereignty and subjectivity itself are increasingly fraught with fissures and erasure.

To return to where we started. The 2012 summer Olympic and Paralympic games offer an opportunity to make real sport's oft-claimed but rarely realised capacity for social and cultural regeneration – both aesthetically, in terms of the physical landscape and environment of East London and the surrounding areas and also existentially, in terms of who we are as co-existing communities. The opening (and closing) ceremony provides London, and by extension England and Britain too, with an opportunity to address the deep-rooted antagonisms of race, nation and empire that so clearly mark the post-colonial, multicultural present. Thus, to paraphrase the Parekh report, the Olympics provide an important public space within which to re-write the national story, as one in which the idea of a multicultural post-national narrative becomes both real and desirable. One that, rather than disavowing Britain's imperial past, acknowledges its painful complexity in forging the present. Englishness, adrift for so long in the multicultural seas, can finally come home, along the Thames and into the Olympic Village, alongside the other 'home nations' that will make up that curious, hybrid sporting nation called 'Great Britain and Northern Ireland'. If that can be achieved then the 2012 Games might just signal the revival of a truly multicultural nation finally at ease with itself.

Previous versions of this essay were presented at the 'Race and Sport Symposium', at the University of Iowa, Iowa City in 2006 and at the University of Toronto's Centre for Diaspora and Transnational Studies in 2007. I'd like to thank organisers and delegates at both institutions for their invitation to speak and for their critical feedback. Mark

Perryman, as ever, provided expert editorial advice and suggestions and Simone Browne, Barnor Hesse and Gary Younge will no doubt recognise some (though not all) of their sage counsel in this chapter. Thank you all for the continuing conversations. A small part of this essay also appears in my co-authored chapter with Ian McDonald entitled 'The Politics of "Race" and Sport Policy in the United Kingdom', in Barrie Houlihan's Sport and Society *(London, Sage, 2008). I'd like to thank Sage for permission to republish that reworked part here.*

NOTES

1. Stuart Hall, 'Conclusion: The multicultural question', in Barnor Hesse (Ed.), *Un/settled Multiculturalisms: Diasporas, entanglements, transruptions*, Zed Books 2000, p213.

2. C.L.R. James, *Beyond a Boundary*, Serpent's Tail 1983, p64.

3. Leader, 'A moment for Britain to glory in the Olympic spirit', *The Independent*, 7.7.05, p36.

4. Melanie Phillips, *Londonistan: How Britain is creating a terror state within*, Gibson Square Books 2006.

5. Trevor Phillips, 'Let's Show the World its Future', *The Observer*, 10.7.05, p5.

6. That is to say, the ways in which black diasporan peoples in Europe have begun to create and forge an identity *as Europeans*. This is an identity that is at once both complexly related to the wider African diaspora but at the same time distinctly European too. This has afforded many black Europeans a way to articulate multiple identifications that resist national assimilation by staking a claim to belong but at the same time challenging racially exclusive forms of European nationalisms. Hence how this 'new' subjectivity can positively claim identification as, for example, 'a Londoner' *and* 'a European', thus negating the nation-state altogether. See Barnor Hesse, 'Afterword: Black Europe's undecidability', in Darlene Clarke-Hine, Tricia Keaton and Stephen Small (Eds.), *Black Europe and the African Diaspora*, University of Illinois Press 2008.

7. Stuart Hall, 'Aspiration and Attitude … Reflections on black Britain in the nineties', *new formations* 33, Spring 1998, p43.

8. Paul Gilroy, 'Foreword', in Ben Carrington and Ian McDonald (Eds.), *'Race', Sport and British Society*, Routledge 2001, p xi.

9. It is interesting how often editors invoke a Habermasian ideal of trying to develop a deliberative democratic space of communicative exchange when faced with accusations of printing racist diatribes that clearly have nothing whatsoever to do with the goal of achieving mutual understanding. Inadvertently revealing the profound depths of racism within the culture of the English cricket establishment, and by extension within *Wisden*

Cricket Monthly itself, editor David Frith's editorial response the following month stated, 'Robert Henderson's article 'Is It In the Blood?' (*WCM* July) did not place a question-mark beside foreign-born England cricketers. It was already there. Reservations have rumbled around the cricket grounds and in the sports columns of the newspapers for several years' (*Wisden Cricket Monthly*, August 1995, p5). From here on we might refer to this as the Habermasian defence.

10. Robert Henderson, 'Is it in the blood?', *Wisden Cricket Monthly*, July 1995, pp9-10. For a critical review of the 'Henderson affair', see Mike Marqusee's 'In search of the unequivocal Englishman: The conundrum of race and nation in English cricket', in Ben Carrington and Ian McDonald (Eds.), *'Race', Sport and British Society*, Routledge 2001.

11. Cited in Ben Carrington, 'Football's Coming Home, But Whose Home? And Do We Want It? Nation, football and the politics of exclusion', in Adam Brown (Ed.), *Fanatics! Power, Identity and Fandom in Football*, Routledge 1998, p118.

12. See Mark Perryman, 'Chapter 5: Red, white and black all over', in *Ingerland: Travels with a football nation*, Simon and Schuster 2006.

13. Paul Johnson, 'The logical end of black racism is a return to Africa', *The Spectator*, 30.12.95, p20.

14. Ambivalent in the sense that racist discourses certainly continued throughout the 1990s and into the present, the fears over so-called Jamaican 'yardies' and gun toting black men being the latest manifestation. Yet more complex and 'positive' frames of reference for blackness emerged in which the black presence was not simply seen as alien and/or threatening. Thus I am trying to indicate the contradictory and in some ways ambivalent nature of this racial reconfiguration.

15. Gary Younge, 'To believe in a European utopia before Muslims arrived is delusional', *Guardian*, 10.12.07.

16. I'm referring here to mainstream, national political discourse. It could be argued with some justification that throughout the 1980s and into the 1990s there was an active local authority politics of multiculturalism within many metropolitan spaces that continues to some degree today. This is true. My argument here concerns how central government has explicitly used multiculturalism both as a conceptual frame to develop progressive social policies and as an ideal through which to give positive meaning to a *new* notion of what it means to be British. In this limited sense I am suggesting that, contrary to most accounts of the term, multiculturalism actually had a very short shelf life within British political discourse.

17. Fran Abrams, 'Tory Conference: Anger as Tebbit questions loyalties of "two-nation"', *Independent*, 8.10.97.

18. David Cameron, 'Call that election. We will fight. Britain will win', Conservative Party Conference Speech 2007: www.conservatives.com/ (retrieved 4.1.08).

19. The Runnymede Trust, *The Parekh Report: The future of multi-ethnic Britain*, Profile Books 2000.

20. All newspaper headlines taken from Eugene McLaughlin and Sarah Neal, 'Who Can Speak to Race and Nation?: Intellectuals, public policy formation and the *Future of Multi-ethnic Britain* Commission', *Cultural Studies* Vol: 21(6) November 2007, pp910-930.

21. Ibid.

22. Ibid.

23. See David Goodhart's essays 'Too diverse?', *Prospect*, February 2004, and 'National anxieties', *Prospect*, June 2006.

24. Ray Pahl, 'Hidden Solidarities', *Prospect*, September 2006.

25. Paul Gilroy, 'Melancholia or Conviviality: The politics of belonging in Britain', *Soundings*, Spring 2005, pp41-42.

26. Michael Hardt and Antonio Negri, *Empire*, Harvard University Press 2000, p128.

27. See Barnor Hesse, 'Racialized Modernities: An analytics of white mythologies', *Ethnic and Racial Studies* Vol: 30(4) July 2007, pp 643-663.

28. Stuart Hall, 'Conclusion: The multicultural question', in Barnor Hesse (Ed.), *Un/settled Multiculturalisms: Diasporas, entanglements, transruptions*, Zed Books 2000, p228.

29. Neil Ascherson, 'Replies to David Goodhart', *Prospect* June 2006.

30. It is worth pointing out that the so-called 'progressive dilemma' is nothing of the sort, being neither 'progressive' – the argument is founded upon a reactionary conceptualization of nationhood and folk – nor a 'dilemma' – there is no inherent contradiction between political solidarity and ethnic diversity. That Goodhart has managed to pass this off as a 'problem' for the left is given the lie by the fact that Goodhart admits in the original essay which sparked the 'debate' that the dilemma was in fact posed by the Conservative politician David 'Two Brains' Willetts. Why Willetts should be accorded such stature to frame the debate for progressives in the first place has rarely been remarked upon. Indeed it is difficult to see why the magazine – co-founded and financially backed by the former Conservative MP Derek Coombs – is still seen to a 'liberal' publication at all when it is clearly a centre-right publication. In a way, *Prospect* itself is symptomatic of how far to the right much of Britain's liberal intelligentsia has shifted.

31. Les Back, Tim Crabbe and John Solomos, '"Lions and Black Skins": Race, nation and local patriotism in football', in Ben Carrington and Ian McDonald (Eds.) *'Race', Sport and British Society*, Routledge 2001.

32. Paul Gilroy, 'Foreword', in Ben Carrington and Ian McDonald (Eds.) *'Race', Sport and British Society*, Routledge 2001, p. xvii.
33. Richard Williams, 'Standard-bearer who influenced people and made an enemy', *Guardian* 22.10.07.
34. Maurice Hamilton, 'The only way is up', *Observer* 7.10.07.
35. Martin Jacques, 'It's the same as Tiger: Nothing will change', *Observer* 3.6.07.
36. Simon Wilde, 'The Big Interview: Monty Panesar', *Sunday Times* 06.08.06.
37. Gary Younge, 'Made in Stevenage', *Guardian* 16.6.07.
38. Simon Wilde, 'The Big Interview: Monty Panesar', *Sunday Times* 6.8.06.
39. Ibid.
40. Martin Jacques, 'A new hero for our times', *Guardian* 22.10.07.
41. Simon Wilde, 'The Big Interview: Monty Panesar', *Sunday Times* 6.8.06.
42. Anna Kessel, 'Race Driver', *Observer* 1.1.07.
43. The advertisement reads: 'The Race is On: Live it fast…Live it large…Live it high…Live it in style…Live it like three-time grand prix winner Lewis Hamilton, and become a living legend'.
44. Stuart Hall, 'The Local and the Global: Globalization and ethnicity', in Antony D. King (Ed.), *Culture, Globalization and the World-System*, Macmillan 1991, p21.
45. Barnor Hesse (Ed.), *Un/settled Multiculturalisms: Diasporas, entanglements, transruptions*, Zed Books 2000.
46. Stuart Hall, 'The Local and the Global: Globalization and ethnicity', in Antony D. King (Ed.) *Culture, Globalization and the World-System*, Basingstoke, Macmillan 1991, p.22.
47. See Mark Perryman, *Going Oriental: Football after the World Cup 2002*, Mainstream Publishing 2002.

Minding our language

Julia Bell

I am English by birth – Bristol, Clifton Maternity Hospital – although when I was six months old my parents moved to rural mid-Wales and I grew up there until I was eighteen. I learnt to speak Welsh, I entered Eisteddfod and recited Welsh poetry, but I am not Welsh. My language skills – I learned Welsh at primary school because everyone spoke it – enabled me to navigate between the Welsh and English in the playground but I was always neither one thing or the other. This bilingual upbringing meant that when I moved to Birmingham in 1989 I was suddenly immersed in a whole new culture, one which had a subtly different set of class expectations and ideas of deference. It was more than just a rural versus industrial shift. Brummies had a different accent and a different experience of their identity, shaped by the Victorian industrialization of the Midlands and the North of England, by a history of Kings and Queens which was very different from the Welsh and Scottish sense of history. Very few people in England know the stories of Owain Glendwr and the Kings of Wales, or the Welsh myths – the Mabinogion.

Birmingham in 1989 was, to put it frankly, a bit of a dump. The loss of industry, coupled with a recession, had left many without much money and jobs were scarce. Added to this was the infamous city centre and the Bull Ring, which by then was a crumbling concrete eyesore of failed 1960s idealism. Here I found a place with a strong sense of class identity, of Brummies sticking it out together – forged also by the fact that Birmingham, apart from nouveau-riche pockets like Solihull, was pretty much out and out Labour. The Conservatives were perceived to have taken away jobs and opportunities, and once again the common man, and woman, was under the thumb of the 'posh' in London.

Added to this, the city that once boasted 'a thousand trades' was a focal point for a great deal of post-war immigration – from Ireland, Poland, the Caribbean, Pakistan, India, China and the Middle East –

who often lived in impoverished communities themselves. Andrea Levy's novel *Small Island* clearly evokes this atmosphere of post-war hardship that many Caribbean immigrants to Britain found in the 1940s and 1950s.[1] Immigrants lived cheek by jowl with each other, and with the English working classes, putting them, too, by default, whatever their social position back home, on the bottom rung of the English class ladder. In the broadest sense this makes the English working classes of the second half of the twentieth century and later a potent mix of cultures and races.

While class is not the only defining characteristic of English national identity, it's perhaps the root cause of the current state of the English identity crisis. In his poem *Men of England*, the Romantic poet-revolutionary and occasional rich layabout Percy Bysshe Shelley exhorts the English workers – the 'bees of England' – to rise up against their masters and create an England of their own making, for their own benefit.[2]

Men of England, wherefore plough
For the lords who lay ye low?
Wherefore weave with toil and care
The rich robes your tyrants wear?

Wherefore feed and clothe and save,
From the cradle to the grave,
Those ungrateful drones who would
Drain your sweat – nay, drink your blood?

Wherefore, Bees of England, forge
Many a weapon, chain, and scourge,
That these stingless drones may spoil
The forced produce of your toil?

This is a revolutionary, proto-Marxist piece, which sees the English as oppressed by their masters, where the produce of their toil goes towards making others rich.

Shelley knew then, as the posh English governing class, still do now, that it's dangerous and *outré* to admit to having a national identity. Irishman Bernard Shaw wittily points this out in his play *Saint Joan*, in which the English Nobleman teases his Chaplain by accusing him of being English: 'Oh! you are an Englishman, are you?' he says. To which the Chaplain responds, insulted: 'Certainly not, my lord: I am a gentleman'.[3] While this was written in the 1920s, this notion that the pursuit of national identity is a poor man's pursuit, and also a potentially treacherous and revolutionary one, still holds in certain quarters of our country to this day. Take, for example, Peter Hitchens's rather hysterical rant against the forces of modernity – in fact mostly liberals and the left – in *The Abolition of Britain*.[4] In his view Britain has undergone a cultural revolution on a par with the Chinese Cultural revolution, in which multiculturalism has gone mad and changed forever the landscape of the Britain he is nostalgic for, cricket and the Church of England. In essence this is just another example of a posh conservative railing against the dangerous forces of social change, the new multicultural working classes. He mistakenly sees 'multiculturalism' as a liberal buzzword, rather than a descriptive term for actual reality.

In Wales, by comparison, this kind of class system is practically non-existent. Based on a more Puritan model and knitted together by a shared language and strong cultural identity the Welsh have a two-tier system – the workers or the *gwerin* – simple country folk – and the professional class which includes doctors, lawyers, teachers, priests, policemen and so on – the community figures who knit the whole together. Perhaps this is a result of being under English rule for so long: the Kings and Queens and noblemen belong to the *Sais*, the English, while the Welsh get on with business pretty much as they always have done, with a distinct resentment of English rule and an adherence to the old language and its poetry, and the mysterious and ancient art of *Cerdd Dant*, singing poetry to the accompaniment of a harp.

For the Welsh, literature and language helped preserve a sense of national identity, whereas the English have, at various times and for generally mendacious reasons, been forced to subsume their identity into the demands of their masters – most latterly to some fey ideas about 'Britishness' at the expense of English as well as Scots and Welsh identity. In the early 1800s Shelley's poem would have been seen as a revolutionary gauntlet to rulers who were terrified of the possibility of a French-style revolution , and as the century progressed Englishness was further suppressed by the explosion of the British, not English, Empire. In the end we were all, as well as instruments and beneficiaries – English, Scots, Welsh, Irish – subjects of the Empire too, and therefore alienated from our identity. And it is the collapse of this Empire and its long legacy that interestingly puts the English question back in the frame.

It seems curious to me as a writer that the nation which gave the English language to the world, and which is acknowledged as produc- ing some of the most exciting and studied literature in the world, does not have a strong sense of its own cultural identity. Perhaps there is partially an answer in the language itself, which is constantly evolving to accommodate other languages. English is spoken by over a billion people worldwide, and is acknowledged as the international language of business and the world's official second language. Its success lies in the flexibility of its grammar, its ability to incorporate new words and meanings, and its reflexive structure, which allows for complex hypothesis and speculation – it's a useful language for philosophy and abstract thought.[5] This flexible structure and evolving lexicon reflects something of its roots – an Anglo-Germanic language which emerged from bits of Old French and Old Norse, with a later large smattering of Latin and Greek which came with the Christianisation of the British Isles. The origins of the language say something about the origins of the English too, which is that they are not indigenous, but a population made up of Celts and Vikings, French, Germans and Danes, to name but a few.

The other interesting feature of the English language in England is that English is at its most linguistically diverse in England – divided into many different regional accents and dialects; although TV and films have to a certain extent homogenized the language, it is still sometimes only a matter of travelling a few miles outside a region to encounter another accent and another subtly different use of the language – consider the difference between a Birmingham and a Derbyshire accent for example.

This diversity reflects something of the basic identity of the English, especially currently, with new mass migration patterns across the globe. The English have always been a nation of immigrants, a diverse concoction of other cultures and languages which mix together to form a patchwork whole. The fall of the British Empire has made England, specifically London and the South East, a destination of choice for many of the former colonies as well as the 'New Europe' too. Coming to terms with Empire and its legacy, for good and ill, is one of the keys to understanding the current state of English identity. Whether we like it or not, England is the parental heart of Empire and London it's global magnet. People are attracted by the opportunity, wealth, tolerance and fluidity of identity that is seen to be possible in a global megapolis such as London, where the streets seem full of the whole world.

This shift is reflected in a great deal of the literature that has been published in the last twenty years. And there have been two noticeable trends. One is the 'post-colonial' novel, which means novels written by and about writers of mixed ethnicity, or those whose origins are in the former colonies. Novels by Monica Ali, Zadie Smith, Hari Kunzru, Kate Grenville, Arundhati Roy, Vikraim Seth, Chimamanda Ngozi Adichie, Andrea Levy and so on are often lumped together in the same category, as 'news from elsewhere' novels. But what is really happening is a reflection of the changing make-up of the country; writers are telling stories and histories of the new global community that we now live in.

The other trend has, ironically, been for more regionalisation. Small independent presses have sprung up in various parts of the country, not so much as a reaction against the global interests of the London editors, but out of a need to disentangle London from the rest of the country; and as a reaction against the media conglomerates who exert a stranglehold over the major London publishing houses. The output of Tindal Street Press in Birmingham provides an interesting example of work that is published by the regions for a national audience. The authors are diverse – Daphne Glazer, Catherine O'Flynn, Austin Clarke, A.E. Markham – and concerned with stories that exist outside the London mainstream. They have consistently invigorated prize lists by publishing work that larger houses find hard to justify – as supposedly too big a profit risk – for example Catherine O'Flynn's wonderful *What Was Lost*.[6] This smaller model – there are many other examples – Telegram Books, Saqi, Egg Box, Dedalus – is a means by which publishing as a creative activity can be celebrated; and shifting the editorial perspective from London to Birmingham shows a subtle shift in taste and viewpoint which is greatly to the benefit of our cultural diversity.

What I am arguing for is just a simple acceptance of our plurality. That the 'bees of England' should feel unashamed of their heritage and identity, and accept that class and immigration have played a large role in shaping the history of this small island, just as the forces of globalisation are shaping it now. And there is much to celebrate. England is popular abroad – a key reason for the scale of the immigration we are witnessing at the moment. As well as the language and literature, English football, comedy and history are popular symbols of English identity abroad, and added to this is the modern financial and cultural centre that is London, one of the Western world's most important cities. The old England that is fetishised by the likes of Peter Hitchens and Morrisey has gone forever, and the navel gazing about the sins of the colonial past is fading.

The English language is favoured by the world because of its flexibility, its intelligibility, its creativity and huge vocabulary. We English could do worse than strive for these virtues in our national identity.

NOTES

1. Andrea Levy, *Small Island*, Headline Review 2004.
2. Percy Bysshe Shelly, *The Major Works*, Oxford 2003.
3. George Bernard Shaw, *Saint Joan: A Chronicle Play in Six Scenes and an Epilogue*, Penguin Classics 2001.
4. Peter Hitchens, *The Abolition of Britain*, Quartet 2000.
5. Melvyn Bragg, *The Adventure of English*, Sceptre 2004.
6. Catherine O'Flynn, *What Was Lost*, Tindal Street Press 2007.

The beautiful North

David Conn

Except in mostly lame or offensive gags, people in England do not talk much about the differences between northerners and southerners, the subtle peculiarities of Geordies or spikiness of scousers. When pundits try, they too often produce a muddle of cliché, get themselves into trouble and end up apologising on local radio. It is slippery to assess how important regional differences and loyalties actually are; they are certainly nowhere near as real as the Labour government thought they were for a time in the late 1990s. Then, bold plans for regional assemblies cooled after local mayoral elections were met with waves of indifference and spoof or oddball candidates, some of whom, like Stuart Drummond, the Hartlepool FC monkey mascot, went on to win.

My own assessment of whether or not regional allegiances could be strong enough to form separate political identities, or undermine a collective sense of Englishness, is a no, on both counts. And that could be a great strength for England, because it suggests that the country embraces historical and cultural differences, yet they are not pronounced enough to create the sort of separatist tensions which test the unity of some other European countries, notably Spain, and more recently France, Belgium and Switzerland.

I have drawn those conclusions partly from my own experience, of lugging my family over the windy Pennines two years ago, when we moved from the grey bosom of Manchester, where I was born and have always, broadly speaking, felt naturally comfortable, across the border into Yorkshire, whose Dales I had never even visited before I met my wife, who grew up there. Moving back with our children to live closer to their maternal grandparents was a journey of just eighty-five miles, up through the sour Lancashire hills and remoter backwaters of Burnley, an hour and a half with no hold-ups, yet in some ways you could be in another country.

In Manchester, for all the grimness which persists in the face of the city leaders' propaganda that the place is wholly resurrected, there is a ducking and diving, a spring in the step, a swagger and a blag. In Yorkshire, to put it simply, people seem to say a lot less. Even young people greet each other with 'Now then?', swap a curt summing-up, then move on. And rather than resenting the stereotype of them as a mean-spirited crew who are extremely careful with money, they seem to quite relish it.

The striking differences between these two clumps of the English nation huddled so closely together has been written about and commented on surprisingly little. That in itself points to a conclusion, that while regional distinctions certainly exist in England, they are not deeply felt – not passionately enough to inspire many writers, nor to create much of a market for their books. The relatively few exceptions, like Stuart Maconie's recent *Pies and Prejudice,* and Simon Armitage's *All Points North,* explore the intricate character and differences between the people and regions of the north in portraits which are wholly celebratory.

Charles Nevin's *Lancashire* is another notable exception, an affectionate, determinedly amused celebration of a region now more accurately, and less winningly, known as 'the North West.' Nevin dives joyfully into a riff contrasting the ribald, have-a-laugh attitude on the rainy side of the hills with the flinty, sense-of-humour-bypass in Yorkshire. 'The Pennines: a boundary far more significant than the Trent,' he writes. 'On the one side lives a warm and whimsical race, ever ready to chuckle, even laugh, in the face of the sheer ridiculousness of life; on the other, a sad and surly people, unable to understand why they haven't been let in on the joke.[1] With persuasive mischief, Nevin then presents two competing lists of celebrities. On the one hand: 'Arthur Scargill, Roy Hattersley, Michael Parkinson, Fred Trueman, Geoffrey Boycott, Alan Titchmarsh, David Blunkett'. And on the other: 'George Formby, Gracie Fields, Stan Laurel, Frank Randle, Robb Wilton, Tommy Handley, Ken Dodd, Les Dawson, Eric Morecambe, Victoria Wood, Steve Coogan, Johnny Vegas, Caroline Aherne, Peter Kay'. 'It is an essential truth,' Nevin concludes, 'that comics come from Lancashire and don't come from Yorkshire.'[2]

Nevin also found surprisingly little literature about this contrast, or its causes, but came across a brilliantly observed passage in a Lancashire guidebook written by Walter Greenwood, author of the 1936 classic, *Love on the Dole.* 'Yorkshire', Greenwood wrote, 'faces the full blast of the easterly wind which may account for the Yorkshire character ... [whereas] The boisterous wind that buffets the land of the

Red Rose is born in the tumbling wastes of the Atlantic. A wild, warm, amorous wind wrenching with fat clouds and leaving them big with rain of which they deliver themselves on the Pennines' westerly slopes.'[3]

It was lucky I hadn't read that before we moved. Who would want to leave a wild, warm and amorous place, which has a Caroline Aherne and a Peter Kay around every corner, for an icy windscape in which the former cricket umpire Dickie Bird (74, Barnsley-born, plain-speaking) passes for a local treasure?

We moved, anyway, and since we arrived, I have found these sweeping, simplistic, patronising generalisations to be ... completely true. The Yorkshire wind does indeed howl in from the Urals. It makes the lips thin and conversation unwise. In Manchester, the clouds rumble and the people hardly stop talking.

And yet, of course, there are many more sides to a proper discussion on local identity. The regions and their people are not as clearly different as that entertaining picture, and they have much more in common than in contrast. Lancashire, for a start, is not the land of whimsy so fondly imagined by Nevin. Even geographically, it was reorganised in 1974, shifted north and west, whilst Greater Manchester and Merseyside took over the metropolitan areas, including St Helens, where Nevin is from. That word – 'from' – is, by the way, important. As Nevin himself says of his beloved Lancashire: 'I left, as you do ... and went to London, change at Oxbridge, holding on to a bit of stage Northernness for distinction and identification purposes among the metropolitan middle classes.'[4] There is a nice self-mockery in that, but its essence is perhaps a truer reflection of regional relationships in England than his portrait of Lancashire's charms. Educated people leave the north for London to build their careers. Very many of the people who triumph northern-ness – their own, or Manchester's music scene of the 1980s and early 90s, or Yorkshire's pride in telling it as it is – do so from their homes in London. Their fond recollections of their northern roots are part nostalgia, part relief that they don't live there anymore.

In Lancashire, the truth is that not everybody is a ribald bundle of whimsy, nor are Mancunians all 24-hour-party-people. Lancashire now stretches to Blackpool, a sinking resort desperately seeking a supercasino, and east to Pendle and Burnley, deprived former mill towns where unemployment is high and the British National Party has a real political presence. Laughs are in short supply.

And the longer you linger in Yorkshire, the more you appreciate some of its virtues; the beautiful, varied countryside, the loyalty and even a seam of gentleness, humour, in the outwardly flinty folk. To talk geography again, Yorkshire is huge, stretching from the Pennines to Scarborough and Whitby out on the east coast, north almost to Durham, south past Rotherham. West Yorkshire, which includes the main cities of Leeds and Bradford, is not so different from the former mining and enduring steel territory of South Yorkshire, which includes Sheffield; but North Yorkshire, wealthier than the rest of the county, is a world apart: agricultural, achingly well-preserved and the place where the former Conservative leader William Hague – another of Nevin's gauche and not-at-all funny Yorkshire-men, presumably – has his Richmond parliamentary seat. In large parts of North Yorkshire, old money and major landownership still set the tone, and Conservative MPs dominate, unlike in the urban constituencies of Leeds, Bradford or Sheffield.

In the Dales and market towns, there is pride, and something genuine, too, in the Yorkshire folk's assessment of the area as 'God's own country'. They appreciate what they have, lovely, well-maintained countryside, historic towns where local farmers and food are still an important presence, where longstanding community institutions are still kept actively intact.

The Yorkshire cities, Leeds, Bradford, Sheffield, are broadly similar, really, to Manchester, Liverpool or Birmingham, as are the people. Perhaps Bradford is most different, because of its very high population of people of South Asian origin, who rather complicate the portrait of the Yorkshire-Lancashire split as Geoffrey Boycott versus Peter Kay. A large part of the generalised differences between the two regions are in fact distinctions between an urban and rural character. English cities in the north – perhaps nationwide – have more in common, good and bad, than any regional characteristics dividing them. Their greatest challenge, probably, is the persistent poverty which co-exists with metropolitan money and style. That is true of all English cities – for all the hype about Manchester's revival, it took a 2007 report, *Breakthrough Manchester*, by former Tory leader Ian Duncan-Smith, to highlight the deep and widespread poverty which persists in the city – 60 per cent of Mancunians live in wards among the 10 per cent most deprived in the country – alongside those relatively few doing well and slurping sushi at that trophy store for all aspirant northern cities, Selfridges. Nowhere, of course, is the divide between rich and poor more extreme than in inner city London – and in that, perhaps the most important urban phenomenon of all, the southern capital has more in common with other English cities than its large middle class would care to accept.

So, Manchester is not that different from Leeds, but it is a world away from the Yorkshire countryside, as it is from the hill farmers of the Lake District – who are on the north-west, warm and supposedly blowsy side of the Pennines, yet are not famously noted for their chuckles and ready wit.

There are some genuine divisions, between the generally wealthier south and relatively impoverished north, which pose serious political and social challenges, but regional differences of character and history sit in the background. People are generally proud of where they come from, but they mostly wear that pride quite lightly. It is felt, not shouted about, and that is why civic leaders like those in Manchester strike the wrong note when they act like US boosters, talking up their city – 'A great European city to rival Barcelona' has been one of the choicest examples – to a degree which departs from the reality in which most of their citizens, struggling along, actually live. That is partly why mayoral elections outside London – and even there the turnout is still woefully low – have not greatly captured the local imaginations, and plans for regional assemblies have been quietly shelved. The local political classes, embroiled in competitive fights against other cities for central government money, major lottery awards for sports events or arts centres, and European Union development funds, work in a world in which geographical difference is very real. The general population feels it much less explicitly, does not understand the bidding wars into which their cities have been pitched as artificial rivals, and does not have much appetite for local mayors or local flags.

Partly, surely, this is a good thing, not just a reflection of apathy. England became a unified, relatively homogeneous country centuries ago, its regional differences steadily reduced to quirks, or the subject of whimsical observation by Maconie or Nevin. This is very different from Spain, for example, where in some principalities, most notably Catalonia, people have felt historically separate, and still push, in a politically organised way, for significant regional independence. However proud people are about their regions – and in England they tend to grumble or self-mock about the problems more than talk up the virtues – that pride never translates into a heartfelt sense of separateness. Only in Cornwall is there any genuine effort to establish some independent identity, and that is confined to a minority view, as compared, say, to the strength of popular Catalan antipathy to the rest of Spain.

The one arena which might seem to contradict that portrayal of England as a place of restrained regional identities is sport. Football grounds have been calmed and spruced up since the clamorous terraces were knocked down in the early 1990s, but still, Manchester United fans – not all of them, obviously – do seem to hate Liverpool, and Leeds. The feelings all being thoroughly mutual. So, when United fans chant 'We all hate the Leeds scum', do they mean it? Are they genuine, expressing extreme pride in their own city and vehement hatred of a city just thirty miles away? On balance, I think not. There are many reasons for hateful chanting at football, but mostly it is men letting off steam and doesn't justify soul-searching analysis. Much of the abuse is restricted to purely footballing rivalry, between two clubs, built up over years of support, and any references to the cities should be seen in that context. Even if there is a fists-clenched local pride at play, the fact that it is contained and expressed through a football medium probably shows it is diluted and manageable. The clincher, though, is so obvious you can miss it. Among the hardcore fans at just about every football club, the bitterest rivalry and cruellest chants come in matches against their closest rivals, which tends to be the other club in the same city. City and United, Liverpool and Everton, Sheffield's Owls and Blades; here there is bitter resentment and defiant proclamations of identity. Yet however you explain it, tribal antipathy or whatever, it cannot be an expression of regional identity because these sporting enemies live next door to each other.

The most striking development of English football fandom in recent years has been, in fact, a rallying around the England national team, with flags of St George sprouting on every car window. That, to some – broadly accurately – represents great progress from the fascist, troublemaking core which used to follow the national team around; but it has also dramatically spread a generally lumpen celebration of Englishness, whether among the hordes of football fans, the cricket 'barmy army', or even the sudden thousands who pitched up in Las Vegas in December 2007 to roar on the boxer Ricky Hatton, a genuine latter day British bulldog. While the nation is gripped in blanket patriotism desperate for an English sporting victory, a quieter portion of the population yearns for a more sophisticated way to celebrate the nation's qualities in the twenty-first century.

What about cricket, the only place left where you will ever hear anybody chant for the historic, pre-1974 county boundaries of Charles Nevin's nostalgic recollection? Here, Lancashire versus Yorkshire is still referred to as a 'Roses Match', which adds some heat to a sporting challenge. But to interpret the county rivalries as any expression of tub-thumping regional identity would mean, most probably, that you have not been to a cricket match recently. Splendid as county cricket is, its championship matches occupy four working weekdays, and so few people have the time to catch any of it that retired people make up at least 80 per cent of the few hundred people who make up 'the crowd' at most matches. The game itself is a proud English invention, but watching it is more in the English tradition of enjoying a nice, gentle day out, than any kind of hotbed of regional separatism.

The generally restrained nature of English regional pride offers, I think, some advantages, which could help to nurture a positive, modern sense of Englishness, in all its human, geographical and cultural variety. In some ways this is already happening, with regional identity increasingly celebrated, in food and other festivals, and an increase in writing and television programmes about the English landscape and coast. There are different histories, traditions and characteristics, yet no concerted, meaningful enmity, no clashing identity to solve, as there has been for centuries in other European countries. The economic dominance of London and the South East is a genuine imbalance which should be recognised and addressed however. In a survey by Centre for Cities, an Urban Policy Research Unit, in December 2007, the three cities with the highest average earnings were London, Cambridge and Reading. Hull, Burnley and Blackburn were among the lowest earning – although Belfast was bottom of the table of 60. Still, it was notable that the south had its blackspots, with Plymouth 54th in the list of average earnings, and Hastings 58th. Bristol was listed with Manchester and Liverpool as the three most socially and economically unequal cities in the UK.

This economic divide is not adequately acknowledged as one which needs a concerted solution – but perhaps because people themselves are not actively complaining about their lot compared with other regions. Culturally, regional differences are still there to discover and enjoy. Southerners who have barely ever been north could do with a trip to see how much of northern England is covered by national parks, and generally the English would benefit from knowing and appreciating more of their own country's history and landscape, which varies so much for so small a place. People may conclude, equipped with a more intimate knowledge of our own country, that Mancs are indeed full of blag and wisecracks, while Yorkshire folk are sharpened by the icy east wind, but, underneath, there is more which binds than separates us. England, for all its differences, is a place where people rub along together remarkably well, and that is a characteristic worth celebrating a little more.

NOTES

1. Charles Nevin, *Lancashire, Where Women Die of Love*, Mainstream 2006, p8.
2. Ibid, p9.
3. Ibid, p10.
4. Ibid, p8.

A short history of the future

The story of the beginning of the break-up of the UK

Gerry Hassan

I think the unravelling, should it come, would probably be a protracted nightmare. It would be a divorce, a division of the spoils on a kind of epic, spectacular scale. If we think of such issues as the army, things like British embassies overseas, Britain's permanent representation on the United Nations – all of these things would have to be unravelled and negotiated and fixed somehow. And I suspect that that would be extremely difficult, it would take a very long time, and I think that maybe for one or two years Great Britain – and I use that term advisedly – would just kind of go out of business in terms of its relations with the rest of the world while all this was sorted.

David Cannadine, *A Beginner's Guide to Separation*,
BBC Radio 4[1]

'Come on', he said. 'It's not a trick question. Just name me one thing he did that Washington wouldn't have approved of. Let's think.' He held up his thumb. 'One: deployment of British troops to the Middle East, against the advice of just about every senior commander in our armed forces and all of our ambassadors who know the region. Two' – up went his right index finger – 'complete failure to demand any kind of quid pro quo from the White House in terms of reconstruction contracts for British firms, or anything else. Three: unwavering support for US foreign policy in the Middle East, even when it's patently crazy for us to set ourselves against the entire Arab world.

Robert Harris, *The Ghost*[2]

The UK is both a space and a location. Where it thinks it is located and positions itself is central to how it sees itself. In part this is about the conversations and stories that all states tell themselves.[3] The UK is a state, but an unusual one – a multi-national state of four

nations, Scotland, England, Wales and Northern Ireland.[4] Its founding
goes back to the 1603 Union of the Crowns and the 1707 Treaty of
Union between Scotland and England. What is less observed is that the
UK is not a nation. While there is a sizeable sociology of 'stateless
nations' such as Scotland or Catalonia, there is no similar body of work
on 'nationless states' of which the UK is one. Other examples, before
they separated into constituent nations, would once have included the
Soviet Union and Yugoslavia.[5]

This in part reflects the bias in research towards 'minority nationalisms' such as the Scots, Welsh, Catalans and Québécois. At the same
time the 'majoritarian nationalisms' of the UK and other big states are
ignored. These 'big state' nationalisms involve the language and
symbols of nationalism but do not see themselves as such. They patro-
nise self-determination movements in their territories on the dangers of
nationalism, the need for stability and the perils of Balkanisation.[6] This
feat is managed without ever stopping to realise the contradictions of
one nationalism trying to question the legitimacy of another; thus
British 'majority nationalism' feels itself confident enough to lecture
the various 'minority nationalisms' in the UK – Scottish, Welsh, Irish –
without seeing itself as nationalist.[7]

The UK is also misunderstood as a unitary state: a place of unfet-
tered central power and conformity, with no checks on that power
through parliamentary sovereignty. This is inaccurate. The UK has
never been a unitary state. It is instead a union state: a place where
national distinctiveness and arrangements different from the centre
occur.[8] The UK has nurtured in large parts of its history distinct
Scottish, Northern Irish and, to a lesser extent, Welsh arrangements
and has never advocated a politics of centralised standardisation.

And yet the mindset of the centre and the political establishment has
always been one of the unitary state. Paradoxically, this has become
more entrenched as the UK has begun to alter and reconfigure. This
misunderstanding of the UK as a unitary state has far-reaching consequences for how power is understood and exercised, and for the future
of the UK.

THE UNRAVELLING OF THE BRITISH STATE

We have travelled a long road since the British constitution was the
envy of the world. In 1953 the American sociologist Edward Shils on a
visit to the UK was surprised to hear 'an eminent man of the left say, in
utter seriousness ... that the British constitution was "as nearly perfect
as any human institution could be"'.[9] This was an age when the UK's
identity, purpose and government had been vindicated by two World

Wars. The Westminster system was viewed as the zenith of political democracy and exported around the world; at the same time proportional representation and referendums were seen as dodgy continental devices beloved of dictators such as Hitler and Mussolini.

Both the self-image and the view of the UK from abroad has changed dramatically since then. In the last forty years the British state has faced a series of internal challenges and external changes which have remade the state and politics. In the decade from the mid-1960s onward a series of challenges coalesced which impacted on the form and language of the ideas of nation, state and territorial politics. These challenges to the British state were both internal, driven by the forces of Scottish and Welsh nationalism, and external, in the growing instability in the world economy in the 1970s. These twin forces are often discussed and studied, but are never understood as dynamics which, in the case of the UK, informed, influenced and altered each other. This is important to any understanding of what has happened to the UK over this period as a state and polity, and the fate of British social democracy as it morphed from Wilsonite to Blairite modernisation.[10]

It is more than coincidence that the junking of Wilson's National Plan in 1966-67 – and with it Croslandite dreams of economic growth, faith in planning and greater equality – happened at the same time as the emergence of the SNP and Plaid Cymru to shake Labour's hegemony in Scotland and Wales. These forces were a long time building. The Nationalist victories at Carmarthen in Wales during 1966 and Hamilton in Scotland during 1967 were not overnight sensations, but products of rising Nationalist tides since the beginning of the decade. They changed the politics in their respective countries, and the UK.

The Hamilton by-election happened sixteen days before Wilson finally bowed to the inevitable and the pound was devalued.[11] The slow death of Croslandite social democracy took nearly a decade, from November 1967 to the culmination of the IMF crisis in December 1976, but the beginning of the end can be traced back to this unhappy ending of Wilson's 1960s honeymoon.

Labour tried to marginalise the Scottish and Welsh challenge with the Kilbrandon Commission, but the internal and external challenges to the state became stronger as the British economy faced the uncertainties of faltering growth, increasing pressure on public spending, and rising inflation. The second wave of Scottish nationalism corresponded exactly in the period 1973-74 with the world economic shock of the same period. Post-Bretton Woods, the seismic shake of the OPEC oil price rise and resulting decade of hyperinflation were intimately linked to the SNP's campaign 'It's Scotland's Oil' after the discovery of North Sea Oil.[12]

British Labour's response to the internal challenge was characterised by timidity and uncertainty. It responded with an embarrassing U-turn, by ordering Scottish Labour to adopt a pro-devolution position – attempting to make concessions while retaining the integrity of the British state. To do this it drew on Labour history and myths found in its roots as a decentralist party in its formative years. This allowed it to present its abrupt change of policy as essentially still consistent with its core values.

Its response to the external challenge of economic change was even more unsure and inelegant: at first trying to ride it out, then facing humiliation at the altar of the IMF in 1976.[13] Here the party had no previous traditions to draw upon. The external challenges questioned just about every social-democratic assumption about economic and social policy: on growth, redistribution, planning, the role of the state and public spending.

The interweaving of the internal and external challenge is pivotal to understanding the last forty years of UK politics: the abandonment by Labour of many of its key beliefs, the onset and triumph of Thatcherism, and the arrival of New Labour and its embrace of the post-Thatcherite consensus. There is a direct relationship between the politics of an unsettled union and the rise of a political consensus around a neo-liberal polity which is unquestioned across the political spectrum. This situation accords a special place to Scotland – given its degree of political and institutional autonomy, and the parameters of its politics.

THE FALL OF LABOUR SCOTLAND AND THE RISE OF THE NATIONALISTS

The emergence of the SNP since the mid-1960s has been matched by the rise of contemporary political and cultural nationalisms north of the border.[14] The SNP has not always enjoyed an easy relationship with these forces. Firstly, the SNP has tended to see political nationalism as synonymous with itself and its own property. However, this nationalism is found across Scottish society, in pro-home-rule forces pre-devolution, in institutional Scotland and civil society, and even, at points in their history, in the Scottish Tories.

Secondly, cultural nationalism has been a fluid force that has been one of the defining elements of Scotland post-1979. It contributed to maintaining a sense of hope, nurturing difference and identity, and asking difficult questions in the aftermath of the first devolution referendum when it looked as if politics had failed Scotland. However, this cultural politics by its very nature has been an uneasy accomplice of party politics, as it is characterised by values largely absent in the fabric of these parties – in particular by ambiguity, transgressing boundaries and the near-constant questioning of traditional certainties.

The SNP has been unable to develop deep roots in large parts of institutional Scotland and civil society; nor can it credibly claim cultural nationalism as its own. This has resulted in the SNP having a degree of positional mobility – as it first exploded onto the scene in the 1960s, then shifted to the left in the 1980s and then flirted with Reaganomics and the Laffer Curve in the late 1990s. Moreover, while this allows the SNP to have a tactical agility, ultimately it is a weakness, as the party lacks a rootedness in genuine, organic social location, classes and movements. In this the SNP is not a conventional 'nationalist movement', but just another political party, while at the same time they invoke and imbue themselves with attributes of the former.[15]

The SNP's arrival in government for the first time in its history has seen it develop as a kind of hybrid party: catch-all and populist in part, social democratic in outlook, and articulating a contemporary nationalism aspiring to an independent nation. This has enabled the SNP administration of Alex Salmond to pioneer a political space which sounds and looks like a national government of the country, rather than the lifeless Labour dominated administrations which preceded it.[16] The first six months of the SNP administration from May 2007 saw them embark on a series of populist measures, at the same time reversing previously unpopular Labour decisions. This only takes the SNP so far and they have yet to develop a thought-out governing strategy which addresses the lack of policy detail in the party. The reality is that the SNP have always been policy-lite, for at their core they are not about policy, but identity and Scotland's status as a nation.

The Nationalists' relationship with institutional Scotland has been revealing – like two ill-at-ease dance partners trying to get the measure of each other. Institutional Scotland, and in particular the statutory public sector, has had a nervousness about the SNP coming to power and disrupting decades of investing in relationships which proffered them access, influence and insider information on how to work the system to their best advantage. In particular, these interest groups have a desire to convince the SNP to prioritise their sectoral demands – whether it is further or higher education, health, law and order or enterprise. The SNP have two possible roads here. One is that their lack of relationships and cosiness will give them a window, with a period of manoeuvre. The other is that they will have a failure of confidence and embrace the institutional and official orthodoxies. These alternatives are not exclusive, and the first could easily lead to the second.

The SNP will for the foreseeable future be perceived as a nationalist party that is different from other parties: as more willing to stand up for Scotland and able to stand above narrow party interests. However, as an autonomous Scottish politics unfolds, we will come to see the SNP's emergence as a governing force as a watershed moment of much greater significance than the narrow 2007 Scottish Parliament election result.

There is a longer backstory to that result. It is the fall of Scottish Labour – the dominant force in politics north of the border for the last fifty years.[17] The Scottish Labour Party was never that powerful a phenomenon in terms of votes – never winning a majority of votes – but it exercised its power through a complex web of institutions, networks and patronage. This was an old-fashioned client state wedded to a party machine.[18] In 1979 Labour Scotland represented three majority parts of Scotland: trade unionists, council house tenants and local councils. These were the three institutional pillars which allowed it to be so powerful and seemingly all-persuasive when it did not win a majority of the votes. Today all three of these areas are now minority parts of Scotland, and Labour is left without a life-support system to maintain a party, losing members and influence.[19]

THE UNIONIST CRISIS OF CONFIDENCE

The establishment of a Scottish Parliament has influenced how England and the UK see themselves and Scotland, particularly in parts of the media. There has been an increase in Scotophobia – with comments from Jeremy Paxman about 'the Scottish Raj', and more virulent statements from tabloid pundits such as Kelvin MacKenzie and Richard Littlejohn. English discussions on Scotland tend to focus on three main issues, the over-representation of Scots in Westminster and the corridors of power in London, the West Lothian Question and public spending levels in Scotland.

First, Scots over-representation at Westminster. In the 1997 Blair cabinet there were six Scots representing seats north of the border out of 24 – including Gordon Brown, Robin Cook and Donald Dewar.[20] In the first Gordon Brown cabinet of 2007 this had fallen to four out of 22 members, and – Brown apart – there were no other Scots in the cabinet at the most senior level.[21] This issue was never just about numbers, however: it touched on fears of a 'McMafia' – particularly in the media and other public arenas – which had roots in the borderline racism and xenophobia that has always been present in parts of English society. Thus, we have had bouts of Scotophobia before, and anti-Irish sentiment has at times been particularly venomous.

Second, the West Lothian Question. This is based on the supposition that post-devolution there is an anomaly whereby Scots MPs can vote on English domestic issues while they cannot do the same on Scottish matters which are the preserve of the Scottish Parliament. This is in many ways a political rather than a constitutional issue. The political impact of this derives from the weight of the block vote of Scots Labour MPs (along with Welsh Labour MPs) – they can sometimes bring undue influence when there is a close English parliamentary result. But the nature of UK politics is not that an 'alien' unpopular Labour government can be foisted on an unwilling England by the Scots and Welsh, since England represents 85 per cent of the UK's population and parliamentary seats, which makes this an impossibility. What can happen is that a close English result could move in a more pro-Labour direction thanks to the Scots and Welsh.

The reality of this in post-war politics is very different from the theory. In only two general elections have Scots and Welsh Labour votes prevented an English Tory majority from forming a government, and both lasted for brief periods: 1964-66 and February-October 1974.[22] Meanwhile, the opposite of the West Lothian Question has also occurred. Tory governments governing Scotland on English votes and with little popular support north of the border have occurred more frequently and for longer periods: 1959-64, 1970-74 and 1979-97.

To date, the West Lothian Question has affected the make-up of UK governments for a grand total of 26 months. UK governments governed Scotland on English votes for a total of twenty-seven years – a significant difference. This does not mean that these contradictory consequences don't matter: they do. But one cannot examine one without the other. There is also a substantial difference between the two: the 1964 and 1974 results happened because the English parliamentary results were perilously close, meaning that Scotland, with its small number of seats, could affect the overall UK result. In contrast, the Tory imposition of governing Scotland with what was seen as 'no mandate' happened despite the Scots increasingly voting one way and England the other. This reached the point in 1987 when Scotland produced a Labour landslide in terms of seats, and England a Tory landslide. Scotland and England seemed like separate nations. Part of this was of course the distortions of an electoral system, which gave a disproportionate dividend to the winning party: the salience of the

West Lothian Question would be minimised by electoral reform that sought to break up such distortions.

Third, Scottish public spending. This has long been perceived as higher than the UK average because of the Barnett Formula – something that has been so over-stated that it has passed into folklore, despite being based on a number of misconceptions. The Barnett Formula, established in 1978, was not set up to maintain higher Scots spending, but to aid eventual convergence. One of the problems here is that the spending levels associated with Barnett are not 'needs' based and transparent, but historically based on the territorial influence of different parts of the UK: Scotland, Wales and Northern Ireland.[23]

Debates about public spending and subsidies north of the border are usually concerned with identifiable public expenditure, and exclude or make questionable assumptions about unidentifiable public expenditure.[24] A recent comprehensive study by Oxford Economics showed that, taking unidentifiable spending into account, Scotland did not have the highest public spending per head, and that the highest public spending, Northern Ireland apart, was to be found in London.[25]

These three issues point to the absence of a common unionist language across the UK, and in particular one which binds together Scotland and England. In effect we are witnessing a unionist crisis of confidence on both sides of the border, where majorities on both sides are pro-union, and yet a number of issues are emerging which are slowly pushing the nations apart.

Gordon Brown's attempts to develop a credo of progressive Britishness in a number of lectures in the long run-in to becoming prime minister has to be seen in this context.[26] These were fascinating on a number of levels: they offered a kind of Ladybird Book version of British history, of good guys and causes, with the downside mostly obliterated. Thus Brown endlessly invokes the NHS and BBC, in an attempt to develop a progressive Britishness which is different from the traditional story of the Church of England, Protestantism and Empire. Moreover, Brown poses Britishness as exclusively about the internal values of the UK, and ignores external relationships such as with the European Union and the Atlanticist project. These latter two factors have become central in how the political classes construct and negotiate Britishness, but are often ones which they choose to remain silent about.

One issue that has been promoted by some has been the notion of 'English votes for English laws' – which is supported by the Conservatives and opposed by Labour. This could, in many imaginable situations, be politically unworkable, for example in a House of

Commons elected by First-Past-The-Post that produced two governments in one Parliament: a UK Labour one and Tory English one. This
is not a political remedy, rather a recipe for disaster and perpetual crisis.
What is surprising is that Gordon Brown once did not only entertain,
but openly supported, 'English votes for English laws'. In a 1980 essay
he wrote that this was a 'prize' worth paying for a 'Scottish Assembly',
even though this would result in 'a semi-permanent majority' for the
Conservatives in England.[27] This is all the more of a shock for those,
such as Brown's biographer Tom Bower, who tend to see Brown in his
early years as a firebrand. They have clearly never taken the time to
read any of the socialist literature of that time.[28]

ENGLAND AWAKENS!
A.J.P. Taylor concluded his *English History 1914-45* by commenting
that at the end of the Second World War few now sang *Land of Hope
and Glory*: 'Few even sang *England Arise*. England had arisen all the
same'.[29] Such declarations of faith have always been close to the surface
in progressive accounts of England, from Robert Blatchford's *Merrie
England* to, more recently, Tony Benn. British Labour usually
conflates English history with that of Britain. Tony Benn's sentimental
evocation of the Levellers, Diggers, English Civil War and so on is a
predominantly English story. Even a Labour politician such as Gordon
Brown, Scottish to the core, has invoked English history and symbols
as British – Magna Carta, the Peasants' Revolt and Orwell's 'English
genius'.[30] Clearly, there is something amiss about the English question
within the Labour psyche.

There are two distinct arguments about the state of England, one
pessimistic, the other optimistic. The pessimistic account believes that
England needs the rest of the UK; without it it will tip over into
permanent Conservative hegemony. Sometimes this borders on an
essentialist caricaturing of Englishness, equating it with reaction,
racism and right-wing bigotry, which it is the duty of the Scots and
Welsh to subjugate. A more measured version of this bases its case on
electoral politics. It states that progressives need Scotland and Wales to
put together a national coalition across the UK, and sees an England
on its own as Conservative dominated.[31] However, this argument is
based on a distortion of the facts. England is not actually an overwhelmingly Conservative nation in political sentiment. The Tories
have in post-war elections only once won a popular majority of the
English vote, in 1955.

The second, more optimistic view tackles the pessimistic argument
head-on and labels it as the stereotype it undoubtedly is. A number of

English commentators have argued that there is a rich lineage of English radicalism and dissent: a counter-strand to the dominant British narrative. This finds present-day voice in the writings of musician and activist Billy Bragg, who poses the case for a progressive, multicultural Englishness that challenges the Whig interpretation of history and is at ease with the Scots, Welsh and Irish making their own arrangements.[32]

Billy Bragg's account offers one possible future of a generous England finding a new role and feeling comfortable with its newly confident neighbours. However, this is a political project and set of aspirations that cannot be guaranteed to represent tomorrow's England. Another England is just as possible, perhaps more likely: one which is anxious about loss and change, fearful about immigration, opposed to sharing powers with the European Union, and resentful of the troublesome Jocks and other non-English peoples of these isles. It is plausible to see such a set of sentiments, which already exist in parts of England, being given encouragement by the Murdoch press and *Daily Mail*, and turning into the scapegoating of Muslims, Polish plumbers and the Scots.

Where the English journey goes in the future has to be seen against the backdrop of the changing nature of English society and the UK over the last thirty years. Some observers like to portray contemporary Britain as a diverse, comfortable, at-ease-with-itself society. But the evident progress that has been made in challenging institutionalised racism and overt homophobia has to be put in the context of a more unequal country, with an increasing sense of indifference about those excluded and left behind. Neo-liberalism is now dominant as both an economic mantra and political ideology uniting all three mainstream UK parliamentary parties. Public institutions are ruled by the marketisation of their structures and commodification of their services. This has had an impact, of course, on every part of the UK, but it has thoroughly transformed England, and the South-East and London have changed more than anywhere else.

A SHORT HISTORY OF THE FUTURE: THE NEXT TWO DECADES OF THE BREAK-UP

Most accounts of the future of the UK either reflect the same viewpoint as Gordon Brown's, founded on the flexibility and adaptability of the UK; or they draw on the *The Break-Up of Britain* thesis first put forward by Tom Nairn over thirty years ago.[33] Nairn's thesis is a rich and complex one, addressing British, English and Scottish identities after Empire and with the rising impact of Europe, while more recent accounts of a break-up tend to concentrate solely on the Scottish dimension.

Instead of looking at the UK through the potential of Scotland to create trouble for the union; it might be more helpful to identify the sources of tensions, forces and movements which could emerge to accelerate the pace of change and challenge the nature of the UK. The following timeline presents one possible set of hypotheses. The trends could be speeded up if the Tories win the next general election, or could be slowed down significantly should the Tory recovery be much delayed. But what needs to be emphasised is that, while the timing of final destination remains open to doubt, the general drift towards a looser, more divided United Kingdom is surely not. The following points only examine the constitutional and political dynamics of the UK, and do not take into account the host of external factors which could impact on the state of the UK. These include how the European Union evolves, how the US exerts its military and economic power around the globe, the nature of globalisation and the gathering environmental crisis spearheaded by climate change.

A SIXTEEN POINT BREAK-UP PROGRAMME

Step 1: 2010 A Labour fourth term:

Despite a worsening economic climate Brown shows a degree of statecraft and competence and wins an historic fourth Labour term against David Cameron's revitalised Conservatives. In spite of Brown increasing Labour's vote from 2005, aided by pulling British forces out of Iraq, his Parliamentary majority is slashed. The Conservative vote rises due to the Liberal Democrats vote being squeezed. Brown faces a similar prospect to John Major in 1992: governing with a small majority and presiding over a party hollowed out and increasingly disunited. While he does not face the fissures of the European issue, he cannot ignore the increasingly salient issue that the Tories have won more English seats than Labour, and Brown's prime ministership is seen as based on Scottish seats.

Consequences: The English question and territorial politics across the union rise up the political agenda.

Step 2: 2011 Scotland, Wales and Northern Ireland elections:

The Scottish and Welsh devolved elections show a further marked swing away from Labour and growing divergence with Westminster. In Scotland the SNP administration win over 40 per cent of the first and second votes and a lead over a disconsolate Labour of more than 10 per cent on both counts. Alex Salmond, from a position of strength, forms a coalition administration with the Lib Dems on the basis of remaking the union and pushing for more powers for the Parliament. In Wales Labour lose votes to all the main parties, who decide to gang up and exclude Labour from power. In Northern Ireland Sinn Fein and the SDLP make significant gains in the Assembly elections.

Consequences: The three devolved nations are increasingly diverging from the politics of Westminster and look likely to grow more assertive in the future.

Step 3: 2012 Welsh referendum:
The Welsh vote on the Welsh Assembly gaining more powers, including primary legislation and tax raising powers along the lines of the Scottish Parliament. The referendum 'Yes' campaign has the support of all the main Welsh parties.

Consequences: A large majority votes in favour, which aids the process of 'catch-up' across the devolved nations, increasing the likelihood that the Scottish Parliament will push for more powers.

Step 4: 2013 Scottish referendum on more powers for the Parliament:
Aided by the Welsh vote, the SNP-Lib Dem Scottish government put forward a referendum which proposes a range of powers to be transferred to the Parliament: ranging from broadcasting, to fiscal autonomy and a number of constitutional issues. The main Scottish parties all support a 'Yes' vote to differing degrees of enthusiasm, with the SNP clear this is the first in a series of proposals.

Consequences: An overwhelming majority in favour which enhances the reputation of the SNP-led administration, and leads to an increasing likelihood of further constitutional change.

Step 5: 2015 The Conservatives return to power:
After eighteen years out of office David Cameron's Conservatives defeat Labour under Ed Miliband who took over from Gordon Brown a year before the election. The Conservatives win a comfortable overall majority, but this masks national and regional variations. The Tories do well across the South and London in their traditional heartlands, while in Scotland and Wales the Cameron effect barely registers. This

means that Cameron's mandate is entirely based on English votes, and, with their platform including a commitment to 'English votes for English laws', future conflict looks likely. Northern Ireland moves further into a different political orbit, with Sinn Fein and the SDLP winning a majority of seats.

Consequences: The union begins to loosen a bit more and English nationalism of a less than attractive kind begins to appear as a serious political force.

Step 6: 2015 Scotland, Wales and Northern Ireland elections:

The SNP win their third election in a row against a Labour Party still losing votes and unsure of itself. Alex Salmond decides to govern as a minority administration as he manoeuvres to win enough parliamentary support to hold an independence vote. In Wales a resurgent Labour Party sweeps back to majority power railing against Tory cuts and insensitivity. In Northern Ireland, Sinn Fein and the SDLP make significant gains in both seats and votes and have a narrow lead over the Unionist parties in both, which foretells the future contours of politics in Northern Ireland.

Consequences: A Scottish independence referendum becomes likely. Irish reunification moves a step closer.

Step 7: 2017 Scottish referendum on independence:

After several years of friction between the Conservative UK government and a SNP administration in Scotland, the SNP decide to move to a referendum on Scotland's constitutional status, and gain support in the Scottish Parliament from the Scots Conservatives to bring the issue to a conclusion. Twenty years after Scotland's last referendum vote, the Scots finally get the chance to have a say on whether they want to be independent. The campaign sees the SNP as the only main party advocating independence. At points in the campaign the vote between the two camps closes, but the result never looks in doubt.

Consequences: A narrow majority in favour of the Union, but the vote is close enough to make the prospect of a second referendum in the near future likely.

Step 8: 2018 European referendum:

The Conservative government calls a UK-wide vote – only the second such occasion in UK history – on taking back powers from the

European Union and opposing any further European integration. The Tories find themselves in the favourable position of being backed by a huge majority of public opinion and most of the press, persuading a reluctant Labour to campaign on the same side, with only the Liberal Democrats making an unapologetic pro-Euro case.

Consequences: The Tories, with Labour support, win a decisive majority. The result institutionalises the UK's semi-detached status in the EU. It contributes to a mixture of anxiety and opportunity in Scottish, Welsh and Northern Irish politicians as they see the rising Euroscepticism of the UK allowing them the prospect of bartering for more influence in the EU while also posing a threat to them.

Step 9: 2019 Scotland, Wales and Northern Ireland elections:

In Scotland the SNP hold most of their vote. Labour shows no sign of recovery and is forced to form a 'Unionist' bloc with Lib Dems and Tories against a rising movement for full independence. In Wales Labour remain the largest party but suffer huge loses to the Lib Dems who emerge as their main challenger, resulting in a Lib Dem-Plaid Cymru minority administration. In Northern Ireland, Sinn Fein and the SDLP make further advances as the Unionist bloc begins to disintegrate with some elements beginning to accept that Irish reunification is inevitable.

Consequences: The politics of the devolved nations diverge even further from Westminster while the health of Labour in its once invulnerable Celtic heartlands looks shaky.

Step 10: 2019 The Conservatives win a second term:

Cameron increases his majority on the back of the European referendum vote against a demoralised, and now much divided, Labour Party. The Tory revival is still geographically concentrated with his election solely due to English votes, and no upswing visible in Scotland or Wales.

Consequences: The progressive case for the union disappears and the UK heads towards break-up.

Step 11: 2020 English referendum:

The Conservative government agree to hold an English referendum on the issue of 'English votes for English laws' and restricting the rights of Scots, Welsh and Northern Irish MPs. In a bitterly fought referendum, the Tories face opposition from Labour and the Liberal Democrats, but have the benefit of several years of press campaigning promoting this as an issue.

Consequences: With a significant majority in favour of 'English Votes for English Laws' the Conservatives enhance their English nationalist credentials. At the same time, the UK faces a future of constitutional upheaval and chaos. Scottish, Welsh and Northern Irish politicians from across the political spectrum condemn the move and pledge to fight it.

Step 12: 2023 third Conservative term:

In a climate of ensuing constitutional and political instability, the Conservatives storm to a third victory and landslide result. This is again based solely on English votes, and aided by divisions in Labour and Liberal Democrats between their Scottish parties and UK party leaderships.

Consequences: The UK seems set on a period of constitutional turbulence.

Step 13: 2023 Scotland, Wales and Northern Ireland elections:

The Northern Irish elections give Sinn Fein and the SDLP a majority of votes and seats and a mandate to begin progress towards Irish reunification, with a significant minority part of the Unionist community now accepting the inevitability of such a vote and decision. In Scotland, the SNP secure a decisive victory in votes and seats which gives them a mandate for a second referendum on independence, while in Wales, the Welsh Labour Party splits in two with the Welsh part winning respectable support and the British part being humiliated; the former announce they are entering into coalition with Plaid Cymru to negotiate a new relationship with Westminster.

Consequences: Scottish and Northern Irish votes on leaving the union become inevitable, while the Welsh are showing signs of mutiny.

Step 14: 2024 Northern Irish referendum on Irish Reunification:

The Northern Irish hold a vote on whether to reunify with the Republic after Sinn Fein and the SDLP win a majority of seats and votes in successive Assembly and Westminster elections. A simultaneous vote is held in the Irish Republic, and with the UK government officially neutral, the Unionist campaign has an air of resignation and defeat.

Consequences: The reunification vote is won and a timetable is agreed to advance towards an united Ireland. The vote is also seen as weakening the union and strengthening the cause of Scottish independence.

Step 15: 2027 Scotland, Wales and Northern Ireland elections:
The last British devolved elections. The Northern Irish vote legitimises the new realities of politics in what was once the province. In Scotland the SNP is returned with a near-majority of the vote and seats with a ballot on independence declared to happen within 100 days of the election. In Wales, the Welsh Labour-Plaid Cymru alliance is returned with an increased majority.

Consequences: The beginning of the end of the UK.

Step 16: 2027 Second Scottish referendum on independence:
The 'neverendum' arrives. The SNP, now with the support of all the other main parties in the Scottish Parliament, secures a second referendum for independence. This is against the backdrop of political crisis and controversy over 'English votes for English laws'. A significant minority of Scottish Labour openly campaign for independence, while a much larger part of the party is known to be secretly in sympathy. All through the campaign the pro-independence forces have a majority in the polls, but at the end there is a closing of the gap between the two options.

Consequences: A majority for independence is won and a process is agreed with the UK government for Scottish independence.

Thus within twenty years or so it is distinctly possible that the United Kingdom as we know it will have broken up, with Northern Ireland reunified with the Republic of Ireland, and an independent Scotland sitting north of the border. This leaves the question of what the Welsh would do in such a situation, and even more importantly, what would the rump remaining be called and what kind of state would it be?

A TALE OF TWO NEW STATES OR ONE?
The United Kingdom is currently situated in a half-way house in 'the twilight of the Westminster model',[34] yet with the political class and system unwilling and unable to kill off the old and embrace the new. The British, as a member of the Nolan Committee on Standards of Conduct in Public Life put it, 'like to live in a series of half-way houses'.[35]

It is possible that this situation could continue for quite a period, but the last twenty years or so have seen significant changes which will shape the future:

- the rise of constitutional questions to the centre of the political stage;
- the establishment of devolved administrations in Scotland, Wales and Northern Ireland at the same time as the excessive centralism of first, Thatcherism, then, New Labour;
- the emergence of judicial power as one of the main checks on the power of the centre;
- the straitjacket of Thatcherite orthodoxy which the political classes adhere to.

The UK is heading in the direction of a loose, more varied set of arrangements which may or may not bring about the break-up of the union but which will look and feel very different to present arrangements. Whatever form emerges will have to address where the UK thinks it is located and how this shapes Britishness. It will have to acknowledge that the UK finds it increasingly difficult to generate a language and statecraft which can adapt to and reflect its constituent parts while providing an over-arching story. Can a union state continue indefinitely without the sense of gut, emotional unionism that held the UK together for so long?[36] Why has the centre-left been so poor at providing a feasible, radical democratizing political project which could provide a progressive narrative for the British state?

The potential break-up of the UK would raise numerous questions:

- Will the Northern Irish and the Scots decide to leave or not?
- Will the English find a political will, whether it is progressive or reactionary?
- What kinds of inter-governmental co-operation and common policy would emerge in a post-UK?
- What would happen to citizenship and nationality and would dual citizenship be possible across the new states?
- Most profoundly, if Scotland leaves what would be the characteristics of the new Scotland and Greater England/Lesser UK: are they one or two new states?

If Scotland leaves the union what does the rest become? Does it become the United Kingdom minus Scotland – a Rest of the UK or does it become something else, new and unnamed? The Greater England/Lesser

UK would in the eyes of some be the successor state to the UK – with the legal rights to continuity of membership of bodies such as the UN Security Council, the G7, the EU and NATO and responsibility for the 13,000 plus treaties to which the UK is signature to.

If it becomes the successor state – the Rest of the UK – it will follow the example of Russia after the Soviet Union fell apart (which it did due to the geo-political realities of the size of Russia in the Soviet Union, the issue of nuclear weapons and international opinion). In this scenario only one new state is created: an independent Scotland which internationally has to apply for membership of the UN, EU, IMF and World Bank.

However, this view is based on the controversial position that the Treaty of Union is just another piece of parliamentary legislation rather than being as close as the UK can get to a kind of fundamental law, and one of the building blocks of the union. The Constitution Unit's comprehensive study of the practicalities of Scottish independence argues that Scotland's position post-1707 is the same as Ireland post-1801, and that Scottish independence would have the same effect on the UK as Irish independence in 1922.[37] This is an astonishingly inaccurate reading of history: Scotland created a union with England in 1707, whereas Ireland was conquered; one was a marriage of equals, the other was a relationship of inequality and submission.

An equally valid perspective states that the emergence of an independent Scotland would see the creation of two new states: Scotland and Greater England/Lesser UK. As Chris Bowlby commented in a recent BBC programme on the Scottish question, after break-up 'what would emerge would not only be a new Scotland but also a new remainder of the UK, in search of a name and a new sense of coherence'.[38] From this perspective Scotland was 'one of the basic building blocks of 'the United Kingdom of Great Britain'.[39] Without Scotland, there is no 'Great Britain' and therefore there is no 'United Kingdom'.

Fundamentally, the nature of break-up comes down to how you understand the character of the UK historically and contemporaneously. If you see the Act of Union as just another piece of parliamentary legislation which continued the process of Greater England, Scotland leaving the union does not alter the glorious tradition of continuity that is England/UK. However, if the Treaty of Union is regarded as being as close to fundamental law as the British can manage, Scottish independence leads inexorably to the end of the UK.

The difference of language between 'Act of Union' and 'Treaty of Union' is central here.[40] Talk of an Act reduces it to parliamentary legislation and prioritises the English Parliament's enactment of 1707, thus continuing the English law and practice in Diceyian fashion. Talk of a Treaty emphasises that was the creation of two consenting states and emphasises the 1707 decisions of the Scottish and English Parliaments.

Both of these perspectives cannot be right, but – strangely in a state that was meant to be 'unitary' – the UK has from its outset contained two entirely contradictory positions, one seeing the UK as Greater England and the other viewing it as a union state, one emphasising parliamentary sovereignty, the other popular sovereignty. Which position will prevail in any break-up process will be determined by wider geo-political realities, power and status, and the finer points of legal interpretation. It seems clear that, whatever the legal position, Greater England/Lesser UK will try to use all of its influence and status in the world of realpolitik to position itself as the successor state to the UK.

There are already going to be many difficult questions: how UK assets such as art collections, museums and embassies are divided, national debt, oil revenues, state pensions and the thorny issue of nuclear weapons. The UK's nuclear weapons are based at Faslane in the River Clyde, and there are potential similarities here with the end of the Soviet Union and the discussions between the Russians and Ukrainians over nuclear weapons and the Soviet Black Sea Fleet being based in Ukrainian ports. Would an independent Scotland tolerate nuclear weapons in its waters? Or could it lease back the base to the Greater English/Lesser UK for a time-limited period? [41]

Whatever the future holds it is going to involve instability, upheaval and argument for a period of time. The break-up of the United Kingdom would be a major historic and international event. The episodes which are likely to unfold along the way, including Northern Irish and Scottish votes on whether to stay or leave the union, will each have significant political consequences.

The potential passing of the United Kingdom into history will invite reflection and remembrance and even a sense of loss and sadness in places far afield across the globe. This is what occurred in Canada in 1980 and 1995 with the Quebec referendums. The same will happen – but more so – with the UK, and it is important that the coming period allows people to have a degree of honesty, reflection, and a sense of the emotion that the UK has invoked in some quarters.

At the heart of the British political system there is still a belief, despite everything, that the British constitution is the envy of the world and close to perfection: the view Edward Shils found such a surprise over fifty years ago. Some of the perspectives which have trumpeted this have included Thatcherism, Blairism and Brownism. It is going to take a political earthquake to dislodge this view.

Post-Iraq, after the Hutton and Butler inquiries into why the UK went to war – and after the details of 25 million British citizens were lost in the post – the British state and its system of government is in deep crisis. In many respects, while functioning like a normal state, it no longer works.

The old British story is nearing its end. A new set of Scottish, Welsh, Irish and English narratives are just beginning.

NOTES

1. David Cannadine, *A Beginner's Guide to Separation*, BBC Radio 4, December 6th 2007, http://news.bbc.co.uk/1/hi/programmes/analysis/7130606.stm.
2. Robert Harris, *The Ghost*, Hutchinson 2007, p251.
3. See: Arthur Aughley, *The Politics of Englishness*, Manchester University Press 2007.
4. To be accurate Northern Ireland is not a nation, but is a part of two states. The Good Friday Agreement identifies Northern Ireland as a place with two nationalities, British and Irish, as a place of devolved government within the UK, and with institutional links to both the UK and the Republic of Ireland.
5. Michael Keating, *Nations against the State: The New Politics of Nationalism in Quebec, Catalonia and Scotland*, Macmillan 1996.
6. See Eric Hobsbawm, *Nations and Nationalism since 1780: Programme, Myth, Reality*, Cambridge University Press 1990. Writing in-between the demise of the Soviet bloc and the end of the Soviet Union, Hobsbawm asks if a 'Europe of nations' in the Wilsonian sense could be a good thing. Looking at a future where the Baltic nations leave the Soviet Union and Czechoslovakia and Yugoslavia break-up, he declares, 'Can it be seriously supposed that such a Balkanisation extended on a world scale, would provide a stable or lasting political system?', p177. Since this twenty-four European and Central Asian countries have become independent nations following the demise of the Soviet Union, Czechoslovakia and Yugoslavia.
7. James G. Kellas, *The Politics of Nationalism and Ethnicity*, Macmillan 1991.
8. Stein Rokkan and Derek Urwin, *Economy, Territory and Identity*, Sage 1983. This was first popularised in James Mitchell, *Strategies for Self-Government: The Campaigns for a Scottish Parliament*, Polygon 1996.
9. Cited in Vernon Bogdanor, 'Conclusion', in Vernon Bogdanor (ed.), *The British Constitution in the Twentieth Century*, Oxford University Press 2003, p689.

10. Gerry Hassan, 'Labour, concepts of Britishness, "nation" and "state", in Gerry Hassan (ed.), *After Blair: Politics after the New Labour Decade*, Lawrence and Wishart 2007.

11. On the 1967 devaluation see: Alec Cairncross and Barry Eichengreen, *Sterling In Crisis: The Devaluations Of 1931, 1949 and 1967*, Palgrave Macmillan 2003 2nd edn.

12. Christopher Harvie, *Fool's Gold: The Story of North Sea Oil*, Hamish Hamilton 1994.

13. Kathleen Burk and Alec Cairncross, *'Goodbye Great Britain': The 1976 IMF Crisis*, Yale University Press 1992.

14. Jack Brand, *The Nationalist Movement in Scotland*, Routledge, Kegan and Paul 1978.

15. Gerry Hassan (ed.), *The Scottish National Party: From Movement to Party of Government*, Edinburgh University Press 2008.

16. The SNP's victory was both an historic one and a very narrow and contested one, The SNP had until May 2007 failed to ever win a national election in votes or seats. It finished the elections 15,853 votes ahead of Labour in the constituency vote and 37,986 votes ahead in the list vote – leads of respectively 0.8% and 1.8% and with a one seat lead over Labour in a 129 member Parliament. There was huge controversy post-election over more than 140,000 votes being ruled invalid due to problems with counting the ballot papers.

17. The phrase is the title of George Dangerfield's *The Strange Death of Liberal England*; Geoffrey Wheatcroft has in recent times used it prematurely about the fate of the Conservatives: *The Strange Death of Tory England*.

18. Gerry Hassan (ed.), *The Scottish Labour Party: History, Institutions, Ideas*, Edinburgh University Press 2004.

19. Gerry Hassan, 'People's party must face the future honestly', *The Scotsman*, 11.8.07.

20. Tim Austin (ed.), *The Times Guide to the House of Commons 1997*, Times Books 1997.

21. *BBC News*, 28.6.07, http://news.bbc.co.uk/1/hi/uk_politics/6247502.stm.

22. In 1964 in England the Conservatives won 262 seats, Labour 246 and the Liberals 3, while across the UK Labour had an overall majority of four. In February 1974 in England the Conservatives won 268 seats, Labour 237, Liberals 9, while across the UK in a hung Parliament Labour had a four-seat lead over the Conservatives. The case of 1950 hung in the balance with the Conservatives winning 253 seats in England, Labour 251 and the Liberals 2, while Labour was returned with a UK majority of seven seats. The Conservatives won more votes than Labour in England in the 2005 election, 35.7% to 35.5%, while Labour won 286

seats to the Conservatives 194 and the Lib Dems 47: a Labour lead of 92 seats. F.W.S. Craig, *British Electoral Facts 1832-1980*, Parliamentary Research Services 1981; Dennis Kavanagh and David Butler, *The British General Election of 2005*, Palgrave Macmillan 2005. Fascinatingly, for protagonists of the 'England's voice is silenced' perspective the Nuffield 2005 election study has index entries for Scotland, Wales and Northern Ireland, and not one for England, choosing to make not a single mention of the above anomaly.

23. Iain McLean and Alistair McMillan, *The Fiscal Crisis of the United Kingdom*, Nuffield College Working Papers On Politics 2002.

24. Identifiable public spending is the spending which is recognized as incurred on behalf of a particular population and allocated to regions or nations in the UK. The non-identifiable expenditure is that part which is incurred on behalf of the UK as a whole such as defence spending or overseas aid.

25. David Leask, 'Why the figures peddled by Scotland's critics don't add up', *The Herald*, 2.11.07.

26. Gordon Brown, *Speeches 1997-2006*, Bloomsbury 2006; Gordon Brown and Douglas Alexander, *New Labour, New Scotland*, The Smith Institute 1999.

27. Gordon Brown and Henry Drucker, *The Politics of Nationalism and Devolution*, Longman 1980, p127.

28. Tom Bower, *Gordon Brown*, Harper Collins 2004.

29. A.J.P. Taylor, *English History 1914-1945*, Clarendon Press 1965, p600.

30. Simon Lees, 'Gordon Brown and 'The English Way', *Political Quarterly*, Vol. 77 No. 3, July-September 2006.

31. See for example: Eric Hobsbawm, 'Some Reflections on "The Break-Up of Britain"', *New Left Review*, No. 105, September/October 1977, http://www.newleftreview.org/?view=680

32. Billy Bragg, *The Progressive Patriot: A Search for Belonging*, Bantam Press 2006.

33. Tom Nairn, *The Break-Up of Britain*, Big Thinking/Common Ground 2003 3rd edn.

34. Pippa Norris, 'The Twilight of Westminster?: Electoral Reform and its Consequences', *Political Studies*, Vol. 49 No. 5 (2001), pp877-900.

35. Cited in Bogdanor, op. cit., p719.

36. Iain McLean and Alistair McMillan, *State of the Union: Unionism and the Alternatives since 1707*, Oxford University Press 2005.

37. Jo Eric Murkens with Peter Jones and Michael Keating, *Scottish Independence: A Practical Guide*, Edinburgh University Press 2002, p109.

38. Chris Bowlby, *A Beginner's Guide to Separation*, BBC Radio 4, 6.12.07.

39. Robert Lane, '"Scotland In Europe": An Independent Scotland In The

European Community', in Wilson Finnie, Christopher Himsworth and Neil Walker (eds), *Edinburgh Essays in Public Law*, Edinburgh University Press 1991.

40. Neil MacCormick, 'Is There a Constitutional Path to Scottish Independence?' *Parliamentary Affairs*, Vol. 53 2000.

41. Malcolm Chalmers and William Walker, *Uncharted Waters: The UK, Nuclear Weapons and The Scottish Question*, Tuckwell Press 2001.

Farewell to the Morris Men

Anne Coddington

When *Guardian* art critic Jonathan Jones reviewed Jeremy Deller and Alan Kane's *Folk Archive* at Tate Britain in 2000 he described it as a 'neat image of what this new museum of national art feels like'.[1] Given that *Folk Archive* is unashamedly unofficial, a collection of folk art from around Britain including gaudy garden ornaments, Morris dancers, cake stalls, sand castles, anti-war protests and graffiti on walls, all created by people who do not even consider themselves to be artists, this might seem like a strange suggestion.

But Jones said this in the context of the break up of the Tate into two separate London galleries (plus two satellite galleries at Tate Liverpool and Tate St Ives). Tate Modern's remit to feature international (including British) art from the twentieth century onwards ties it to the global, the cutting edge, the cosmopolitan – it is an institution looking excitedly towards the future. In comparison, Tate Britain, as the museum of British art, is resolutely associated with the past, struggling to find popular and relevant ways to connect this vital cultural resource to the present. 'Tate Britain feels like stepping into a folk song, an old ballad, and encountering homely images we thought we'd left behind,' wrote Jones. 'We're so far removed from the rural culture that produced Stubbs's paintings of horses or Gainsborough's rustic portraits' that, as images of Britishness, 'they are strangely at odds with how we see ourselves'.[2]

The range of English festivals, banners, murals and more that *Folk Archive* has collected together indicates a much more open and accessible example of what a modern museum of national English art might feel like. For a start it breaks with the narrow patriotism that characterises much old English art. Hogarth may have been the first artist to describe 'the peculiar manners and characters of the English nation',[3] but his approach was also typically xenophobic. He presents foreigners – and the French in particular – in the most jaundiced of ways. Think of his image of starving Frenchmen salivating at the sight of

171

English sirloin steak in *O Roast Beef of Old England*. This version of patriotism represents an Englishness trading on claims of unquestionable superiority to other nations. An internal, class-based version of this deeply situated cultural trait is seen in Reynolds's lofty portraits of the aristocracy, with their equally exclusive preoccupations of blood, birthright and property – the assumption that this group is somehow born to rule.

In Deller and Kane's alternative account there are few references to England's imperial past; the stock images of royalty, flag-waving or bulldogs are absent. Furthermore they purposefully do not set out to provide a worked-out definition of a modern-day nation – either of England or a broken up Britain. What they present instead is a mishmash of local community practices loosely grouped around headings such as 'Tea and Cakes', 'Seaside', 'The Street' and 'Politics'. Their version of the state of England seems to be a collection of communities, localities and regions unproblematically patchworked together into nationhood. In Haxey, Lincolnshire the local community plays a strange, archaic football game on 6 January every year; at the Egremont Crab Fair in Cumbria there is a gurning (face-pulling) competition (loosely based on the Medieval tradition of imitating the village idiot); in Birchington, Kent the locals are treated to elaborate April Fool's day practical jokes (by unnamed jokers) at the Monkey's Tea Party.

Deller and Kane make no attempt to explain what these practices might have in common, how they connect to some predetermined idea of 'the nation'. As Jeremy Millar explains: '*Folk Archive* does not perpetuate – or even allow for – any coherent sense of what might be meant by community, although many different communities are represented'.[4] Deller and Kane have abandoned analytical rigour – and the fixity it demands – in favour of enabling us to see our national identity in the broadest possible terms. We are encouraged to simply look at ourselves – in all our strangeness and particularity – rather than drawing on narrow stereotypes and assumptions about who we are.

Deller and Kane are re-examining folk art as an important part of present day culture. *Folk Archive* is not seeking to catalogue or explain the provenance of individual folk traditions – to track an authentic folk culture – like the Compton Verney Museum of Folk Art in Staffordshire. But that should not undermine its significance in terms of cultural practice. It is an important attempt to re-evaluate folk art, to see these practices as more than 'charming' or 'quaint' examples of our pre-industrial past that have little relevance today. Deller describes *Folk Archive* as, 'an alternative portrait of all the energetic and enthusiastic things that happen when people make and improvise ... and are creative on an everyday level'.[5] Although he does admit they favour material that represents a counter to the status quo, Art historian Rachel Withers, writing in the *New Statesman*, has questioned Deller's choice of subjects: 'Given the presence in the archive of everything from Northern Irish republican murals to unionist propaganda, environmental protest leaflets to a Made-in-China whoopee cushion, and slavishly hand-copied soft porn to a Women's Institute cross-stitched sampler, it is hard to know precisely what they understand the status quo to be.'[6]

Withers is suggesting that Deller and Kane ought to have a more coherent definition of national identity. But this failure to be specific in their selections is a key part of the appeal of *Folk Archive*. As Deller puts it: 'it's what surprises us. What we were not expecting to see. When you see an item that is a variation on something maybe taking it forward or sideways'.[7] It is this looser definition of national identity that helps us to understand how Englishness might evolve. It shows people enjoying, celebrating their communities, taking pride in local traditions and their connections with the past. This suggests a flexible sense of belonging – where no one tradition is more important than the other, where there is room for all the different and in some cases competing versions, but all are welcoming to others. In a broken up Britain, we can begin to understand our specific identities by having the space and confidence to take part in these popular practices of reimagining. The loose, undefined space in *Folk Archive* is a place for experimentation and questioning as well as preservation and celebration.

In effect Deller and Kane are helping us to understand and appreciate the natural inclination of most people to love their country. It's a sentiment that echoes George Orwell's view in his essay *The Lion and the Unicorn*. 'Economically, England is certainly two nations, if not three or four. But at the same time the vast majority of people feel themselves to be a single nation and are conscious of resembling one another more than they resemble foreigners. Patriotism is usually stronger than class-hatred and always stronger than any kind of internationalism.'[8]

In seeking to understand who we are, accepting that folk art is an important part of everyday Engish culture is key. The success of Tate Modern may well be evidence of the importance of high culture – set-piece installations, cutting edge conceptual statements of artistic intent, high volume exhibitions – as symbols of a new cosmopolitan Britain. But such aims require a cultural practice to accompany them. Otherwise arts policy descends into a crass populism. Or worse.

Commenting on Gordon Brown's foreign forays to China and India in January 2008, historian Tristram Hunt compared Brown's mission to the selling of a modern version of Elizabethan mercantile adventurism. 'A Mansion House version of Britain as a trading nation dominated by the City, the docks and a broadband, coffee-house culture. Gordon Brown has embraced a Brand Britain strangely devoid of industrial heritage, political inheritance, or socialist virtue'.[9]

Seduced by commerce, national identity in the hands of Brownite Labour is firstly divorced from the politics of devolution. Hence the obsession with Britishness, and increasing divorce from politics entirely; locality, community and most of all class become categories to jettison in favour of bright shiny new logos. Meanwhile a resurgent right seeks to entrench a vision of the nation in an unproblematic settlement with the past. In 2006 the New Culture Forum was founded by Cameron-type Conservatives to 'challenge the discredited left/liberal cultural orthodoxy and change the terms of debate'. The challenge was defined as 'to affirm and celebrate the canon of Western cultural achievement and our own national history, rather than resile from them in ill-considered shame and embarrassment. To promote a new flowering of excellence in the arts, motivated by aesthetic honesty, not box-ticking or political indoctrination'.[10] In the make-believe world of the right, the Enlightenment has been entirely overtaken by an ideological coalition of relativism and multiculturalism, national identity is under threat via an assault on historical achievement and cultural values, and 'political correctness gone mad' explains every faultline in Britishness and Englishness.

In such a contest of dull alternatives, Deller and Kane's work begins to provide a colourful alternative. *Folk Archive* is suggestive of another version of Englishness that lies outside of the official art practices that Brownite Labour would seek to commodify and the right would preserve unchallenged by the pressures of social change. In this sense Deller and Kane's practice and their subject complement each other. Many of the displays are a kind of popular art or low culture that might be mocked by the art establishment. (The very fact these displays have been exhibited in major galleries is because the curators – Deller a Turner Prize winner and Kane a well-established artist – have the cultural capital to make this happen.) The photos of cake sculptures or protest banners have not been produced by academically trained conceptual artists aiming to deconstruct Middle England or political political culture; rather they are drawn from everyday life. They are the images of ourselves as a nation that we all recognize and are familiar with, a reimagining from below.

As Orwell put it, the English are not gifted artistically; they are, 'a nation of flower-lovers, but also a nation of stamp collectors, pigeon fanciers, amateur carpenters, darts players, crossword puzzle fans'.[11] It is these popular symbols and pastimes that *Folk Archive* draws upon and indeed celebrates. The exhibits may be considered lowbrow by the majority of cultural commentators and exhibition curators, but they are an integral part of our traditions and culture.

Deller and Kane are asking why these popular and mainly local practices should not be considered art. After all, like other forms of art, they were all intended for an audience. As they state in the preface to *Folk Archive*: 'Our artists are mostly quite clear on how their work will be read, and we have simply transposed the works from one form of public display to the more traditional presentation of an art gallery'.[12] They are not examples of 'outsider' art where the author has no interest in appealing to a wider audience. The difference between the works in *Folk Archive* and other exhibitions may simply come down to the fact that, 'they have been authored by individuals who would not primarily consider themselves to be artists'.[13]

But *Folk Archive*, as the collective embodiment of these works, does raise other important themes. Does this popular art suggest that our national imagination is primarily backward looking with its focus on recreating age-old traditions? It is a crucial point. After all, a modern, global nation must be inclusive – all citizens must feel they belong. Folk practices that draw on the local and the regional are most likely to appeal to those who through blood or family ties are able to make that connection. How easy is it for a first-generation Afro-Caribbean resident of Padstow in Cornwall, say, to feel included in maypole dancing, in a celebration of 'old' English heritage?

As Stuart Hall explains: 'A shared national identity depends on cultural meanings which bind each member individually into the large national story ... The National Heritage is a powerful source of such meanings. It follows that those who cannot see themselves reflected in the mirror cannot properly belong.'[14]

This is an issue Deller and Kane appear to side-step. The catalogue to the exhibition at Tate Britain acknowledges that 'these activities help to define individuals and communities', but they also see the aim of *Folk Archive* as providing a resistance to 'the homogenous effects of mass consumer culture manufactured by global capitalism'. The concern is that 'certain grass-roots activities were in danger of being eclipsed by the ubiquity of dominant consumer culture', and that exemplars of contemporary folk art should be documented, 'before they become extinct'.[15]

But after looking at *Folk Archive*, a more complex understanding of national identity is revealed. A modern nation cannot simply purge itself of its past, of its traditions. Indeed it loses something if it does. Having respect for the past does not necessarily mean a desire to preserve it in aspic: to create a static museum society. Deller and Kane have a vision of national identity that is fluid and changing rather than fixed. It echoes Stuart Hall's view that: 'what the nation means is an on-going project, under constant reconstruction'.[16]

Folk Archive pioneers a representation of the nation that welcomes competing claims to authenticity rather than the traditional approach which settles these claims via codification and hierarchies that privilege some at the expense of others. Instead older rural traditions – the hobby horses of Banbury – sit alongside the newer urban festivals like the Notting Hill Carnival, a reflection of the West Indian culture of those who settled in West London in the 1950s. Both are equally valid. Crucially, the older, rural tradition is not, because of its history, considered more authentic, more essentially English. This postmodern soup of traditions is an inclusive version of national identity. It doesn't judge, analyse or define – all contributions are welcome.

Some of the communities represented have a strong single voice, suggested by the trade union banners. Others feel at ease to draw on the traditions of the past and recycle them. We see the traditional Mayday celebrations based around ancient ideas of fertility and growth reinvented in the Mayday protests of anarchist guerilla gardeners, who sought to plant flowers in Parliament Square as part of the Anti-Capitalist protests in May 2000. They were transferring the older rural traditions into a modern urban environment.

Folk Archive offers an alternative to official constructions of national identity, which seek to create a (single, unified) story of the nation through a selective process. As Stuart Hall puts it: 'heritage inevitably reflects the governing assumptions of its time and context. It is always inflected by the power and authority of those who have colonized the past, whose versions of history matter'.[17] *Folk Archive* then is proudly unofficial, it's a democratic space of many versions of the nation – indeed it remains an online resource to which people are encouraged to contribute.[18] In the traditional Marxist sense it is a people's history, yet minus all the ideological baggage. And it is never complete or fixed, but always developing and growing organically.

As Jeremy Millar explains: 'there is no such thing as the *Folk Archive*. Rather, it is a concept instead of a material fact, an actively organizing (and disorganizing) idea instead of a passive accumulation of objects, that it is able to represent more accurately the cultural productions of contemporary communities, rather than being hampered by any perceived lack of methodological rigour.'[19] As well as showing us a picture of present-day England, it is also a forward-looking vision of what we might become as a nation.

NOTES

1. Jonathan Jones, 'Tate Modern gets a million visitors in just six weeks. Meanwhile at poor old Tate Britain...', *Guardian*, 28.6.00.

2. Ibid.

3. Mark Hallett, 'Hogarth's Variety' in Mark Hallett and Christine Riding (Eds), *Hogarth*, Tate Publishing 2006, p21.

4. Jeremy Millar, 'Poets of their Own Affairs: A Brief Introduction to the Folk Archive', in Jeremy Deller and Alan Kane, *Folk Archive: Contemporary Popular Art from the UK*, Bookworks 2005, p152.

5. Iain Aitch, 'Hot Stuff', *Guardian*, 11.5.05.

6. Rachel Withers, 'Gurning and embroidered knickers', *New Statesman*, 23.5.05.

7. Iain Aitch, 'Hot Stuff', *Guardian*, 11.5.05.

8. George Orwell, *The Lion and the Unicorn, Socialism and the English Genius*, Penguin 1982, p48.

9. Tristram Hunt, 'Merchant Adventurer', *New Statesman*, 28.1.08.

10. New Culture Forum founding aims, June 2006, see www.newcultureforum. org.uk.

11. George Orwell, *The Lion and the Unicorn, Socialism and the English Genius*, Penguin 1982, p39.

12. Jeremy Deller and Alan Kane, 'Preface' in *Folk Archive: Contemporary Popular Art from the UK*, Bookworks 2005, p2.

13. Ibid.

14. Stuart Hall, 'Whose Heritage?' in Jo Littler and Roshi Naidoo (Eds), *The Politics of Heritage*, Routledge 2005, p24.

15. Julian Stallabrass, 'Clever clogs', in the *New Statesman*, 18.9.00.

16. Stuart Hall, 'Whose Heritage?' in Jo Littler and Roshi Naidoo (Eds), *The Politics of Heritage*, Routledge 2005, p25.

17. Ibid., p26.

18. www.folkarchive.co.uk.

19. Jeremy Millar, 'Poets of their Own Affairs: A Brief Introduction to the Folk Archive', in Jeremy Deller and Alan Kane, *Folk Archive: Contemporary Popular Art from the UK*, Bookworks 2005, p152.

Three world cups and no more wars

Markus Hesselmann

Stephanie says that she is plagued by being born in Germany

F.S.K.[1]

What Nick Hornby claims for football clubs holds even more true for national teams. You don't choose them, they choose you. You are born into this loyalty. But you have to be at least a bit of a patriot in order to accept this born-into loyalty. And patriotism was a bit of a problem for German post-war generations – at least for those who did not belong to the far right. 'There are difficult fatherlands. One of them is Germany', said Gustav Heinemann in 1969 in his inaugural speech as President of the Federal Republic. Steve Crawshaw quotes this famous presidential saying at the beginning of his *Easier Fatherland: Germany and the Twenty-First Century*;[2] and this book title, from a British writer who has lived in Germany, shows us Germans how much more easygoing we seem to have become. It is an irony that a Brit of all people is putting forward such a view, and encouraging us Germans.

Crawshaw describes the decades after the Second World War in Germany as an era of double psychological repression. At first German war crimes were taboo and could not be discussed in public. Then, after the left-wing revolt of 1968, German victims of the war were hushed up. Crawshaw feels that the right balance has now been struck. Books such as *Crabwalk* by Günter Grass[3] – which dealt with the sinking of the Wilhem Gustloff, a huge German refugee ship – or *The Fire* by Jörg Friedrich[4] – which concentrated on Germany's victims of aerial bombardment – have contributed to this balancing. According to Crawshaw, 'Germany came to find such subjects embarrassing; only those with pronounced right-wing views highlighted tragedies like that of the Gustloff. Grass showed that it need not be that way'.[5] Germans seem to be ready now to take on the responsibility for their history without 'surmounting the past' (*Vergangenheitsbewältigung*), or drawing the much-discussed 'final stroke' (*Schlusstrich*). These were two key terms in the debate on German approaches to its history: *Schlusstrich* was a means to finally get rid of the guilt, while *Vergangenheitsbewältigung* was a more moderate concept, accepting the guilt but somehow also trying to overcome it, through dealing with it for a time and thus eventually disposing of it. Both terms have been used to criticise those who – to varying degrees – were unwilling to accept Nazi crimes as a legacy of German history that was there to stay. While now fully taking on this responsibility, Germans, according to Crawshaw, also seem at last to be ready to commemorate their own victims – without denying that many of their people had actually been culprits and not victims of the Nazi era and the war. Germany thereby finds a new self-conception: a revived yet softer patriotism.

When patriotism was discredited after the war, there was also a loss of national rituals. In 1954, at Bern's Wankdorf Stadium, after Germany's World Cup Final victory against the favourites Hungary, German fans defiantly sang the national anthem's tabooed first verse (*Deutschland über alles*), which had been discredited because of its use by the Nazis. Twenty years on, in 1974, before the kick-off of what was to become Germany's second victorious World Cup final, the players on the pitch of Munich's Olympic Stadium would not even sing *Einigkeit und Recht und Freiheit*, the post-war German anthem. This was a generation of long-haired football players who, if not politically then surely aesthetically, was influenced by the 1968 revolt, whose protagonists wanted, and in many ways succeeded, to get rid of everything suggestive of nationalism in West Germany.

Accordingly, many German football fans in those days did not accept loyalty to the national team they were born into supporting. They became fans of other national teams: England most of all, but also Scotland, Argentina or Brazil. Later Ireland and Cameroon also became our promised lands of international football. West German leftists would rather support the Soviet Union or the GDR than their own country. There was a lot of cheering in these quarters when the GDR beat the Federal Republic 1-0 at the 1974 World Cup. Meanwhile, behind the wall, many ordinary East Germans were happy about the victory of Beckenbauer, Maier and Breitner, who they saw as the greater sporting heroes, or as representatives of the free Germany on the other side of the much-hated wall.

However, two years before Nick Hornby's *Fever Pitch*, the German popular theoretician Diedrich Diederichsen laid out the mechanisms of following football the right way in an essay for the magazine of *Die*

Zeit.[6] He recalled his experience from his World Cup initiation in 1966: 'It was only logical that I "was" "for" "Germany" as much as I had been for Hamburger SV before, whose following I was born into'. He stuck to that over the years: 'Even as a Hippie or Commie I kept being "for" "Germany" at World Cups and Euros … This was my team, right or wrong, I had no choice'. Diederichsen went on to castigate those intellectuals who do not understand the essence of football:

> Just abominable were those fellow students who celebrated Algeria's victory out of vulgar-left sympathies. They don't know anything about the seriousness of this game, which is the only remaining mass-engaging metaphor of life. How can anyone think, simply out of their political disposition, that they had nothing to do with it, and could support some-one else more likeable?

Reunification, however, proved too much for Diederichsen. What appeared to him to be a country free of nationalism, the good old comfy Federal Republic, now took on a dangerous new dimension. To support Germany at the 1990 World Cup was difficult for him:

> The word 'Deutschland' does not mean a two-syllable, chantable fiction that no one links to atavistic national sentiments, but rather now stands for everything ranging from the Wehrmacht to re-unification to economic world power: for a force and its subjects who are suddenly not a free, frenetic mass any more, fuelled by nameless fury and unleashed energy, but war volunteers.

Diedrichsen's radical manifesto, introduced as such by the *Zeit Magazin* editorial as a warning to its readers, culminates in a stupid *Faschismusvorwurf*[7] – a nonsensical comparison of the newly united Germany with the Third Reich, which lacked the analytical depth of the rest of the text. He suggested that the solution was to 'wait until the next all-German team gets their arse kicked in 1994 in the USA, as much as the first one in 1938 against Switzerland'. Thankfully, while his predic-tion of failure for the German team at World Cup '94 was proved right, no Fourth Reich came into being. Terrible events did occur on both sides of the former border however. There were racist attacks on foreigners in Hoyerswerda, Rostock-Lichtenhagen, Solingen and Mölln, some of them lethal. But the mass of people stood up against all this with huge demonstrations and the famous *Lichterketten* (candle-lit demonstrations). That does not mean that there are no longer any disturbing events, particularly in the East: for example in Summer 2007 a xenophobic mob chased a group of Asians through the small town of Mügeln in Saxony. But the United Germany has turned out to be anything but a threat to its neighbours. Whereas the old West Germany was an economic giant and a political dwarf, the new Germany's slow political growth has been accompanied by economic decline. It is only now regaining some of its economic strengths, and some analysts still maintain that this is not a lasting recovery, since Germany still lags behind in future key sectors such as service and finance. Meanwhile, German soldiers are back on foreign soil, in the Balkans and Afghanistan. Ironically we are criticised for not providing enough soldiers – that is what our former World War enemies Britain and the US now demand of us!

Interestingly, football has gone through a roughly parallel development. At first predictions of success were overblown. Franz Beckenbauer managed to make himself look even more ridiculous than Chancellor Kohl, who had claimed that there would be no unemployment or deindustrialisation in the East as a result of reunification: in a TV address in 1990 he anticipated 'blooming landscapes', achieved through 'a common effort'. Beckenbauer managed to surpass even this faultless optimism by claiming that the future united German football team would beat any opposition for years to come. Here, not Beckenbauer but Diederichsen was right. The united German team really did get their arses kicked. Germany was eliminated in the quarterfinals of World Cup in 1994 and 1998, and failed to get beyond the Group Stage at Euro 2000 and 2004. (Every England fan would surely add to this litany a certain 5-1 thrashing by England in 2001. However, though this has become part of English football folklore, frankly speaking this does not matter so much in Germany as a defeat on that kind of scale against the Netherlands, our real favourite enemy.) There were some successes during this period, however, including the wonderful exception when Germany became European champions in 1996 – at Wembley of all places.

It was not until World Cup 2006 that Jürgen Klinsmann showed the Germans the unifying and mobilising power of the national team, in a new way, that was appreciated by broad sections of our population. With meticulous planning, a modern approach to training, an attacking philosophy and an appeal to both individual skills as well as collective team effort, Klinsmann managed to lead a team with very few stars but many talents into the World Cup semi final. An overflowing of soft patriotism accompanied the progress of the team: 'It's like another country: Hundreds of thousands in the stadia and millions in front of their TV sets and in the streets celebrate football and themselves – with

Mediterranean joy and a relaxed, cosmopolitan patriotism', said *Der Spiegel* in its review of the tournament.[8]

For me, this was a refreshing experience. It took me a long time to learn to love the German team – and Germany as my home country for that matter. To support other teams – including England – was much easier than to argue with friends at a peace march or a punk concert, who simply would not understand if someone like me supported Jupp Derwall's teutonic Germany team during the 1980s. Amongst your left peers you could easily become subject to a *Faschismusverdacht* (suspicion of fascism) in those days. Everything could be denounced as 'fascist' then: the *Hausmeister* (caretaker), the Hippies and the Helmuts (Schmidt and Kohl). 'God save the Queen, it's a fascist regime' bellowed the Sex Pistols. 'California über alles' roared the Dead Kennedys. 'We don't need this fascist groove thang', chorused Heaven 17. These bands spoke directly to us. Their anti-authoritarianism was expressed in being against all things fascist, and they became our heroes in Germany because of it. The German band *Kolossale Jugend* (Colossal Youth), an early precursor of the Hamburg school of German guitar pop, printed a t-shirt with the slogan 'Shut up Germany'. I bought one of these shirts but I did not wear it that often.

By 1989 I was becoming bored by this constant self-hatred. I came to England, and encountered there a progressive, internationalist thinking and popular patriotism that did not necessarily exclude others. To put it mildly, it is inhibiting to constantly look only for the negatives in your own country's culture and identity. The English taught me to love Germany. Like Diederichsen and Hornby I do not believe in choice any more when it comes to your favourite football club. It's destiny. You are born into it, with no chance for escape. Therefore my football teams are, and can only ever be, in this order: Schalke 04 (home region), Rot-Weiß Oberhausen (hometown), Middlesbrough FC (twin town of hometown).

It was town twinning that brought me to Ayresome Park and the Northeast of England – otherwise an unlikely place for a holiday trip. I went there twice with groups of German youths in my early teens and I enjoyed it. The place was familiar to me from the beginning, and not only because Oberhausen is like Middlesbrough minus the sea. England was the land of football –'Das Mutterland des Fuáballs' as the Germans say, avoiding the more familiar term 'Vaterland'. And for me, England was also the motherland of pop. Manuel, the Spanish waiter in *Fawlty Towers*, says: 'I speak English well, I learned it from a book', but I add: 'and I learned it from pop songs'. When I was young I taped them from the radio on my cassette player – one of my favourite stations being British Forces Broadcasting Service. I tried to make sense of the lyrics even before I went to grammar school at the age of ten to learn proper English. And I wrote down the titles in the idiosyncratic Pop Pidgin spelling that I and my cousin Michael had developed. 'Stand by me' became 'Stan Barney'. For every English word, there is still a song I remember. Whenever 'Holidays' are mentioned I can only think of the Sex Pistols' track 'Holidays in the Sun' and Johnny Rotten snarls his way through the lyrics in my head.

Now I was there, finally. And what a paradise it was! The mothers of the families we stayed with knew as much about the pop charts as their kids (my parents at home listened to instrumental muzak by the likes of James Last or Richard Claydermann). I was particularly fond of Madness in those days. It impressed me that their singer Suggs was as much into football as singing. The songs from the British charts from those days are still in my head: songs like The Jam's 'Going Underground', 'Turning Japanese' by an obscure band called The Vapors, or even more bizarrely 'Together we are Beautiful' by one hit wonder Fern Kinney. And what impressed me even more than this wonderful music were the spacious public parks everywhere, that were open to everybody to play football whenever they liked. It appeared to me that the English put the little boxes they live in so closely next to one another so that they could leave as much space as possible for these parks, with their football pitches. In German cities, even as a youth player in organised club football, you were trying your best not to scratch your knees on a clay pitch. Playing football on the grass in a German park? Verboten! Not so in England, football paradise.

Like so many things, all this has become much more relaxed in Germany now. And, conversely, the English seem to put up more 'Verboten' signs these days than we Germans ever did, not to mention the selling off of these playing-fields for the short-term profit of property development. In England, in the early 1980s, I liked the football, the music, the sea, and the sense of humour. Most of all I liked my new favourite football club, though I soon had to learn that since the prehistoric beginnings of English professional football Boro had never been league champions. And I learned much later that a certain Herr Hitler had prevented Boro from winning the one championship where it had a chance of success. He started his war exactly in the year when Boro had its best team ever. I also learned a bit later that Coventry City, which I only knew as the opposition at my first Middlesbrough match, had another – very violent – relationship with Germany, a link from an era that made Anglo-German projects like town-twinning and youth exchanges all the more important.

After my first stay 'on the island', I developed a fascination with all things English, as so many other Germans of my generation have done. (The English, on the other hand, have a rather focused fascination with Germany. Ask most people in England to name the three most famous Germans and it would be Hitler, Hitler and Hitler. If we are lucky, Beethoven, Beckenbauer and Boris Becker come before Göring, Goebbels and von Ribbentrop. Followed perhaps by Claudia Schiffer and Heidi Klum.) In order to become an official German England expert I crossed 'den Kanal' to visit 'die Insel' many times, and also spent two terms as a student at Reading University. And this had another effect too. When you live abroad for a while you learn to love your own country. You really get to know where you come from. I had to go to England to become a German fan.

I still like the English team but I would always want Germany to beat them now. I would have most liked that to happen in Berlin – Germany vs England, my perfect 2006 World Cup final. But that did not work out for either team. I learned a bit of healthy patriotism in England, where many of my friends would be very critical of their government on certain social and political issues, but would always be loyal to their country. They would make a lot of jokes, sometimes cruel jokes, about Germany and the Germans. But they would also show a lot of respect for a country that had achieved so much in its history, and had come back from the ruins of total defeat.

I still admire England now that I work here as a correspondent. I was lucky to have come here in the year after a World Cup that had changed Germany's image for the better. I never experienced the adversities faced by other colleagues during their tenure in London. Matthias Matussek of *Der Spiegel*, in May 2006, just before the beginning of the World Cup, wrote a piece about his bad experiences for *The Guardian*:

> When I was dispatched to London for two years to report for *Der Spiegel* magazine, and my nine-year-old son was chased around Richmond Park by some English teenagers shouting, 'Nazi, Nazi', I admired the English sense of fair play and enthusiasm for sport. 'Running in the fresh air will do you good', I explained to my son, and quietly dispatched him to karate classes.[9]

But no raised right arms and no 'Heil Hitler' greetings for me so far – phenomena that I used to encounter quite often during my earlier stays in this country. And on top of that there is hardly any German-bashing in the newspapers any more, at least for the time being. That seems to have to do with the World Cup as well. It must mean something when so many people are keen to assure me of how great an experience the World Cup in Germany was for them and their friends, and what a nice bunch of people the Germans are after all. It also went down as a rather pleasant surprise when German fans and journalists were greeted by a huge *Danke für 2006* banner at Germany's friendly against England at the new Wembley in August 2007 – and so nice that England allowed us to win there again.

But the most intriguing thing for me in my current stay in England was to learn that there is an identity debate going on in this country right now. Wasn't that something for Germans, a people who had always been inclined to brooding? A late nation, whose identity had been crushed by having to come to terms with the greatest atrocities in the history of mankind, and then being a divided country, part of which was again a dictatorship. If national identity is a process of amnesia (as Ernest Renan in his lecture 'What is a Nation?' famously put it, 'the essential element of a nation is that all its individuals must have many things in common but it must also have forgotten many things'[10]), then the Germans would never have a chance of being a nation again, since their crimes were too outrageous to ever be forgotten. But England? The oldest democracy, on the right side of history for most of the time? 'It is a mark of self-confidence: the English have not spent a great deal of time defining themselves because they haven't needed to. Is it necessary to do so now?' asks the *Newsnight* presenter Jeremy Paxman.

THE LEITKULTURDEBATTE

Germans are experts on debates about national identity, so perhaps it is richly appropriate that we should be asked to contribute to yours. Our very own *Leitkulturdebatte* (debate about defining culture) peaked around the turn of the millennium. Interestingly, the term was coined by an immigrant scholar, Bassam Tibi, and it was brought to bear not so much on Germany alone but on European or Western identity as a whole. 'The values for the desirable Leitkultur must come from cultural modernity and they are: democracy, secularism, enlightenment, human rights and civil society.'[11] This was then adopted particularly by conservative politicians in a German debate about immigration and integration. And it also catered well for a popular appetite for self-discovery. *Nabelschau* (navel-gazing) is one of the terms used to criticize this supposedly typically German inclination.

The 2006 World Cup contributed to loosening all this up. It was a collective celebration of playful patriotism. It cleared the air for a while and will hopefully last. Before the tournament's opening match

I wrote in *Der Tagesspiegel*, the newspaper I work for, and also in a book I edited before the World Cup with Christopher Young, about my problems with German patriotism. But I also added that a World Cup in our own country without patriotism would neither be fun nor would make much sense.[12] Then, over the next few weeks, I felt a pride in all those black, red and gold flags that were seen all over Germany for as long as the tournament lasted. 'The whole of Germany is surprised and the world around it even more', commented the serious Swiss newspaper *Neue Zürcher Zeitung*. 'No one would have expected from the Germans so much happy patriotism and enthusiasm in black, red and gold, combined with open-hearted hospitality.'[13] There had been a bit of this in 1990, after the World Cup victory, and again in 1996 after the victorious European championships final. But that had been more about simply celebrating football victories. This time it was not only about winning games, but also about playing with style, being good hosts and joining in the great party of the football nations gathered in our country. The flags became more of a symbol of this easygoing reassurance than of any victory. In his book about his World Cup documentary, *Deutschland. Ein Sommermärchen* (*Germany. A summer's tale*), director Sönke Wortmann explains his experience with patriotism, which in large measure corresponds with mine. He calls himself a post-68er who had had these same difficulties with supporting Germany: 'I approached the German anthem and the German flag with a scepticism that was typical for my generation. That had to do with German history and a feeling that its darker parts were still repressed'. The 2006 World Cup was the final stage for him in challenging these attitudes: it 'proved my changed attitude towards Germany'.

Wortmann's film *Das Wunder von Bern* (The Miracle of Bern), a Hollywood-style treatment of Germany's unexpected victory in the 1954 World Cup final, had already contributed to a new perception of Germany by its people. Historian Wolfram Pyta interprets the renewed interest in everything Bern after German unification to the need for a founding myth that any nation state has. The 1954 final stands as 'the most impressive example of how a depressed people can manage to find their feet again through hard work'.[14] One might add that the World Cup 2006 finally taught this formerly depressed people how to party too.

But there is more to it than partying. For us soft patriots it is becoming easier and easier to support Germany. Jürgen Klinsmann, the Californian-German cosmopolitan, fielded a team during the World Cup that featured four out of six forwards who were not born in

Germany: Miroslav Klose (Opole, Poland), Lukas Podolski (Gliwice, Poland), Oliver Neuville (Gambarogno, Switzerland), Gerald Asamoah (Mampong, Ghana). Added to this was the Westphalian Mike Hanke and David Odonkor, a Westphalian-born player of Ghanaian descent. The *Nationalmannschaft* is becoming more and more of an *Internationalmannschaft*. Here we are again late. While England, France and the Netherlands have been relying on players originating from their former colonies for years, Germany has had no such option. It was stripped of its colonies after the First World War. But it is also fair to say that the German Football Association for a long time made little effort to include players from minorities in the national squad. German-Turkish players, for example, were (and still are) enticed away by Turkish scouts to play for the country of their forefathers. All this is changing for the better now.

It seems to me that football provides at least an element of a model for identifying with a modern multicultural German society. There are none of the exclusions there used to be when Germany was in denial of being a nation founded on waves of immigration. But there has also to be a certain disposition, a will for identification, by all those we should be making welcome to join in. This identification does not function along the lines of ethnicity, ancestry or 'blood' any more, but around the acceptance of achievements such as democracy, women's rights, free speech, free trade, entrepreneurship, social security, functioning public services and infrastructures, tax solidarity, consensus, charity, volunteering, tolerance. This sounds very much like an expanded and more detailed list of Bassam Tibi's *Leitkultur* elements. But there is a bit more, and that is at least a sense of a national heritage or culture, which of course includes football. Culture in the sense that T.S. Eliot understood it in *Notes Towards a Definition of Culture*, where he listed 'Derby Day, Henley Regatta, Cowes, the twelfth of August, a cup final, the dog races, the pin table, the dart board, Wensleydale cheese, boiled cabbage cut into sections, beetroot in vinegar, nineteenth century Gothic churches and the music of Elgar' as elements of English culture.[15] This identification is less about integration, which means more or less having to give up other inherited cultures, and more about a sense of inclusion, inviting others to bring inherited cultures to add something new to the continually, but also carefully negotiated, *Leitkultur*, without alienating those unfamiliar with these new additions, or suppressing what is perceived as the original culture. Is not our present *Leitkultur* nothing but an amalgamation of past inclusions? I agree with what Billy Bragg wrote in his book *The Progressive Patriot* about 'the urge of the majority to assert itself', and what can happen if that urge breaks out from a real or imagined suppression and 'is taken to the extreme'.[16] Nazi Germany is one of his examples for the terrible consequences such an outburst can have. Billy Bragg calls for new narratives to be developed to foster a progressive, non-exclusive patriotism and to 'challenge the Right's monopoly on patriotism'.[17] In a certain sense, and in all due modesty, Germany's World Cup 2006 offered one of these narratives – not just for ourselves but for England too.

NOTES

1. F.S.K. or Freiwillige Selbstkontrolle (Voluntary Self-Control) were the favourite German band of the BBC's legendary DJ John Peel. 'Das schlechteste Land der Welt' (The worst country in the world), the song quoted here, satirises German self-doubts and self-flagellation. The original German verse from the song runs: 'Stefanie sagt, dass es sie plagt, in Deutschland geboren zu sein'.

2. Steve Crawshaw, *Easier Fatherland: Germany and the Twenty-First Century*, Continuum 2004.

3. Günter Grass, *Crabwalk*, Faber and Faber 2003.

4. Jörg Friedrich, *The Fire: The Bombing of Germany, 1940-1945*, Columbia University Press 2006.

5. Crawshaw, op. cit., p171.

6. Diedrich Diederichsen, 'Ernster als Leben und Tod', *Die Zeit, Magazin*, 8.6.90.

7. This is another classic term in the debate. It could be translated as 'blame for having fascist ideas'.

8. 'Deutschland, ein Sommermärchen', *Der Spiegel* (25) 2006, p68.

9. Matthias Matussek, 'Beethoven, Claudia Schiffer, Willy Brandt? No, the British are only interested in Germany when it involves Nazis', *The Guardian* 23.5.06. Germany's and Arsenal's goalkeeper Jens Lehmann told me in an interview that his son was called a 'bloody German Nazi' at a rugby school match in 2007. See: 'Ich werde bei der EM spielen', *Der Tagesspiegel* 24.12.07, p26.

10. Ernest Renan, 'What is a Nation?', in John Hutchinson, Anthony D. Smith (eds), *Nationalism*, Oxford University Press 1994.

11. Bassam Tibi, *Europa ohne Identität*, 1998, p154.

12. Markus Hesselmann, 'Deutschland lieben lernen', in Markus Hesselmann and Christopher Young (eds), *Der Lieblingsfeind, Deutschland aus der Sicht seiner Fußballrivalen*, Verlag Die Werkstatt 2006.

13. Gerd E. Kolbe, 'Ein Land badet in Schwarz-Rot-Gold', *Neue Zürcher Zeitung am Sonntag* 25.6.06.

14. Wolfram Pyta, 'German football: a cultural history', in Alan Tomlinson and Christopher Young (eds), *German Football, History, Culture, Society,* Routledge, 2005, p18.
15. T.S. Eliot, 'Notes Towards the Definition of Culture', in Frank Kermode (ed), *Selected Prose of T.S. Eliot,* Faber and Faber 1975, p298.
16. Billy Bragg, *The Progressive Patriot, A Search for Belonging,* Bantam 2006, p12.
17. Ibid., p14.

The great escape

From Enoch Powell to Hope Powell and beyond

Paul Gilroy

One of the most peculiar features of race politics in Britain is the fact that many of our most powerful, influential and ambitious people and institutions cannot leave the vexed memory of Enoch Powell alone. Anybody committed to improving social life here will eventually have to delve into what it is about the legacy of this duplicitous and eccentric politician which makes his forty-year-old fantasies of a racial war in our country such an enduring touchstone for smug xenophobia and thoughtless hatred. Surely by now his ideas should have passed their sell-by date? The fateful twenty years of his predictions have now elapsed and the black man doesn't seem after all to have gained 'the whip hand over the white'. But, despite that obvious failure, Powell's name commands awe. This is true even among younger politicians and commentators who can have no personal memory of the incendiary force of his carefully calculated intervention in April 1968. Their overly respectful invocations of Powell and his project are best approached as a political device that shuts down access to the history of struggles to make this into a multicultural and postcolonial country at ease with itself and its past. Instead, we are required to revisit Enoch Powell periodically in order to avoid having to engage in that belated and necessary reckoning.

The immortal power of his prophecy is therefore a symptom. It points to deeper problems that bedevil the pursuit of a more habitable and comfortable Englishness. It was Powell who first designed and then brandished the demotic cloak that has reappeared regularly to work its special magic in assembling populist electoral blocs since his bid for the Tory leadership foundered. His apologists are legion. They applaud his supposedly peerless statesmanship and his blunt, honesty which is judged – miraculously in this anti-intellectual climate – to be simultaneously both ethnic and cerebral. The guardians of his brilliant contribution assert that he has been misunderstood. They then spin any embarrassing evidence about the scenario described in his famous 'immigration' speech so that its author's absurd claim to have acted in good faith can stand unchallenged.[1] To say anything unflattering about Powell is to violate our narrowing political world's basic codes of politeness. Refusing to bend the knee in his direction is an objectionable act of surrender to the anti-democratic pressures of what is risibly known as 'political correctness gone mad'.

Powell's legacy assumes this primal significance because it symbolises the contested integrity of British nationalism. As a result it can never be racist. In that distorted world, the wogs *do* begin at Calais and racism is only ever a Germanic thing. Anti-racism and any aspiration towards a 'progressive patriotism' must confront what we can call the Enoch Powell problem. Until it has been dealt with, the door to more wholesome or just more realistic forms of nationalism will remain impassible.

I had just finished reading Eric Clapton's autobiography which skates embarrassingly over the guitarist's own visceral attachment to Powell's view of post-colonial English life when Nigel Hastilow, a plain-speaking ex-journalist and would-be Tory candidate from the West Midlands let the tired, old, racist cat out of the English nationalist bag yet again. The cat looks decidedly scrawny these days. It is old and slow but still intermittently agile. I couldn't help noticing that Hastilow had been an undergraduate in Birmingham at the time of Clapton's celebrated racist outburst from the stage of the New Street Odeon. I wondered whether young Nigel had attended that famous concert? Whether he was a punk or a Clapton fan? At the same time, I was surprised that the old political line originally drawn by Ted Heath when he sacked Powell from the shadow cabinet had held firm. That principled definition of what counts as acceptable political speech in Britain was enforced subsequently by Rock Against Racism and others who persistently unscrewed the cultural hinges which held the frame of racism to the traditional oak doors of Englishness. David Goodhart, Trevor Phillips, Margaret Hodge and Powell's various other updaters, translators and apologists were presumably uncomfortable at this instance of needless retreat. However, David Cameron, as alert as Heath before him to the pragmatic as well as the philosophical dimensions of this populist challenge, put his foot down, and Hastilow was pressured into a reluctant resignation.

The recurrence of events like these raises difficult questions that go beyond Powell's mythic significance as a talisman of authentic English nationalism and a cipher for acceptable xenophobia. Powell's own duplicity provides some of the best evidence we have about the deeply xenophobic cast of English nationalism and its fundamental associations with a version of national culture which can only make sense in exclusionary, racial terms. The quest to understand his enduring appeal has to be connected with other, broader lines of inquiry into the character of English nationalism during this pivotal moment in the process of national decomposition he feared and foresaw. Those inquiries must discover what Powell's authority, celebrity and beguiling example might now reveal about the obstacles to any progressive politics in an area which urgently needs to be able to align local, regional and national attachments with more worldly and possibly more cosmopolitan ones that can withstand the dubious allure of an imperial revival.

We were forced to endure the tide of nostalgic identification with and rehabilitation of Powell that accompanied the fortieth anniversary of his horrible prophecy. In those conditions, the very least any would-be salvagers of Englishness must do is ask *when* those rivers of blood were supposed to foam and flood? We should also try to clarify exactly *whose* blood was supposed to be pulsing away in portentous Roman torrents. The blood of immigrants has certainly flowed in England's streets, but it has seldom been present in the quantities that Powell predicted with such fake, theatrical gravity. Let's be clear. That wasted blood has mostly come from the bodies of isolated and frightened people of colour. They were caught out, usually late at night, by various freelance implementers of Powell's nightmare vision, who felt that they had a patriotic duty to bring his morbid tableaux to life whenever they could act with impunity. It is still the case that the only place to read the full text of the 'Rivers Of Blood' speech online is on an old National Front web site.

I am reluctant to accept that I am the only person who is bothered by the threat of violence that those frequently repeated words contained and can still be made to convey. If the dodgy Jamaican Imam, Abdullah Al Faisal, can be convicted of 'non-specific incitement to murder', couldn't our ancient law, or perhaps just Britain's famous national sense of fair play, pay some belated attention to the perlocutionary force of Powell's hateful performatives? At the MacPherson inquiry, Stephen Lawrence's killers seemed clear enough about what their espousal of Powell's political outlook had enabled them to accomplish.[2] In other words, isn't the element of incitement to murder that is audible in Powell's words something that we could acknowledge and perhaps even disapprove? That task seems more urgent and important than being able to discover that the hidden name of the shit through the letter box woman may have been Druscilla Cotterill – somebody who seems never to have actually had that particular form of harassment happen to her.[3]

Of course, liberal racial realists, neo-patriots, clash of civilisationists and practitioners of joined-up thinking all thrill at being able to use an expurgated Enoch as a sock puppet with which to enact their own growing anxieties about swamping, security, failed multiculture, social cohesion and home grown terrorists. A new-found love of Powell's works and statesmanship facilitates the return of those no-longer-lefty prodigals to the bosom of a conservative nation they thought they had lost. Their circuitous political journey now requires them to argue that his concern with the corrosive effects of immigration was prescient and that years of immigration-talk can, exactly as David Cameron has himself proposed, be effectively 'de-racialised' at a stroke without giving attention to the political baggage that has been accumulated. This aspiration is also potent because it reassures the commentariat, the info warriors and all who dwell comfortably within the bubble of official politics, that they are right to believe they can make anything mean exactly what they want it to mean.

The substance of a counter-history that could drain the emotional and psychological energy away from this complex nationalist formation is not, at present, to be found either in the reformed history syllabus or in a mediascape policed by twenty- and thirty-something gatekeepers from Oxbridge, who know next to nothing of the recent history of this country and care even less about the post 1945 politics of race and nation. For that cohort, racism was placed firmly in the past by the likes of Wrighty, Tim Westwood, Moira Stewart and Andy Peters. At a safe distance now from those dangers, we are, in a sense, obliged to return to Enoch Powell in order to see where he might be able to help us with contemporary problems. His lonely old woman's victimisation at the hands of those malevolent piccaninnies and his figuration of the nation in her vulnerable, feminine form is connected to a vivid new projection of Powell himself as an unjustly persecuted Englishman: a man who really and truly wished that he had perished on the battlefield. If only he had been granted that wish!

English Enoch saw the US as the enemy of the British Empire, a view which was sharply inverted in John Sturgess' 1963 film *The Great Escape*. The movie's continuing popularity is not just the result of Elmer Bernstein's viral theme tune. No less than Powell's immortal influence, the film's resurgent appeal reveals something about the social psychology of its many fans and also about aspects of the historical condition of a nation that has become steadily more anxious about what now binds it together. The quest for an answer to that question presses us all back towards a simplified sense of identity as radical sameness. That national seriality can be imagined best through a heavily filtered and idealised invocation of the anti-Nazi war. It generates a version of the battle of Britain that is conducted without the aid of Polish, Indian or Caribbean pilots. It summons a different England, which unfolds most smoothly when it is understood to be an all-white, anglophone affair. No darkies, coons or *kit-e-kat* eaters are present to sully the glorious unanimity of tea drinking and hokey cokey dancing that takes place safely down in the underground while the solidarising adversity of the blitz bursts overhead.[4] The pursuit of security, safety and consolation via those familiar images is worth exploring, even if we acknowledge that the affection in which Sturgess' film is held today has been tinged with irony. The re-figuring of the nation in exclusively masculine form is a significant component of its popularity. Today, that shift returns us to a pre-feminist world where quiet men proved and tested their manhood in battle and women knew their places and made their own clothes. This is the fantasy of England celebrated in the popular fiction of Tony Parsons and boldly repudiated by Mike Leigh in *Vera Drake*. Among other things, *The Great Escape* dramatises the transition from European – specifically British – world domination to the emergent alternative order dictated by the US Empire. The gum-chewing, mit-wearing, motor-bike-riding Steve McQueen is the avatar of a novel imperial arrangement: the nomos of the earth.

The fumbling, stoic, blindness of Donald Pleasance personifies the strengths and the weaknesses of the order that is being left behind. The transition identified here is comforting because it celebrates the idea of Britain – synonymous now with England – as endlessly resourceful and plucky. The historical defeat of the nation to which the escapees mostly belong dovetails neatly with the larger victory against Nazi evil on which it signifies. We have learned to get pleasure from the enactment of the larger historical change which, in Dean Ascheson's famous Cold War phrase, saw Britain lose its Empire but prove unable to find another role.

I want to suggest that there is also something about the idea of escape itself that has become deeply pleasurable. The mythology of that thwarted wartime breakout and the peculiar mixture of failure and triumph that it articulates, provides ways to make the nation's painful geo-political and economic transition psychologically bearable to many who experience its unhappy consequences without appreciating their underlying cause. There is also something else at stake. It can be interpreted as a repressed desire to be able to escape from the grip in which the invented memory of that anti-nazi war has held us. Somewhere, against the odds and in opposition to the logic of our national melancholia, many people do want to work through the past. Half of the country is desperate to move on.

The principal alternative site of Britain's national palingenesis is another, different, contest with Germany: England's World Cup victory of 1966. The question that moment raises for us is whether Wembley in 1966 represents the continuation of the war against the Nazis by other means. That issue has not been settled and may not be until the competition returns to these shores. The meaning and memory of the war itself are very different now that a further forty-two years have elapsed. The easy, unthinking substitution of England for Britain defers other problems that arise in trying to identify and conserve the country's ebbing cultural core.

1966 was also the year that Hope Powell was born in South London. She is currently manager of the England women's football team, in which she had previously distinguished herself as a creative attacking midfielder. The black, dreadlock-wearing sister of Pete Docherty's sometime drummer Gary Powell, Hope is a creature seemingly plucked from Enoch Powell's worst nightmares. Her life and success are absolutely unimaginable from within his system of thinking about nation, culture and identity. She was not one of those Wolverhampton piccaninnies, but she is certainly their racial, generational and cultural kin. In striving to make England more healthy and more habitable, we can try the thought experiment of borrowing Hope Powell and using her personal achievements on and off the football pitch, as well as her contributions to our collective national life, to invent another variety of patriotic attachment. It's not just that Hope's real English tale has nurtured the variety of feel good multiculturalism affirmed by Gurinder Chadha's epochal contribution *Bend It Like Beckham*. It's that all the advocates of Enoch Powell's wisdom must be acquainted with his namesake and made to reckon with her twenty-first-century English presence. They will have to face the fact that the process they see as failed multiculturalism is in fact an irreversible accommodation of postcolonial difference that demands more from us than merely recycling the nightmares of a sour and twisted old man who thought he could employ popular racism to further his own political ambitions, and almost managed to pull it off. The well-named Hope stands for more than the belated prospect of being recognised as being both black and English. Unlike the underperforming men's team, which, as we all know, plays for money rather than honour, her underfunded England footballers are amateurs. That means that somehow, in spite of their frustrations, they play for their evolving country essentially out of love.

NOTES

1. Paul Gilroy, *There Ain't No Black In The Union Jack*, Routledge Classics 2002.

2. See the 30th June 1998 discussion of the surveillance video shot by police in 1994.

3. Fiona Barton, 'Widow in Enoch Powell's Rivers of Blood speech really did exist', *Daily Mail*, 2.2.07.

4. Maev Kennedy, 'Sex, fear and looting: survivors disclose untold stories of the Blitz: New history based on interviews gives unvarnished account of bombings and air battle', *Guardian*, 5.10.06.

A green and pleasant land

Nicola Baird

It is a rare person indeed who admits to disliking the English countryside. Many of us feel closely connected with it, wherever we live
– loving the patchwork mix of arable and livestock, the village dramas
and connections with the past. But as the price of country homes soars
– and the cost of farmland has rocketed to a new thirty year high – few
but the very rich get to buy up their own pastoral slice.[1]

As a result we've learnt to connect with our English soil in a different way, a process that has been made easier as we convince ourselves
that rural life is a compromised option anyway. All the good things
about country life – the springtime lushness, the native wildlife, the
footpaths, the cosy pubs and the traditions – don't offset the inconve-
nient truths of rural living. These include the absolute necessity of
owning a car because of the non-existence of rural public transport that
can link home, bus and railway station in anything resembling a
timetable, the endless frustration of finding a newspaper, stamps or
fresh bread (thanks to pogrom-like closures of village shops and post
offices), and the challenges of finding a dentist for your kids in the
same county as the one where you currently live.

Yet it wasn't that long ago that abandoning city living for the sticks
to do wholesome work, the sort advocated by Tolstoy because it was
as good for you as it was for others, was the only way to be green. It
was as if you couldn't live an eco life in a city – a window box of herbs
was a signal that you were soon to sell up and try out agriculture on a
bigger scale rather than sometimes add parsley to your omelette or
homegrown basil to your pesto. One inspiring example of a rural move
is Satish Kumar's departure from London to a tiny Devon village to let
his children go barefoot at the Small School while he edited the spiritual green magazine, *Resurgence*. Another is radio producer, now
master baker, Andrew Whitley, who gave up growing a few square
metres of wheat on his tiny north London allotment to set up the
highly successful Village Bakery in the Lake District. Many urban

emigrees were inspired by John Seymour's 1975 publishing sensation, *The Complete Book of Self Sufficiency*,[2] to step away from conventional jobs and choose the life they really wanted – complete with laying hens, compost toilets and Land-Rovers held together with imaginative twists of bailer twine. The 1970s TV sit-com, *The Good Life*, was an enjoyable send up of this trend, ironically set in a South London suburbia, then the nadir of green aspiration.

Three decades later there's just as powerful a desire to reconnect with the land, but few of us are doing it by owning a chunk of English pastoral. In 2007 the Commission for Rural Communities found that just 19.3 per cent (9.5 million) of the English population lived in rural areas (mostly in a country town).[3] And only 3 per cent lived in places that are smaller than a village – and just 1 per cent in even more sparse areas. It is hard to tell if it is just cash that's the problem, or simply a modern desire to do the green thing wherever we live, whatever our financial means.

The new green thinkers, often urban based, have a different take on self-sufficiency: it is collective not individualistic. These people use their eco-thinking to underpin everything they do, whether it's getting around by pedal power, swapping sofas for bread makers on www.freecycle.org or campaigning against out-of-town shopping centres. Most typically they are resistant to a globalisation that spreads the corporate superbrands to country after country, and in so doing crush the special flavour associated with place, to produce what Andrew Simms has described as 'Clone Towns'.[4]

For starters they want self-sufficiency at a neighbourhood level, so that communities will be able to feed and heat themselves whatever the impacts of climate change. They want food that travels just a handful of miles to their plate – thereby slashing its embodied carbon emissions and getting tastier, healthier, seasonal produce. They want to transform rat runs into streets which are safe to cycle, and quiet enough to chat to a neighbour. They want their parks to be orchards hedged with edible greenery that lets kids pick up blackberries, and birds feed during the harshest months. The added bonus is that this obsession with neighbourhood looks set to turn urban England into the new green and pleasant land.

Paul Kingsnorth, anti-globalisation campaigner and author of the hugely successful *One No, Many Yeses*, has interestingly turned his attention in the last couple of years to the link between environmental activism and the increasing sense of a place called England.[5] In his latest book, *Real England*, he identifies environmentalists inspired to act because of their commitment to locality as 'heroes of place-based resistance';[6] and he defines these heroes as 'communities all over the country who refuse to lie down before the juggernaut of a spurious progress, or to sacrifice the landscapes and cultures that matter to them for the benefit of a global economy'.[7]

ONE SIZE DOESN'T FIT ALL

This change is happening all over England, yet expressed in a wide variety of ways. Within fifteen minutes walk of where I live in North London there is a decidedly old-fashioned community vibe that works just as well for the iPod generation – three street markets, three weekly farmers' markets offering produce that is less dependent on agrochemicals, many independently owned shops where goods bought with a local loyalty card are discounted, a members' car club and some traffic-calmed streets that are excellent for walking beside or cycling.

In many places resistance starts with the carrying of a reusable bag – admittedly an unlikely totem. But since May 2007, when the little Devon town of Modbury banned plastic bags (the only ones offered in any of the town's shops had a price tag and were made from corn starch that can biodegrade or cotton shopping bags), more than fifty other English towns are following its lead, from Hebden Bridge in Yorkshire to the one-shop village of Amberley in West Sussex.[8]

Modbury's initiative was inspired by local resident Rebecca Hosking's film, *Hawaii: Message in the Waves* shot for the BBC Natural History Unit, which showed how the Pacific tides gather humankind's plastic junk to the lethal detriment of the wildlife.[9] The impact back home in Devon has been a surprise win for reducing waste. 'It's made such a difference', says one of the volunteers in the charity shop as I buy a couple of secondhand books to entertain my kids on the long train ride from Plymouth to Darlington, Yorkshire. 'The film helped us realise that plastic bags kill 2 million sea animals a year, but now there's no plastic bags given out here, the hedgerows roundabout are so much cleaner.'

LET'S IMAGINE

It is our sense of what England should look like – those clean landscapes the TV cameras pan across and holiday snaps of thatched-roofed villages, wild Lakeland, or the big-sky East Anglian views fringed by black poplar trees that Constable would have known – that still inspires people to use their spare time to resist inappropriate change. Slowing change is why people are willing to make time to reject what they see as poor planning decisions, such as changes to a nearby green space, attempts to build out-of-town supermarkets or Heathrow airport's expansion.

Such campaigners, once maligned as small-minded NIMBYs (a person who is pro development so long as it is 'not in my backyard'), are increasingly enjoying the status of local heroes as they try to stop the sort of development that is leading us all to use the world's resources as if we had the eight planets we need to keep up this wasteful pace of unsustainable economic growth.

'If I had my way the term NIMBY would be consigned to the nearest waste bin marked 'not conducive to a socially just democracy', says Ann Coleman, a granny from Greengairs in Scotland who started out campaigning trying to prevent the open cast mine near her home becoming a vast landfill for the rubbish you and I have chucked out:

> I feel very strongly about this term – it's an arrogant put down – used by those who stand to gain financially from a proposal but who will not have to live with the consequences. It allows for the avoidance of asking the real questions like; why are the public so afraid of development? The term NIMBY seems to me to fuel the argument that the public are against development when we are not ... The public need to care about their local environment now and not sit back and wait until something happens – and they need to let it be known that they are not going to be called NIMBYs when what they are doing is challenging our Planning Law, which has no provision for justice, lacks any measures to ensure public accountability and equality and, as a consequence, allows for discrimination against communities who lack financial, social or voting power. It has never been so crucial for the public to take an interest, become informed and active in planning. The planning reforms have the potential to reduce their local influence if they don't act now to ensure they have genuine influence over their own environment.

After all a local – who lives and maybe even loves their area – is the best one to speak up against inappropriate location, bad design and practices that deny communities any come-back if their health is compromised, or traffic increases, or recycling is rendered pointless by the creation of new landfill sites, or air quality tumbles. Falling house prices are the least of it.

And now there are two extra fillips to act like a NIMBY. The first is our fear of how England's timeless views and even plant life could change because of global warming unless action is taken now. The second is anxiety about how we will cope with peak oil – the point when oil supplies start to decline, thus ending a long period of cheap oil.

NEW INCENTIVES

Government has noticed the trend too. That's why in late 2006 the recently-appointed Environment Minister David Miliband, speaking at a Fabian Society event, explained that the meaning of citizenship is changing:

> Our conception of politics has been Whitehall and Westminster based. It has been about managing not mobilising, governing not campaigning, based on active government and passive citizens. The environment shows how outdated this is. People don't want the remote influence of lobbying their representatives through the occasional tick in the ballot box. They want to be players.[10]

And where better to play at making the world a better place than on your doorstep? Not just resisting developments such as new towns and new power stations because of their negative impact on sustainability and climate change, but dreaming up the solutions that make life in the here and now better for you – and others.

This partially explains the rapid spread of the Transition Town movement, appropriate for a country town or a medium-sized city like Bristol, and motivated by a very human characteristic –survival instincts. Transition Initiatives (TIs) help towns plan ways to tackle the likely problems they will face when oil production peaks – which will lead to price crashes and food shortages, and quite possibly the end of suburbia.

Permaculture teacher Rob Hopkins, the dynamic activist behind this campaign, is based in Totnes, Devon. He has helped inspire people to find ways to make their neighbourhoods more sustainable with his version of the Kinsale 10-step Energy Descent Action plan. Instead of hyping the horrors of adapting to a world without oil, he writes on his website that: 'People are starting to see peak oil as the Great Opportunity, the chance to build the world they always dreamt of' (see http://transitionculture.org). The Transition Towns 10-step plan lists the following priorities:

1. Raise awareness
2. Lay the foundations
3. Have an official unleashing
4. Form groups
5. Use open space
6. Develop visible, practical manifestations of the project
7. Facilitate the great reskilling
8. Build a bridge to local government

9. Honour the elders
10. Let it go where it wants to go and reflections.

In Totnes, points five and six have led to nut trees being planted to provide emergency food and timber (and as carbon sinks to reduce the town's footprint of carbon dioxide emissions). Residents are also printing their own money for use locally only, a revival of the LETS system (local exchange trading systems), whereby individuals bank their time or swap skills and produce for a locally devised currency. Though LETS' drawback remains the plethora of aromatherapists (or a lack of plumbers), swapping things you want for things you need is an inevitable part of strong local communities.

Another small town in the process of adopting the action-plan is Lewes in Sussex. Here there's a push to help locals learn practical skills such as basket making, bike maintenance, foraging for food and altering your clothes. Such skills have a dual purpose: they will be essential for a world obliged to use less energy when oil reserves shrink and will make those who know them more resilient and independent.

Rob Hopkins argues that Transition Initiatives inhabit the territory between idealism and practicality. They are about developing a vision of a low energy future as something positive and then working out practically how we might get to it: 'It is a positive and optimistic approach, seeing the unleashing of hope as a powerful tool, going way beyond just campaigning against things'.

In Leeds David Midgley is working at the civic level to help create a sustainable city, popularising the TI model through public events and the Leeds Eco-village initiative. 'We want to challenge this enormous momentum for development which is unsustainable,' explains Midgley. 'Climate change is one aspect – it's by far the most prominent but it's a much broader problem than that – our industrial economy has now passed the limit of what the Earth can support so we see crises in many aspects of the economic system. There may be surprises in what may sneak up on us.' It sounds bad, but Midgley is positively looking forward to meeting these challenges:

If you present the idea that you can influence government policy on the one hand by joining a protest campaign, and you can change your individual behaviour by changing to a more energy efficient light bulb, you are limiting action to two fields – national/international and purely personal – which I believe makes people feel powerless ... People think if they cut their carbon emissions by 50 per cent it won't make the difference in getting the Prime Minister to change. But if we engage people at community level, even a relatively small group, people can easily influence their local community and take initiative themselves.

Examples range from people's willingness to stand as local councillors (particularly for an increasingly electorally successful Green Party); the take-up of DIY streets, where local people transform difficult roads into something approaching the home zones so beloved in Holland and Germany, which ensure a safer mix of pedestrians, playing kids and cars moving slowly and carefully through residential streets; and the growing number of entire towns now declaring themselves to be plastic bag free.

BUCKING TRADITION

The people finding ways to make their areas more sustainable are not traditional little Englanders. They are individuals with a backpack of green housekeeping skills who have been shocked into action by the negative impact of globalisation. What's more, they find it incomprehensible that in a sustainably-aware world we continue wasting our natural resources.

As Rob Hopkins explains, 'something very powerful is stirring and is taking root the world over. People are choosing life and are manifesting that in their lives and their communities. This is about transition to where we want to get to, how do we do it and what might it look like.'

It's this knowledge about what's going on globally that is inspiring people to act locally. The result is an imaginative new vision for England as a trend-setting world leader, with a downshifted, non-commuting, less stressed population, eating better food, sourced here, rather than over there.

The idea of practical sustainability has a long history amongst alternative and green thinkers. Their guru is maverick economist E F Schumacher, best known for his book *Small is Beautiful*. Schumacher adapted his thinking after visiting Burma as an economic consultant. In Burma he devised a set of principles that he dubbed 'Buddhist economics', because he felt that people need good work, and that 'production from local resources for local needs is the most rational way of economic life'.

Midgley acknowledges the influence of Gandhi on Schumacher, and argues that a lot of the ideas within the transition towns initiatives have come from these sources. He points to Gandhi's reconstruction programme, based on rebuilding economies in villages to turn around the impoverishment of the countryside by returning production to the local level, using sustainable methods that weren't dependent on industrial technology. His argument is that Schumacher brought Ghandi's ideas up to date, and applied them to the Western context, 'where huge scale dehumanizes, and there is massive pollution and destruction of nature'. Midgley admits that Schumacher was seen as 'a woolly thinker', but argues that what we are seeing now is a paradigm shift away from the technological scientific convention that dismisses small scale:

> I think its time has come, as people are getting more and more extreme with free market technological triumphalisms – just look at the American economy. They are building skyscrapers still in Las Vegas. But the Hoover dam which provides water for Las Vegas is nearly empty. What will they do then? … Sustainability is a huge thing now – people in local government have got that message. But in Yorkshire the region is focusing on bio-fuel production and carbon burial storage, which we'd have major problems with. Food is responsible for 40 per cent of carbon emissions – by relocalising food supplies we are well on the way to solving that problem. We also have a pioneering eco-village project in an area of multiple deprivation – the first to be built in an urban regeneration area. If you are looking at relocalising the economy this is a good way. People will build houses of good quality and get employable skills. If we grow food people can be involved in its production and improve their health.

PATRIOTIC TWISTS
The shift from personal improvement to an insistence on social solutions, which is becoming increasingly central to eco-politics, clearly stems from environmentalists' growing fear of the ticking clock. They see meltdown Britain queuing for price-hiked oil; they fear building-site Britain coated in housing estates where the car is king. Yet we are not necessarily descending into an irreversible crisis: instead this could be the best chance we've had to find new solutions to get the thriving world and the lifestyles that we want.

As Kate Soper argues in her essay on green hedonism in *Red Pepper*, that doesn't mean going without. She argues: 'the progressive dimension of a certain nostalgia for the pleasures that have been lost or pre-empted through the advance of consumerism, and… newly emerging green sentiments [show us] attempts to live differently in response to the humanly and environmentally destructive aspects of what is currently presented as progress'. [11]

My belief is that this represents a new vision for England, which is more and more being taken up by a caring society, impatient to be underpinned by ecological sustainability rather than sub-prime mortgages, built-in obsolescence and unsatisfying shopaholic spending sprees in climate-controlled malls. You don't need to be a good person to be green, you just need to understand that with climate change, life's long game requires the sort of co-operation that used to see us all in the same hay meadow sharing tasks. This time, though, we're not working for a bullying money lender or the lord of the manor; we're bucking global capitalism and doing it for ourselves. This is a constituency largely unrepresented by the mainstream parties with their MPs in Westminster. It is unashamedly patriotic for the most part, with an uncomplicated commitment to a global internationalism co-existing with their growing passion for the local.

Paul Kingsnorth is convinced that it is correct to consider this local-global activism central to environmentalism as a new version of patriotism:

> Patriotism – in the truest, most fiery and most radical sense of that misused word. Institutions and values can divide us: the place we live in can unite us, wherever we initially came from, whatever our politics, our class or our religion. Urban, rural, suburban – the landscape we inhabit is the one thing that can bind us together, the one thing in which we all have an interest: it is the real source of belonging ... In an age of global consumerism, corporate power and the dominance of a homogenising placeless, economic ideology, the one truly radical thing to do is to belong.[12]

This type of belonging requires neither a membership card nor a ready-made and centuries old ideology. Instead we join in when we open our front door and step into the street that we share with our neighbours. Here the discontented mutterings about speeding traffic or the enthu-siastic plans for a community festival are the earliest starting-points towards not only a greener England but more pleasant social spaces too. And as a result, in that fine old English tradition of bottom-up, we might slowly win over those who the political class – red, blue and even green – wouldn't normally expect to worry about their carbon foot-print. This is a popular patriotism of place, both at home and abroad.

NOTES

1. Amol Rajan, '"Lifestyle farmers" force up the price of Britain's farmland', *Independent*, 17.11.07.
2. John Seymour, *The Complete Book of Self Sufficiency*, Dorling Kindersley 1975.

3. Commission for Rural Communities, *State of the Countryside* 2007. See full report at www.ruralcommunities.gov.uk/files/socr2007-fullreport.pdf

4. Andrew Simms, Petra Kjell, Ruth Potts, *Clone Town Britain*, New Economics Foundation 2005.

5. Paul Kingsnorth, *One No, Many Yeses*, Free Press 2003.

6. Paul Kingsnorth, *Real England*, Portobello Books 2008.

7. Paul Kingsnorth, 'Know Your Place', *New Statesman*, 5.9.05.

8. John Vidal, 'From Scotland to the Channel Islands the cry goes up: "Banish the plastic bag"', *Guardian*, 22.9.07.

9. See www.messageinthewaves.com.

10. David Miliband, short version in The Guardian http://www.guardian.co.uk/environment/2007/jan/03/labourparty.society. Full text of the speech at http://fabians.org.uk/events/dmiliband-environment-06/speech.

11. Kate Soper, in *Red Pepper*, October/November 2007.

12. Paul Kingsnorth, 'Know Your Place', *New Statesman*, 5.9.05.

Half of some and half of the other
The racialised (dis)contents of Englishness

Daniel Burdsey

My mother was half English and I'm half English too
I'm a great big bundle of culture tied up in the red, white and blue
I'm a fine example of your Essex man
And I'm well familiar with the Hindustan
Cos my neighbours are half English and I'm half English too.

Billy Bragg and The Blokes, 'England, Half English'[1]

My name is Karim Amir, and I am an Englishman born and bred, almost.

Hanif Kureishi, *The Buddha of Suburbia*[2]

In October 2006, the England men's football team played Macedonia in a qualifying match for the 2008 European Championships. I watched the match in an ordinary pub in Brighton's leafy suburbs. After the game two young men were involved in a lengthy argument over manager Steve McClaren's team selection. Initially their dispute centred on predictable, mundane tactical issues, such as the benefits of 4-4-2 or 4-5-1 formations, and the respective qualities of Stewart Downing and Shaun Wright-Phillips. Yet their dialogue soon moved towards the specific physical and cultural attributes they expected England players to possess, and the issue of race eventually reared its head. As the dispute developed, one declared that, 'The day an England player runs onto the pitch wearing a turban is the day I leave this country'.

I immediately thought of Cyrille Regis, one of the pioneering black stars of the 1970s, who made his name alongside Laurie Cunningham and Brendan Batson as one of the so-called 'Three Degrees' at West Bromwich Albion. In 1982, before he was due to make his England debut, Regis infamously received a letter containing a death threat and a bullet from a racist opposed to his selection. Looking back on that incident, more than a quarter of a century later, the appearance of an England team with a majority of black or mixed race players is now a refreshingly unremarkable facet of the modern game. Nonetheless, the conversation I witnessed in that pub suggests that, amongst sections of the population, a demotic resistance to an inclusive, multicultural national identity, together with a belligerent, racist interpretation of Englishness, remains alive and still very much kicking.

THE PAREKH REPORT AND THE RISE OF THE LITTLE ENGLANDER

The racialisation of English national identity is not a new phenomenon. It is ingrained in history – from the inter-relationship between Englishness, nationalism, imperialism and whiteness that characterised the British Empire, via the racist political machinations of Oswald Mosley, Enoch Powell, the National Front, the Thatcherite New Right and the BNP, to populist opposition and resistance to immigration and asylum. By the end of the twentieth century, the fusing of notions of race, nation and culture meant that the dominant narrative of national identity remained a racially exclusive one. Englishness and minority ethnic identities were perceived to be oppositional and incompatible, with Paul Gilroy remarking in the 1990s that, in the popular imagination, 'to speak of the British or English people is to speak of the *white* people'.[3]

This state of affairs provided the context for the 2000 policy report, *The Future of Multi-ethnic Britain*, known more colloquially (after the commission's chair) as the 'Parekh Report'. One aspect of the commission's wide-ranging remit was to address the possibility of a broad, civic conceptualisation of national identity, rather than a narrow, ethnic one. In this regard, it signposted the formulation of a multiethnic Englishness and Britishness, whilst also outlining the existing impediments to achieving this goal. Most significantly, the report highlighted the marginalising, racialised aspects of national identity, stating that

> Britishness ... has systematic, largely unspoken racial connotations. Whiteness nowhere features as an explicit condition of being British, but it is widely understood that Englishness, and therefore by extension Britishness, is racially coded.[4]

This statement was widely misreported, purposefully confusing the terms 'racist' and 'racial', and a vehement backlash was led by right-wing ideologues and prominent newspapers, particularly the *Daily Mail* and *Daily Telegraph*. In one of many similar captions, the former headlined one story, 'British is racist, says peer trying to rewrite our history'.[5] The Home Secretary, Jack Straw, responded by combining a trenchant defence of Britishness with an attack on the perceived lack of patriotism amongst left-wing liberals. By reacting to the backlash rather than focusing on the issues actually raised in the report, Straw and others neatly sidestepped the real problem – the enduring racialisation of Englishness – and, with it, the opportunity to address it that the commission had provided. History shows that this failure to engage with the imperative of anti-racism has been an enduring feature of Labour in government ever since.

When Tony Blair's modernising New Labour regime came into power in 1997, it helped popularise the branding of *Cool Britannia* – a concept which Culture Secretary Chris Smith told us was 'here to stay'.[6] Blair's successor, Gordon Brown, has concentrated on developing the idea of a progressive Britishness, arguably a smart move for a Scottish prime minister governing a state in which the vast majority of the population live in England. Both Blair and Brown have continually employed the rhetoric of Britishness, especially after the terrorist atrocities of 11 September 2001 and 7 July 2005, and again after the attempted car-bomb attacks in London and Glasgow during the summer of 2007, in order to facilitate community cohesion and citizenship, and to fight a bogus 'war on terror'. For example, in his 2006 address to the Fabian society, entitled 'The Future of Britishness', Brown stated that: 'We the British people should be able to gain great strength from celebrating a British identity which is bigger than the sum of its parts and a union that is strong because of the values we share and because of the way these values are expressed through our history and our institutions'.[7] Despite the rhetoric of inclusion – through the attempted inculcation of minority ethnic groups into a consensus around spurious, state-regulated core values – in practice this discourse acts as 'a blueprint for the demarcation of those who belong and those "others", the barbarians at the gate ... who must be kept out and controlled'.[8]

Notwithstanding their close associations and the fact that they are frequently conflated by the English, the notion of Englishness has taken on a different political and cultural trajectory to Britishness. In many respects, the former has come to be a byword for racism, chauvinism, jingoism and indeed sexism. This is most publicly demonstrated by small-minded, defensive Europhobes campaigning against immigration, or belligerent, xenophobic football supporters singing about world wars and hurling plastic chairs around the plazas of continental Europe. As a result, centuries after the liberal middle classes embraced English nationalism as a means of articulating their opposition to British imperialism – a notion of national identity coinciding with the geographical confines of England itself was seen to signify a rejection of the global excesses of the empire – the majority on the left have now withdrawn from, and disengaged with, it. As Jonathan Rutherford points out:

> Who wanted the risible, sometimes ugly, baggage of Englishness? Everything which signified Englishness – the embarrassing legacy of racial supremacy and empire, the union jack waving crowds, the royalty, the rhetoric about Britain's standing in the world – suggested a conservative deference to nostalgia.[9]

This particular standpoint is perhaps most notably articulated by leftists during sporting contests. We cheer on India, the Republic of Ireland or the West Indies, for instance – colonised rather than (neo-)coloniser – as solidarities are forged with sections of Britain's minority ethnic populations in backing *anyone* but England.[10] It is a position I have long supported. In contrast, those on the centre-right are subsumed by what Paul Gilroy labels a 'postimperial melancholia'.[11] They protest that they are no longer permitted to promote their Englishness, due to the influence of those they invariably label the 'politically-correct brigade' – just as they claim that they are now prevented from talking about Christmas or celebrating St George's Day, despite never actually elaborating on the exact sources of this censure. *Daily Mail* columnist Melanie Phillips has, for example, bizarrely posed the query, 'How long will it be before Christianity becomes illegal in Britain?'[12]

Discourses of Englishness have been subsequently appropriated by the far right, who employ them to promote their disingenuous claim that they are advocating 'rights for whites' and representing a putative oppressed white English ethnicity, rather than preaching racial hatred. Far right activists present their ideas as a defence of a mythical English identity – in an *ethnic* or *cultural* sense – that is under threat by enemies not just from outside, but now from within, in the form of 'homegrown' jihadists and an 'open-door' immigration policy.[13] As Michael Treacy of the BNP stated, unconvincingly, after the urban unrest in Oldham during 2001, 'I have no qualms against Asians or people of any colour. It's a matter of the country losing its identity and culture'.[14] Whilst the BNP is most prominent in this sense, it is no coincidence that other far right groups call themselves The England First Party and The English Democrats.

Narrow, racialised articulations of Englishness are not simply the preserve of the far right though. This 'white backlash'[15] is increasingly embodied by Little Englanders up and down the country – from northern mill towns to Home Counties commuter belts – who adopt a siege mentality centred on the extraordinary belief, perpetuated especially by the *Daily Mail*, that they are becoming a minority in their own country. This is a worldview that arguably transcends the political spectrum, and one that, through their draconian policies on immigration, Blair and Brown have done little to discourage.

These different political positions often have the effect of being mutually reinforcing. Thus they serve to highlight the potential contradictions of the 'anyone but England' position. Emblematic of this state of affairs is Jonathan Rutherford's admission that 'my involvement in radical politics on the left taught me to disavow the racial exclusivity of white ethnicity, but never to analyse it or try and understand it'.[16] Whilst the recognition and renouncement of white privilege by those that embody and profit from it is a crucial step towards achieving racial justice, the unmitigated rejection of Englishness as a *topic for debate* has evidently buttressed its adoption by malevolent, reactionary sections of society. Put simply, ignoring something does not make it go away or cause its pejorative characteristics and connotations to instantly disappear. Instead it facilitates the creation of a political vacuum – precisely the sort of territory that extremists are able to exploit. Consequently, rejecting associations with England and Englishness is one thing, but then to bemoan the fact that they have become the preserve of the far right is hypocritical, and does little to disrupt this state of affairs. Whether or not Englishness is an identity worth rescuing – or has the capacity to be reappropriated and articulated under a new banner of multicultural inclusivity that recognises its contradictions and ambiguities – are key questions currently facing the left.

LOOKING FOR A NEW ENGLAND: MULTICULTURAL ENGLISHNESS OR MISSED OPPORTUNITIES?

Krishan Kumar identifies that England's dominant position within the British Empire and its hegemony over the British Isles have meant that the English have traditionally existed in a position of comfort and privilege. Unlike other nations, they have not been forced to ask uncomfortable questions about themselves, in terms of their history, culture and traditions.[17] Yet the impact of Scottish, Welsh and Northern Irish devolution in subverting the role of Britain as a coherent political entity, membership of the European Union, changing demographics of immigration, and the gradually increasing influence of post-colonial critiques in historical studies of the nation, have meant that these questions are now paramount to the future of England as a multiethnic entity.[18] The hedgerows and dry-stone walls which have steadfastly protected the vacant space in which Englishness existed have gradually been dismantled, and for the first time ever, 'the English have had to turn the mirror directly to themselves to see who they are and where they may be going'.[19] In saying this, it is important, nevertheless, to challenge the uncritical reproduction of the idea that there was once a fixed, consistent model of Englishness. Jeremy Paxman, for instance, claims that 'once upon a time the English knew who they were',[20] and that 'being English used to be so easy',[21] but, as Phil Cohen argues, this serves to 'underwrite the invented tradition of Englishness itself, to accept at face value its own myths of origins and destiny'.[22]

Mike Marqusee correctly points out that 'Englishness is a category vague enough to accommodate radically opposed ideas of what being English might be'.[23] In recent years, various sections of the left have sought to cultivate the ground prepared by the Parekh Report and to re-engage with notions of Englishness. One notable intervention was in 2005, when the then Home Secretary David Blunkett gave a speech entitled 'A new England: an English identity within Britain'. He argued that a renewed sense of English national identity is 'a progressive and generous force' and, in doing so, shifted the terms of debate towards the belief that it is *too little* rather than too much national identity that has blighted England and Englishness in the past.[24] According to Blunkett, a shared identity is important to the integration of a nation – but this is a discourse that, through the government's community cohesion and anti-terror policies, has already revealed itself to be problematic and at times antithetical to multiculturalism; and he also tried to reconcile patriotism and internationalism, ideologies mostly regarded by the left as incompatible. He then proceeded to outline the components that a modern multicultural Englishness might entail, thus giving himself the opportunity to challenge the interpretation enunciated by John Major in his 1993 St George's Day address. (Major's vision of village cricket, warm beer and bicycling maids was a white, middle-class, rural utopia, and represented a view of England which, as Michael Billig sardonically notes, was 'empty of motorways, mine-shafts and mosques'.[25]) Yet Blunkett's selection was similarly racialised and gendered, paying homage to the England of Orwell, Eliot and Betjeman; it too failed to engage with the possibility of a multicultural national identity. He spoke of Englishness as being about the National Trust and National Parks – long regarded, like much of bucolic England, as excluding and alienating environments for minority ethnic groups. He cited the literary works of Chaucer, Shakespeare, Milton, Keats and Owen, along with contemporary poets Tony Harrison and Wendy Cope, but made no mention of Benjamin Zephaniah, Lemn Sissay, Zadie Smith or Monica Ali. His musical inspirations were long-dead classical composers, such as Purcell, Elgar, Williams and Britten, not Lemar, Craig David or the Sugababes. His humour was Hancock, Round the Horne, Fawlty Towers and Monty Python, rather than Shazia Mirza, Gina Yashere or Andi Osho.[26] Sport was conspicuous by its absence, but one might predict that his choices would have been more Moore, Boycott and Coe than Panesar, Khan and Holmes. Whilst this was unapologetically a *personal* account, by drawing solely on the national *past*, rather than the national present and future, his portrait represented a failed opportunity to delineate an inclusive, de-racialised national identity, solidifying the uneasy relationship between Englishness and multiculturalism in the process.

This intervention is symptomatic of a wider trend within a Labour Party that has an essentially inconsistent and contradictory stance on race and racism. The Public Inquiry into the murder of Stephen Lawrence and the introduction of the 2000 Race Relations (Amendment) Act on the one hand, but an increasingly discriminatory approach to immigration, refuge and asylum on the other.[27] Through its move rightwards Labour has jettisoned a core idealism that would not only facilitate the promotion of a popular politics of anti-racism, but would also be capable of engaging with its contemporary complexities. To make this shift to the political centre without forcefully embracing anti-racism as a core value is potentially catastrophic. Effectively Labour is likely to end up validating the racialisation of Englishness and Britishness, and continue to marginalise minority groups, such as British Muslims, as the parameters of citizenship and belonging are constricted.

Other individuals have made more meaningful, if still somewhat nebulous, attempts to destabilise racialised concepts of Englishness. Paul Kingsnorth, for example, has called for a new, positive English nationalism. For him, this would resemble 'an anti-racist, forward-looking but rooted nationalism that all of us who think that place matters should be able to embrace'; 'one that takes our country back from the sneerers on the left and the bigots on the right'.[28] Similarly, Billy Bragg, who describes himself as a 'progressive patriot', argues for the need to re-engage with an Englishness that is 'outgoing and friendly, rather than inward-looking and hostile'.[29] Key to the positions adopted by these and other individuals is the symbolic role they ascribe to the St George flag.

FLAGGING UP ISSUES OF ENGLISHNESS

Overt public displays of English and British flag-waving have traditionally been associated with royal weddings, the Last Night of the Proms, travelling English football fans and, more insidiously, National Front marches and BNP rallies. They remain at the forefront of debates around Englishness and Britishness.[30] Specifically, the soft patriots on the left argue that one of the main reasons why Englishness retains its pejorative connotations is because the St George flag has been 'hijacked' by the far right. Its 'ownership' is believed to be central to a progressive politics of nationhood, and the pragmatic response to this, we are told, is an act of reclamation. For example David Blunkett stated that 'the reclaiming of the flag ... must be sustained if we are to see off the BNP and the National Front',[31] whilst in 2007 Gordon Brown encouraged more public flag displays as a way of encouraging a sense of citizenship.

For such arguments, the supposed 'evidence' that this process can contribute towards a tolerant, multicultural Englishness is frequently taken from sport. That England teams have facilitated a re-engagement with the flag of St George is unsurprising, for they represent some of the few specifically English as opposed to British institutions.[32] The 'Raise the Flag' initiative involves supporters at England matches holding up cards, which together form a huge St George cross, sometimes emblazoned with an anti-racist message. Mark Perryman, one of the organisers (and editor of *Imagined Nation*), argues that 'the St George Cross has become a sign of a newish England, with a make-up we're increasingly at ease with ... St George offers the unfulfilled potential for England's national liberation'.[33] Similarly, Billy Bragg views 'the resurgent popularity of the St George's Cross as emblematic of a broadening of the English identity, accessible to anyone who wants to be part of it'.[34]

Both Billy Bragg and Mark Perryman are certainly right to point out that a flag is a site of cultural contestation. Like the identities they reflect and represent, symbols possess meanings that fluctuate over time and space, and thus there is no necessary relationship between any given subjectivity and a national flag. For example, in France the National Front and the Communist Party both march behind the tricolour, with each party laying claim to its ownership. George Alagiah is, therefore, partly correct in stating that the Union Jack we see wrapped around the shoulders of Kelly Holmes or Amir Khan 'cannot be the same flag my father and mother might have noticed fluttering in an imperial wind over the governor's residence in Colombo'.[35]

However, whilst access to, and inclusion in, the symbols and institutions of the nation is theoretically open to all, in practice it remains unequal and contingent. As Mike Marqusee states, 'recasting English national identity as forward-looking, inclusive, free of chauvinist aggression is a more complicated business than merely "reclaiming" the St George's flag from the far right'.[36] Putting this in context, Paul Gilroy points out that the failure of England and Britain to disconnect themselves from their imperial and colonial past means that the 'ambiguities and defects' of this period continue to influence contemporary racial politics.[37] Attempts to subvert the connotations of a flag do not – perhaps cannot – therefore eradicate centuries of imperial atrocities carried out in its name. In this regard, Alagiah is mistaken in his claim that 'it may look the same, but its meaning has changed entirely, redefined by the people who hold it now'.[38] For even the best clean-up operations cannot entirely remove the blood of subjugation, exploitation and oppression with which the St George Cross is indelibly stained. Although growing numbers of minority ethnic groups have begun to embrace England's flag, many others are still instinctively repulsed by it, and painfully recall the fear and terror that it has caused them.[39]

There are at least two further problems with the position adopted by the 'reclaimers'. First, whilst some of the 'soft patriots' have rebutted the belief that the flag can be claimed by one ideology or set of values over another, many others assume that its 'ownership' can be fought over, in a metaphorical tug-of-war, to become the exclusive possession of the progressive side of the political pendulum at the expense of the far right. But the re-engagement with the flag by sections of the left has by no means led to a loosening of the right's mucky grip on it. Take for instance the Afghan man repeatedly stabbed outside Barking tube station in May 2006. The final act of his attackers was to drape him in a St George flag.[40] On this very same night, in this very same borough, the BNP achieved an unprecedented number of council seats with the campaign led locally by Richard Barnbrook, who has infamously dressed up as St George as part of his political campaigning. Joseph Harker is therefore right to warn of the potential for far right extremists to take advantage of the flag's new availability and popularity. Remarking upon the frenzy of flag-waving that occurred before and during the 2006 men's football World Cup, he stated that, 'right now I can't help thinking that the BNP's leaders are secretly smirking every time they see the flag'. [41] With football fans and fascists both claiming to fly the flag as a badge of national pride, the danger of the former inadvertently playing a part in legitimising BNP's politics is very real.

Second, there is a belief that the increasing engagement by minority ethnic groups with the St George flag represents an unequivocal affiliation with Englishness. As Paul Bagguley and Yasmin Hussain demonstrate in their study of young British Pakistanis in Bradford, however, the relationship is not nearly so straightforward. Whilst these young people often displayed the flag, usually in conjunction with their growing support for the England football team, it was, ironically, as a symbol of their attachment to British citizenship – in the context of perceived neo-Nazi associations of the Union Jack – rather than pride in an English national identity.[42] Nevertheless, various commentators continue to proclaim the cultural and political significance of the increasing number of St George flags being flown from curry houses or by British Asian taxi-drivers. That this represents a move towards a truly multicultural sense of nationhood or the elimination of the racialised and racist aspects of Englishness is highly debatable, however. They may look the same as the flags fluttering from the windows of pubs, clubs and housing estates, but the meaning is different. The flag outside your local tandoori might reflect a feeling of participation in, or desire to be part of, the national collectivity. But it may equally be a matter of self-protection. The restaurant whose window displays a flag may be less likely to have it shattered with a brick than the one that does not, when England crash out of a major football tournament. Similarly, the racist murders of Mohammed Sarwar, Tariq Javed, Sarfraz Khan, Israr Hussain and Mohammad Parvaiz are surely still in the minds of fellow taxi-drivers in northern England as they attach flags to their cars. In other words, for some, flying the flag of St George can be an act of survival as much as one of national celebration.

Despite the position of those who would claim that flags are sites of contestation, questions remain as to whether the historical symbolism of the St George cross can ever be truly subverted, to leave a symbol free from presumptions of definitive meaning, and whether it is worth contesting at all. The answer to the latter is most likely yes, but the response to the former is far less clear-cut. The sight of British Muslim sport fans adorning the flag with the Islamic star and crescent, or of Khan's Army (the supporters of boxer Amir Khan) joining together Union and Pakistani flags, earmarks the potential for subverting dominant associations, albeit ephemerally.[43] They also demonstrate that if the flag is to contribute towards a progressive politics it must be seen as a work-in-progress rather than a finished article – open to multicultural annotation, embellishment and modification.

TOWARDS A MULTICULTURAL ENGLISH NATIONAL IDENTITY: BEYOND ELEVEN PLAYERS AND BALL?

Stuart Hall argues that the reproduction of national identities occurs through 'the *narrative of the nation,* as it is told and retold in national histories, literatures, the media and popular culture'.[44] The role of popular culture in articulating a progressive politics of nationhood remains especially pertinent at present, given the Labour government's effective refusal to embrace the imperative of anti-racism. Sport is central to this project, with Eric Hobsbawm famously declaring that the identity of a nation of millions 'seems more real as a team of eleven named people'.[45] But what does this mean for the people and the communities who are not in the team, or those that may be in the team but are not represented in the stands?

Paradoxically, sport remains both a prominent arena in which minority ethnic groups are excluded – both physically and figuratively – from the national collectivity, and a sphere in which younger members of minority ethnic groups perform their diasporic identities.[46] It is thus one of the primary means through which notions of 'Englishness' and 'Britishness' are constructed, contested and resisted. It was the decision of many minority ethnic supporters to support their country of ancestry rather than England in Test cricket that provided the context for Norman Tebbit's attempts to implement a narrow, prescriptive model of British citizenship. More recently, boxing – or more specifically boxer Amir Khan – was used by Labour peer Valerie Amos to counter Tebbit's test, when she quoted Amir's declaration that 'I'm Asian, but I'm British – I was born here, I went to school here, all my mates are British, and I'm proud to represent my country'.[47] The development of a multicultural Englishness – if it is to become possible – certainly cannot be limited to the realm of sport, yet it is here that the first tentative steps might be taken.

For instance, young British Asian football players and supporters – still discriminated against in, and excluded from, so many other aspects of the game – are exhibiting a hitherto unwitnessed level of affiliation with the England team.[48] Evidence also points towards increasing numbers of minority ethnic groups actively supporting the team, with some attending matches, home, away and at European Championships and World Cups.[49]

However, the optimism offered by these trends must be countered by a degree of caution. They do not signify a universal, unconditional embracing of Englishness by young British Asians (or other minority ethnic groups), any more than their support for India or Pakistan in cricket necessarily represents a rejection of British citizenship and values, as is frequently claimed. Likewise, white England cricket supporters wearing false bushy beards and headscarves may be heralded as a form of harmless reverence to Monty Panesar, but it represents an all-too-close brush with the odious latter-day Black and White minstrelsy of Sacha Baron Cohen and Little Britain rather than a move towards multiculture. Whilst England cricketer Sajid Mahmood, as he playfully cups his ear to the 'traitor' taunts of British Pakistani fans, may be seen as embodying the 'good Muslim' figure championed by the government, it only serves to highlight the large numbers of young minority ethnic people who feel alienated and excluded from the national collectivity.

From whom or where is the desire for a new Englishness coming from? As Steve Fenton points out, the majority of recent literature on Englishness has reproduced the assumption that national identities are powerful and enduring, but there has been little consideration of why, in an era of migration, globalisation and hybrid identities, people might still be expected to attach such prominence to the country in which they were born or live. Indeed, the young white participants in his study exhibited a strong degree of apathy and indifference – a 'so what?' factor – towards English national identity. This rejection stems from a variety of factors, including a sense of moral universalism, and the celebration of their individual or supranational identities.[50] Attempts to reconfigure Englishness come from a wide variety of political and social positions, but for many a compelling reason does not go not much beyond a form of simple 'me too-ism'. The articulation of multiple identities – 'new ethnicities'[51] – by diasporic groups has created a multitude of specific categorisations with which they can identify, whilst the white English majority are left facing an identity crisis and a partial share in a broad, pluralistic British identity. As Kobena Mercer points out, 'identity only becomes an issue when it is in crisis, when something assumed to be fixed, coherent and stable is displaced by the experience of doubt and uncertainty'.[52]

The viability of a multicultural Englishness is an important topic for debate over the next few years. It may well be unachievable, but if an answer is to be found we must engage in further rigorous discussion rather than ignore the emergence of a politics of English national identity. However, it must first be acknowledged that the task of outlining the specific components of a multicultural Englishness is not only difficult, but also not necessarily desirable. As Tariq Modood argues:

The idea that there has to be a schedule of 'non-negotiable' value state-ments to which every citizen is expected to sign up to is not in the spirit of an open, plural citizenship. National identity should be woven in debate and discussion, not reduced to a list.[53]

A starting point would surely be the convivial multicultural future that Paul Gilroy describes – a time characterised not by an absence of racism or the existence of universal tolerance, but one in which multi-culture becomes an unremarkable feature of British metropolitan life.[54] Or perhaps the last word is best left to Slavoj Žižek, who reminds us that 'the final answer is of course that *nobody* is fully English … every empirical Englishman (sic) contains something "non-English"'.[55] Or, as the song goes, 'England, Half English'.

NOTES

1. Billy Bragg and The Blokes, 'England, Half English', from the album *England, Half English*, BMG Music Publishing Limited 2002.
2. Hanif Kureishi, *The Buddha of Suburbia*, Faber & Faber 1990, p3.
3. Paul Gilroy, *Small Acts: Thoughts on the Politics of Black Cultures*, Serpent's Tail 1993, p28.
4. Runnymede Trust, *The Future of Multi-ethnic Britain: Report of the Commission on the Future of Multi-ethnic Britain*, Profile Books 2000, p38.
5. Andrew Pilkington, *Racial Disadvantage and Ethnic Diversity in Britain*, Palgrave 2003, p269.
6. Stuart Jeffries, 'So how did he do?', *Guardian*, 2.5.07.
7. Gordon Brown, 'The future of Britishness', speech given at the Fabian Society, London 14 January 2006. http://fabians.org.uk/events/new-year-conference-06/brown-britishness/speech.
8. Claire Alexander, 'Embodying violence: "riots", dis/order and the private lives of the "Asian gang"', in Claire Alexander & Caroline Knowles (eds.), *Making Race Matter: Bodies, Space and Identity*, Palgrave 2005, p207.
9. Jonathan Rutherford, *Forever England: Reflections on Masculinity and Empire*, Lawrence & Wishart 1997, p5.
10. Ben Carrington, '"Football's coming home" but whose home? And do we want it?: nation, football and the politics of exclusion' in Adam Brown (ed.), *Fanatics! Power, Identity and Fandom in Football*, Routledge 1998; Mike Marqusee, *Anyone but England: an Outsider Looks at English Cricket*, Aurum Press 2005.
11. Paul Gilroy, *After Empire: Melancholia or Convivial Culture?*, Routledge 2004.

12. Melanie Phillips, 'How Britain is turning Christianity into a crime', *Daily Mail*, 7.9.06.

13. Arun Kundnani, '"Stumbling on": race, class and England', *Race and Class*, 41(4), pp1-18, 2000; Bridget Byrne, 'England – whose England? Narratives of nostalgia, emptiness and evasion in imaginations of national identity', *Sociological Review* 55(3), pp509-30, 2007.

14. Jeevan Vasagar, David Ward, Abigail Etim and Matt Keating, '"No go for whites" in race hotspot', *Guardian*, 20 April 2001.

15. Roger Hewitt, *White Backlash and the Politics of Multiculturalism*, Cambridge University Press 2005.

16. Jonathan Rutherford, *Forever England: Reflections on Masculinity and Empire*, Lawrence & Wishart 1997, p5.

17. Krishan Kumar, *The Making of English National Identity*, Cambridge University Press 2003.

18. Kevin Davey, *English Imaginaries: Six Studies in Anglo-British Modernity*, Lawrence & Wishart 1999.

19. Krishan Kumar, *The Making of English National Identity*, Cambridge University Press 2003, p251.

20. Jeremy Paxman, *The English: A Portrait of a People*, Penguin 1998, p1.

21. Jeremy Paxman, *The English: A Portrait of a People*, Penguin 1998, p.ix.

22. Phil Cohen, *The Last Island: Essays on England and the Dreaming of 'Race'*, Centre for New Ethnicities Research, University of East London 1998, p4.

23. Mike Marqusee, 'In thrall to St George', *Guardian*, 27.6.06.

24. David Blunkett, *A New England: an English Identity Within Britain*, speech given at the Institute for Public Policy Research, London 14 March 2005, p3.

25. Michael Billig, *Banal Nationalism*, Sage 1995, p102.

26. David Blunkett, *A New England: an English Identity Within Britain*, speech given at the Institute for Public Policy Research, London 14 March 2005, pp8-9.

27. Liza Schuster & John Solomos, 'Race, immigration and asylum: New Labour's agenda and its consequences', *Ethnicities* (4, 2, pp267-300, 2004).

28. Paul Kingsnorth, 'Reclaim our Englishness and throw out the burgers', *New Statesman*, 15.11.04.

29. Billy Bragg & Martin Linton, 'George on our mind', *Guardian*, 24.4.04.

30. Paul Gilroy, *There Ain't No Black in the Union Jack*, Routledge 1987; Sarfraz Manzoor, 'A cross to bear', *Guardian*, 10.6.04; Denis Campbell & Anushka Asthana, 'The flag is everywhere. But what does it mean to you?', *Observer*, 4.6.06; Nick Groom, *The Union Jack: a Biography*, Atlantic Books 2006.

31. Alan Travis, 'Fly the flag against racism says minister', *Guardian*, 27.6.02.

32. Ben Carrington, 'Too many St. George crosses to bear', in Mark Perryman

(ed.), *The Ingerlund Factor: Home Truths from Football*, Mainstream 1999; Krishan Kumar, *The Making of English National Identity*, Cambridge University Press 2003.

33. Mark Perryman, *Ingerlund: Travels with a Football Nation*, Simon & Schuster 2006, p133.

34. Billy Bragg, *The Progressive Patriot: a Search for Belonging*, Bantam Press 2006, pp277-8.

35. George Alagiah, *Home from Home: from Immigrant Boy to English Man*, Little Brown 2006, p265.

36. Mike Marqusee, 'In thrall to St George', *Guardian*, 27.6.06.

37. Paul Gilroy, *After Empire: Melancholia or Convivial Culture?*, Routledge 2004, p2.

38. George Alagiah, *Home from Home: from Immigrant Boy to English Man*, Little Brown 2006, p265.

39. Helen Carter, James Meek, Oliver Burkeman & Lucy Mangan, 'I no longer view the flag with suspicion', *Guardian*, 10.6.04.

40. Denis Campbell & Anushka Asthana, 'The flag is everywhere. But what does it mean to you?', *Observer*, 4.6.06.

41. Joseph Harker, 'Flutters of anxiety', *Guardian*, 18.5.06.

42. Paul Bagguley & Yasmin Hussain, 'Flying the flag for England? Citizenship, religion and cultural identity among British Pakistani Muslims', in Tahir Abbas (ed.), *Muslim Britain: Communities Under Pressure*, Zed Books 2005; see also Bhikhu Parekh, 'Reasoned identities: a committed relationship' in Margaret Wetherell, Michelynn Laflèche & Robert Berkeley (eds.), *Identity, Ethnic Diversity and Community Cohesion*, Sage 2007.

43. Daniel Burdsey, 'Role with the punches: the construction and representation of Amir Khan as a role model for multiethnic Britain', *Sociological Review*, 55(3), pp611-31, 2007.

44. Stuart Hall, 'The question of cultural identity' in Stuart Hall, David Held & Tony McGrew (eds.), *Modernity and its Futures*, Polity Press 1992, p293.

45. Eric Hobsbawm, *Nations and Nationalism since 1780: Programme, Myth, Reality*, Cambridge University Press 1990, p43.

46. Ben Carrington, '"Football's coming home" but whose home? And do we want it?: nation, football and the politics of exclusion', in Adam Brown (ed.), *Fanatics! Power, Identity and Fandom in Football*, Routledge 1998; Les Back, Tim Crabbe & John Solomos, *The Changing Face of Football: Racism, Identity and Multiculture in the English Game*, Berg 2001; Daniel Burdsey, '"If I ever play football Dad, can I play for England or India?": British Asians, sport and diasporic national identities', *Sociology* 40(1), pp11-28, 2006.

47. Michael White, 'Try boxing test, says Lady Amos', *Guardian*, 27.10.04.
48. Daniel Burdsey, '"If I ever play football Dad, can I play for England or India?": British Asians, sport and diasporic national identities', *Sociology* 40(1), pp11-28, 2006.
49. Mark Perryman, *Ingerlund: Travels with a Football Nation*, Simon & Schuster 2006.
50. Steve Fenton, 'Indifference towards national identity: what young adults think about being English and British', *Nations and Nationalism* 13(2), pp321-39, 2007.
51. Stuart Hall, 'Old and new identities, old and new ethnicities', in Anthony King (ed.), *Culture, Globalization and the World System*, Macmillan 1991.
52. Kobena Mercer, *Welcome to the Jungle: New Positions in Black Cultural Studies*, Routledge 1994, p259.
53. Tariq Modood, 'Multiculturalism and nation building go hand in hand', *Guardian*, 23.5.07.
54. Paul Gilroy, *After Empire: Melancholia or Convivial Culture?*, Routledge 2004.
55. Slavoj Žižek, *For They Know Not What They Do: Enjoyment as a Political Factor*, Second Edition, Verso 2002, p110.

A political imaginary for an English left

Andy Newman

The paradox for understanding England is that we must learn from Scotland. As Iain McLean and Alistair McMillan observe, the Treaty of Union was passed by two sovereign parliaments, and distinct civil and religious institutions were preserved in both countries.[1] Thus the Scottish state was only interrupted, not extinguished; and the sovereignty of the pre-existing English parliament could not have been fundamentally extended to Scotland, as it could be repealed, like any other act of parliament.

As Tom Nairn argues, the defining feature of the United Kingdom is therefore not that the English and Scottish nations were merged; it was their states that were; and the relative disparity of size and power between England and Scotland required that the English state totally absorbed the Scottish state. The purpose of the 1707 treaty was subordination, not elimination, because the 'subordination of the non-English periphery was a necessary condition of Britain's power base and imperial ambition'.[2]

The Scottish nation never ceased to exist, and Scotland's economy benefited hugely from the Empire. As Angus Calder has remarked: 'The Scottish past was wonderfully lively, an incomparable source of song and story, but self interest dictated that Scots should abandon heroics and lost causes and accommodate themselves with commerce, industry and the British imperial project'.[3] Or, as Scottish Socialist Party theorist Murray Smith argues:

> It is mistaken to describe the Union that gave birth to the British state as an annexation. It was an agreement between two ruling classes, two oligarchies. Of course it was done without consulting the people (who consulted the people in the 18th century?) ... It was a lop-sided agreement, given the relationship of forces, but it was an agreement that the Scottish ruling class ultimately gained from.[4]

But now that the Empire has gone we are left with only the pomp and circumstance of a late capitalist monarchy, and the pretensions with which Britain seeks to maintain a bloated sense of its own international importance. Here Scotland is out of step: the most concrete example of this is the application by Scottish First Minister Alex Salmond for Scotland to join the Nuclear Non-Proliferation Treaty talks, to oppose Britain's renewal of its Trident nuclear weapons. [5] (Both the Scottish parliament and a majority of Scottish MPs in Westminster voted against Trident, yet the British nuclear warheads would be based in Scotland.)

Unlike in England, the majority of Scottish socialists feel comfortable in identifying themselves with their country. A generation ago, the Communist Party in Scotland played a key role in winning arguments for devolution, based upon arguments that workers in Scotland were more left-wing than workers in the rest of Britain.[6] They even went so far as organising bagpipe bands on labour movement demonstrations, complete with kilts.

The pro-independence Scottish National Party includes a number of socialists; Bill Wilson MSP, for example, makes a strong case for the left to support the SNP government: 'A fairer tax system, democratic access to education, public services to serve the public rather than for private profit … An SNP government does not offer nirvana, but it does offer a vast improvement on what has gone before'.[7] Gregor Gall argues that socialists participating in the SNP give it 'a veneer or complexion of radicalism', providing 'another link in the chain tying radicalism and Scottishness together'.[8] The Scottish Socialist Party believes that 'Scotland would be economically, politically, culturally and socially better off making our own decisions and standing on our own two feet. We look forward to … an independent socialist Scotland.'[9]

Many Scottish socialists have embraced the cause of independence, because they understand that 'it is not just the issue of independence, but of what sort of independence'.[10] Frances Curran and Murray Smith of the SSP have argued: 'Support for Independence is stronger among the working class and youth. It is therefore natural to fuse this democratic aspiration with the aspiration for social transformation. In this fusion is found the key to every project for emancipation in Scotland'.[11]

Gregor Gall believes that the existence of a Scottish national consciousness reinforces a culture of greater militancy: the Scottish working class believes it is more radical than the English, and may therefore act more radically. To this degree Gregor sees Scottish national consciousness as progressive, as an ideological reservoir for retaining the memory of past struggles, even in periods when collective class consciousness is weak:

> Red Clydeside and John Maclean have become part of the heroic iconography on the left in Scotland, not only in terms of image ... but also as history. [During] the Tories years of office ... – the most sustained offensive by the ruling class since the 1920s – those on the left looked back to the past to help inform their present.[12]

The common sense belief that Scotland is more egalitarian than England played an important role in strengthening the resolve to resist Thatcherism in the 1980s, which was seen as essentially English and alien. Scottish national identity was expressed in the ideological rejection of the Poll Tax. Of course it was also a class-based rebellion, but that class consciousness was mediated through ideological expression in terms of national identity.[13]

The attempt by Ron Davies (Labour's architect of Welsh devolution) and John Marek (a former Labour MP who is now an independent in the Welsh Assembly) to construct a distinct Welsh left has not flourished so well. But the automatic Labour voting of the Valleys has been undermined, as New Labour is seen as alien to Wales. As Chris Harvie SNP MSP recounts:

> In Blaenau Gwent, at the heart of Welsh Wales, a New Labour attempt in 2005 to force in one of its clones provoked a revolt by the former Assembly Member, the ailing Peter Law, who got in as an independent. Law died and in the subsequent by-election the seat remained independent. In the campaign a friend driving a Plaid Cymru van was halted by an immense ex-miner: 'Plaid? There's OK. If you'd been New Labour, we'd have smashed your fookin' windows in.' This was once, as Ebbw Vale, the constituency of Nye Bevan and Michael Foot.[14]

NEW LABOUR, OLD BRITAIN

A peculiarity of the English government at the time of the 1707 Union was that sovereignty did not lie with the people but in parliament. This was because decisive battles against feudalism happened in England in the seventeenth century, before ideologies of democracy had fully flourished. The elite social strata of England and Scotland combined into a common imperial ruling class, and, as Nairn explains:

> 'Britain' was a multi-national social class before it was a multi-national state, and the latter remains in essence a manifestation of the former.

Britishness was a stratum phenomenon rather than a mass or popular one, but later on the elite-mass linkage was greatly fortified [by mass participation in Empire, which] gave this class-forged link an iron durability.[15]

The form of the British state is peculiarly pre-Modern, and was created in specific and contingent historical circumstances. This pre-modernity of British institutions was famously commented upon by Perry Anderson in 1968, as an explanation of why Britain did not see the same level of student radicalism as other European countries. Anderson argued that this was the reason that Britain had never developed a major school of sociology or Marxism that sought to explain our society – a phenomenon he described as the 'missing centre'.[16] That prevailing empiricism and lack of interest in constitutional issues endures today, and has its root in the pragmatic origins of 'Britain' as a marriage of convenience that was subsequently mystified.

This indifference affects the political far left as well as the general population. During the 1990s the constitutional reform group Charter 88 had a big impact on shifting public opinion towards support for proportional representation, and helped shape devolution in Scotland and Wales. But the far left failed to grasp how reforms in the here and now can pave the way for deeper change later. Dismissing Charter 88, leading Socialist Workers Party member Lindsey German simplistically counterposed revolution to achievable reforms: 'A political movement which fought not for narrow constitutional change but for a real upheaval in society – with a new form of democracy – might seem harder to get, but it also seems much more worth fighting for.'[17]

As Britain has been a rapacious imperial political project, the support of the Conservative Party for conserving the British union is self-explanatory. Yet Tom Nairn has made the interesting observation that New Labour is also a political phenomenon based on the current unitary state (especially with Gordon Brown's current exaggerated emphasis on Britishness). As he says:

'Britain', the Empire's rump state, can only be kept going by some new regulating and stabilising cadre, one really capable of taking over from the gentlemen ... One should not judge [New Labour] solely in terms of the former Left-Right spectrum. Seen rather in terms of curatorship, as a form of state survival kit, it becomes more comprehensible.[18]

Ron Davies has explained this phenomenon:

The timidity of New Labour is preventing us from making even more gains. Timidity in not just philosophical terms but in policy terms as well ... Because they believe ... that the solutions to the problems of Wales [and Scotland] are to be found in exactly the same mechanism as the problems of the North of England or wherever. The answer is a strong Labour government in Westminster who will legislate all these problems away.[19]

The support for the unitary British state is deeply embedded in the Labour Party, on both the left and the right. Devolution was supported, in effect, because it was thought it would be just enough to conserve the Union. As Douglas Alexander, who ran Labour's campaign for the 2007 Scottish Parliament, said: 'The great outcome of devolution is it allows people to demonstrate their identity within the United Kingdom and, at the same time, not break up the United Kingdom'.[20] Labour Party figures as far apart politically as Tony Blair and Tony Benn oppose Scottish independence.

THE ESCALATING EFFECT OF DEVOLUTION
Devolution, the reform designed to save the union, has started a seemingly irreversible dynamic towards further separation. Michael Keating has examined the growing policy differences between England, Scotland and Wales:

The Labour Party may be the dominant political force in London, Edinburgh and Cardiff. But Scotland and Wales have stuck more to the traditional social democratic model of public service delivery. This has led them to stress non-selectivity, professionalism and uniformity, while rejecting foundation hospitals, star-rated hospitals, school league tables, beacon councils, elite universities and selective schools. Scotland also scrapped up-front university tuition fees and rejected top-up fees. At the same time, free care for the elderly has been introduced north of the border.[21]

In Wales, there are no NHS prescription charges. The 'One Wales' agreement between the Welsh Labour Party and Plaid Cymru, which underpins their coalition government, is designed, in the words of First Minister Rhodri Morgan, to put 'thick red water' between Cardiff and London; and it includes a commitment that: 'We firmly reject the privatisation of NHS services or the organisation of such services on market models. We will guarantee public ownership, public funding and public control of this vital public service.'[22]

So far the differences have largely been driven by Cardiff and Edinburgh resisting policy initiatives originating from Westminster, but with the SNP and Plaid Cymru both now in government we may start to see divergent policies positively introduced in Wales and Scotland.

What is more, policies which only affect England are voted through the Westminster parliament by Labour MPs representing Scottish and Welsh constituencies. The danger is that the debate resulting from these anomalies will focus upon resentment of the Scots and Welsh, and that the right wing will benefit. For example, former *Sun* editor Kelvin Mackenzie writes: 'It is the political issue for England and there is a great prize for Cameron if he can prove to the poor of the northeast, northwest and parts of London that he will look after them rather than the overfunded, feather-bedded Scots'.[23] The English Democrats, a political party that advocates an English Parliament, has made a conscious decision to position itself on the political right, to compete with UKIP and the BNP for votes.

FAREWELL TO LITTLE BRITAIN
When we talk of a Scottish left, or a Welsh left, this generally means more than just the left who happen to be in Scotland or Wales. It refers to a form of progressive politics that identifies with the national culture and political context of those countries. But there is not yet an equivalent English left; there are only socialists and progressives who happen to be in England.

Yet as the break up of the UK becomes more of a mainstream political issue, there needs to be a response from the left to the specific consequences that only affect England. As the likes of Garry Bushell and Kelvin MacKenzie traduce the Scots and Welsh for higher government spending and better social services, we need to endorse and support the more progressive direction from Cardiff and Edinburgh, whilst arguing that these policies need to be extended to England. This combines making the case for a similar improvement in working and social conditions for people in England with undercutting the arguments of the reactionaries who so resent the advances made in Scotland and Wales.

The Scots and Welsh are very clear that being English is not the same as being British, but the majority of the English people have yet to find an independent voice. As Tom Nairn argues:

England has refrained from speaking because a British-imperial class and ethos have been in possession for so long of its vocal chords. A class has spoken for it. This is the evident sense in which England has been even more affected and deformed by imperial globalisation than other parts of the archipelago![24]

The dynamic towards independence for Wales and Scotland could leave England as just Little Britain: with little changed. But instead the left could create a positive agenda for English independence. To do so we need to imagine life without Britain, and what policies would benefit working people who live in England.

Firstly, the economic policy of the *British* government prioritises the maintenance of London as a major financial centre, even though, according to a recent report by Goldman Sachs, this has led to the pound being overvalued by 12 per cent in recent years – one consequence of which is the loss of a million manufacturing jobs in the English regions, Scotland and Wales since 1999.[25] In a celebrated public relations gaffe, the Governor of the Bank of England, Eddie George, actually conceded that regional inequality is deliberate, when, asked if job loss in the north was an acceptable price to pay for the control of inflation in the south, he was reported to have said 'yes, I suppose in a sense I am'.[26] A progressive priority for England should be to distribute employment fairly, instead of encouraging population movement to the South East.

Secondly, successive *British* governments have overheated the economy in the South East, based upon house price inflation. The consequent equity withdrawal and private debt has driven the economy, rather than strategic investment in infrastructure and manufacturing capability. Today, one third of the EU's entire consumer debt is in the UK: nearly all of it in England. This has a further policy implication, as Labour's failure to provide adequate social housing is designed to prop up these exaggerated house prices. The left needs to explain that the housing crisis is linked to the lack of integrated regional planning; an English parliament needs to give equal voice to the regions outside the South East, and produce an equitable housing policy.

Thirdly, the English left needs to argue for raising public expenditure per head to Scottish levels. To take one example: smaller class sizes, and greater emphasis on teaching rather than testing, has led to pupils in Scotland being 50 per cent more likely to progress to higher education. As a result, more than 37 per cent go to college or university, compared with just 25 per cent of English students. And Scottish schoolchildren are also up to a third more likely to get good grades at age sixteen.

Fourthly, an independent England should play a more modest role in the world. The English left should highlight the obscenity that Britain now has the world's second largest armaments expenditure. It stood at 5 per cent of the global total in 2006 ($59,200 million at 2005 prices) – above Israel, China and Russia.[27] The demand to close down the Faslane nuclear submarine base and remove these weapons from their soil, and seas, is already central to Scots nationalism. An English left should similarly pledge to abandon our nuclear weaponry, which would amount to a saving of £85 billion over the lifetime of Trident.

And finally, an independent England should make a virtue of being one of the most multicultural societies in the world, and we should remind ourselves that England in the past was proud to be a refuge from tyranny. We should be proud that immigrants want to come and share England with us.

A LEFT OUT OF TOUCH WITH ENGLAND

Left-wing politics in Britain has been moulded over the last two decades by the enormous transformation of the Labour Party. As long ago as 1990 Beatrix Campbell pointed out that the Labour Party was becoming a party of opinion rather than a party of activists in a movement.[28] Although the party still has a broadly progressive electoral base, and links with trade unions, it no longer articulates the aspirations of those supporters. Jon Cruddas MP has argued:

> New Labour has quite consciously removed class as an economic or political category. It has specifically calibrated a science of political organisation – and indeed an ideology – to camp out in middle England with unarguable electoral successes. Yet the question remains as to whether the policy mix developed to dominate a specific part of the British electoral map actually compounds problems in other communities with different histories and contemporary economic and social profiles.[29]

As a consequence of Labour abandoning working-class politics, the party no longer has an active membership base at a local level; and this means that in many progressive campaigns, for example against the war in Iraq, against the fascist BNP, or in defence of council housing, the relatively small forces of the far left, most notably the Socialist Workers Party, have a disproportionately important role. The SWP are large enough, and well organised enough, to initiate and staff various campaigns, while their placards and newspapers give them a high profile on demonstrations. So in some contexts they might seem to be the most prominent advocates of socialist ideas.

Two of the campaigns that the SWP is prominent in, the Stop the War Coalition and Unite against Fascism, are focused on just the kind of issues where a sophisticated understanding of the place of national identity and patriotism in politics are most vital. Yet the SWP is determined to actively ignore the growing political significance of the English national question, and consequent demands for English independence. The SWP even denies that there is such a phenomenon as an English national identity. According to Paul McGarr: 'Ordinary people in England may live on the same piece of land as the rich, but they have nothing else whatever in common.'[30] Martin Smith, National Secretary of the SWP, in a review of Billy Bragg's book *The Progressive Patriot*, argued that Bragg 'throws together a number of disconnected historical events, myths and anecdotes and tries to make a case for an English national identity'.[31] He has also written that:

> Waving the St George flag is not about inclusion – it's all about exclusion. What are we supposed to celebrate? The Empire? Or the fact that we live in a society where the levels of inequality continue to grow? All you are left with is David Beckham, Jonny Wilkinson and big profits for the breweries. Not much really … BBC London News conducted a survey. It asked viewers what made them proud to be English. The answers make interesting reading. Multiculturalism, free speech and the NHS were the top three. And they are things to be proud of. But none of them have anything to do with being English.[32]

For Martin Smith the ideology of Englishness has a content that is always reactionary. Yet multiculturalism, free speech and the NHS are also very much something to do with being English. Indeed, our historical understanding of how these gains were won, however mythologized, is a key building block towards a shared national consciousness. To surrender these aspects of Englishness, and allow the right-wing to interpret Englishness as narrow national chauvinism and nostalgia for backwards-looking social attitudes on race and immigration, would be a historic defeat. Many millions of people connect with English national identity without necessarily making these right-wing associations.

This automatic association of national identity with far right politics is a commonplace of the SWP and similar groups, and it has practical consequences. As the editor of the anti-fascist magazine *Searchlight*

Nick Lowles has written:

> Starting from the premise that patriotism is intrinsically wrong immediately puts you at odds with the majority of people in this country, the vast majority of whom can easily balance loving their country with supporting a modern multi-cultural Britain. As soon as you place yourself in opposition to the idea that people can love their country you are creating a barrier which cannot easily be overcome. Searchlight's most successful campaign image was of the England football team with the black players 'whited' out. The BNP, meanwhile, refused to support England because of the very presence of these players and it hurt them in the public's mind. The vast majority of English people identify with modern England so let us embrace it rather than denounce it.[33]

UNDERSTANDING NATIONAL CONSCIOUSNESS

A more sophisticated argument than Martin Smith's comes from fellow SWP member Neil Davidson: 'Identities are the ensemble of all the external signs through which people show to themselves and to other people that they have chosen to be identified in that particular way'.[34] Davidson clearly, and helpfully, accepts that national identity exists as a collection of shared ideas, behaviours, myths and attitudes. He cites the contribution of Russian psychologist Valentin Voloshinov, who argued that 'consciousness is not an individual but a collective attribute. It is produced by people internalising the meaning of the ideological signs that their social group has used over a time in the process of interaction'.[35] The forms of consciousness available to individuals are those that have been collectively developed, and a national identity could be seen as an example of a collective identification of this kind.

Otto Bauer, an Austrian socialist who lived in the multi-national Austro-Hungarian Empire, argued that a nation is the product of a common historical experience, ultimately based upon mankind's struggle against nature, but also on political struggles within the nation and against other nations; this creates an unfinished outcome, a process of constant change. This has two important implications for national identity. Firstly, as Bauer puts it, the nation is a piece of history frozen in collective consciousness. But secondly, the nation does not exist as a set of identifiers, and a consciousness, that its members simply accept; rather, the nation is always in the process of discovery. Hence the ideological content of the nation is always part of a contested process, reflecting the different class interests of those who identify with it. Bauer's approach – seeing the nation as a process of constant reinvention – also has the advantage of explaining how nations can embrace new cultural influences through immigration, and how new immigrants can be part of their new nation while retaining identification with their original culture and nation. This is particularly important for understanding England, a nation built on successive waves of immigration.

An example of such changing national self-perceptions is given by Arthur Aughey in his discussion of the ways in which Britain's progressive struggle against European fascism transformed English intellectual attitudes.[36] In the 1920s the predominant view among the intellectual class was that England was decadent and repugnant, but after the Second World War many who had previously ridiculed and abhorred patriotism began to see themselves as patriots. What produced this transformation was mass participation in the popular front to defend democracy against Mosley's fascists during the 1930s, and the ultimately successful campaign by the left during the Second World War to open a military second front directly against the Nazis, instead of concentrating the British war effort on defence of the Empire. Popular patriotism shifted the whole political climate in a progressive direction, while redefining national consciousness in terms of egalitarianism rather than Empire loyalism.

Unfortunately, Neil Davidson's approach assumes that national identity is always an unchanging obstacle to progress, and must be judged against the standard of a working-class revolution. He argues that it is the capitalist system that generates nationalism, and that it is part of the 'reformist consciousness' of the working class, which must be rejected by revolutionaries.[37] National consciousness must be opposed because it is a distraction from revolutionary class consciousness. For Davidson, acceptance by Scottish workers of British nationhood, though not wholly positive, has involved 'recognition of the collective interests of workers on both sides of the border – interests formed at the level of civil society', and has therefore offered the possibility of achieving socialism, and of 'escaping from the prison of nationhood altogether'.[38] In effect he is arguing that British national consciousness is more progressive than Scottish, Welsh, and certainly English national consciousness. Davidson also argues that, as nationalism is reformist, so internationalism is a component of revolutionary consciousness; it involves 'workers in one nation giving solidarity to workers in other nations, even at a cost to themselves: for example, the support given to the Liverpool dockers from as far afield as the United States and Australia'.[39] But surely, most of the dockers in Australia and America did not reject their national identity as Australians and Americans as a precondition of international trade union solidarity? And surely only a tiny minority of them have what Neil Davidson would consider 'revolutionary class consciousness'? It seems that the more appropriate lesson to learn is that national identity, and even patriotism, can coexist with working-class solidarity.

Since the demise of the Communist Party, the SWP has been England's main far left organisation. It is in a position to shape political initiatives, but because of its devotion to the unchanging template of revolutionary socialism on a 'Leninist' model, it remains very conservative about social changes that don't fall within this very particular template of analysis and action. As a result the SWP ignores the development of English and Scottish national consciousness and underestimates the importance of the declining identification with Britishness. In the abstract the SWP supports the break up of the British state, but it opposes actively campaigning for a democratic English parliament and Scottish independence. Yet it is precisely this rising English and Scottish national consciousness that promises to actually subvert the power of the British Empire state, and open up new political possibilities for significant social change.

IMAGINING A PROGRESSIVE PATRIOTISM
Writing in *Marxism Today* in the immediate aftermath of the 1982 Falklands war, Eric Hobsbawm surprised many leftists when he outlined the progressive potential in patriotism:

> The dangers of patriotism always were and still are obvious, not least because it was and is enormously vulnerable to ruling class jingoism, to anti-foreign nationalism and of course in our days to racism. These dangers are particularly great where patriotism can be separated from the other sentiments and aspirations of the working class, or even where it can be counter-posed to them: where nationalism can be counterposed to social liberation. The reason why nobody pays much attention to the, let's call it, jingoism of the Chartists, is that it was combined with and masked by an enormous militant class consciousness. It's when the two are separated, and they can be easily separated, that the dangers are particularly obvious. Conversely, when the two go together in harness, they multiply not only the force of the working class but its capacity to place itself at the head of a broad coalition for social change and they even give it the possibility of wresting hegemony from the class enemy.[40]

Eric Hobsbawm argues exactly the opposite to the SWP. Most workers, even in periods of heightened radicalism, have a strong attachment to their nation, which coexists with class consciousness and progressive aspirations towards international solidarity. If the left abandons the ideological battleground of defining national consciousness, then we hand over the appeal of national identity to become the exclusive property of the far right. An error borne of extraordinary strategic timidity.

If, on the other hand, socialists contest the ideological content of patriotism and claim it for the left, then we resist the unnecessary polarisation that forces a choice between the competing consciousnesses. Instead we can reinforce class consciousness as being a characteristic of our national culture, and can begin to mobilise liberal patriotic opinion way beyond the left and trade unions, in support of progressive ideas identified as part of our past, present and future national culture.

The English left should learn from Scottish socialists who seek to combine the democratic aspiration for national independence with the campaign for greater social equality and emancipation.

The contribution that the SSP has made is to understand that progressive and social democratic aspirations are often couched in terms of national identity.[41] This gave an immediacy to their arguments for socialism, that resonated with how working-class Scots see themselves. As former leader of the SSP Tommy Sheridan put it: 'The people of Scotland actually believe in the redistribution of wealth, they believe in trade union rights. We have shown that socialism is alive and well in Scotland'.[42] The SSP's success was predicated upon overcoming the historical divisions between socialists, uniting a critical mass of the Scottish left in one united organisation, and combining this with a commitment to the hard slog of community campaigning over day-to-day issues. The result was that the SSP grew to 3000 members in a population of just five million, and six SSP members were elected to parliament in 2003, with 7.7 per cent of the national vote. Subsequently the SSP has suffered a tragic implosion, following a splenetic dispute over a libel action by Tommy Sheridan, but this should not distract the English left from learning lessons based on what they achieved.

Scottish identity is fundamentally linked to egalitarianism – 'We are all Jock Tamson's bairns' (meaning we are all the same, with the same interests)[43] – and the self-belief of a tradition of political radicalism.

English national identity is not so clear cut, but we can learn from Billy Bragg when he says, 'I believe in this country and in those traditional values which served my ancestors so well in the past. Through their constant struggle to be treated fairly they were able to bequeath to me the liberties that I enjoy today'.[44] England is a nation where class difference, them and us, is at the heart of our self-awareness. George Schöpflin argues that the English subordinate ethnicity to class, and this explains why there are such strongly competing notions of Englishness – the radical England of Billy Bragg and the conservative England of Roger Scruton.[45] This has two important messages for the left. Firstly, as Schöpflin argues, our national consciousness being dominated by class rather than ethnicity has helped to make the country relatively open to migrants, exiles and other foreigners; and secondly, we can build upon the instinctive Robin Hood strand of English identity – robbing from the rich to give to the poor.

The left in England is not yet an English left. The decay of the Labour Party, and the fractious and conservative diaspora of the far left groups, means that progressive opinion is spread across a mosaic of different organisations and political projects, including Compass and the Labour Representation Committee in the Labour Party, Respect, the Green Party, and others outside of it. An English socialism cannot proceed by counterposing itself to these existing organisations. Nor do we have any unifying national-popular dynamic, which existed in Scotland when the SSP was founded.

The first step is that those who wish to see an English left must network together, without organisational pre-conditions, to promote a sustained debate with the rest of the left, which remains in general distrustful of any progressive potential in English national identity. Our weight in having this argument is helped by our common cause with socialists in Scotland and Wales.

Secondly, the left needs unashamedly to participate in and support some of the constitutional and cultural initiatives that it currently seems to reject. These include the Campaign for an English Parliament, the increasing demand that England should have its own National Anthem, and local efforts to celebrate St George's Day in ways which are both popular and inclusive. The alternative is that legitimate democratic aspirations will be hijacked by the far right.

Thirdly, we need to participate in a general left renewal underway both inside the Labour Party and outside, particularly following the fallout with the SWP in Respect. This means building trust though practical cooperation, and focusing back onto the day-to-day community campaigns that connect with peoples' lives. Socialists who understand and sympathise with a common sense patriotism instead of denouncing it have an important role to play here.

Finally, there is an audience for a left-wing English culture. Billy Bragg is the supreme representative of this process; his music might perhaps appeal to a relatively narrow audience, but his achievement is to have marked out the cultural potential of a progressive patriotism. Another example is the fan-led campaign to begin to ensure that supporting the England football team is for all, with spectacular results in rapidly growing Black and Asian identification with team and the flag at the time of major tournaments. The left needs to become unafraid to promote a progressive Englishness as a core element in an emerging national-popular culture.

We are starting from where we are, and we can only do what we can. But an English socialism which finds its own authentic voice could begin a process towards helping to move the whole political culture to the left in the country we are learning to call England.

NOTES

1. Iain McLean and Alsitair McMillan, 'England and the Union since 1707', in Robert Hazell, *The English Question*, Manchester University Press 2006.

2. Tom Nairn, *After Britain, New Labour and the Return of Scotland*, Granta 2000, p5.

3. Angus Calder, 'Imperialism and Scottish Culture', in *Scotland, Class and Nation, editor Chris Banbury*, Bookmarks 1999, p146.

4. Murray Smith, 'The National Question in Western Europe', *Frontline*, Issue 11, 2000.

5. Eddie Barnes, 'Salmond's bid for seat at UN', *Scotland on Sunday*, 21.10.07.

6. Gregor Gall, *The Political Economy of Scotland*, University of Wales Press 2005, p134.

7. Bill Wilson, 'Give Change a Chance', *Scottish Left Review*, Issue 41, July/August 2007, p16.

8. Gregor Gall, *The Political Economy of Scotland*, University of Wales Press 2005, p137.

9. http://www.scottishsocialistparty.org/.

10. Murray Smith 'The National Question in Western Europe', *Frontline*, Issue 11, 2000.

11. Frances Curran and Murray Smith, 'The Scottish Socialist Party – the rise of a new Socialist party', *Socialist Outlook*, June 2000, p10-11.

12. Gregor Gall, *The Political Economy of Scotland*, University of Wales Press 2005, p139.

13. Andy Newman, 'A Conversation About National Identity', http://www.socialistunity.com/?p=959, 3.11.07.

14. Chris Harvey, 'Red Flag, Red Dragon', *Scottish Left Review*, Issue 40, May/June 2007, p12.

15. Nairn, *After Britain*, p176.

16. Perry Anderson, 'Land of Opportunity', *New Left Review*, July-August 1968.

17. Lindsey German, 'Not long to reign over us?', *Socialist Review*, Issue 180, November 1994.

18. Nairn, *After Britain*, p58.

19. Andy Newman, 'Interview with Ron Davies', http://www.socialistunity.com/?page_id=851, January 2005.

20. BBC News, 'English parliament "unworkable"', http://news.bbc.co.uk/1/hi/uk_politics/6267305.stm, 16.1.07.

21. Michael Keating, *Policy convergence and divergence in Scotland under devolution*, http://www.devolution.ac.uk/pdfdata/Keating_rsa_03.pdf.

22. 'One Wales – A Progressive Agenda for the Government of Wales', An agreement between the Labour and Plaid Cymru Groups in the National Assembly, June 2007.

23. Kelvin Mackensie, 'Sun debates UK Break Up', *Sun*, 30.10.07.

24. Nairn, *After Britain*, p79.

25. Donald Adamson, 'Celtic Tiger/Celtic Kitten', in *Scottish Left Review*, Issue 38, January/February 2007.

26. Kevin Morgan, 'The English Question. Regional Perspectives on a Fractured Nation', in *Regional Studies*, Issue 36, Number 7, October 2002.

27. Military Expenditure, 2006: http://nfpb.gn.apc.org/milsp07.htm; Stockholm International Peace Research Institute, http://www.sipri.org/.

28. Bea Cambell, 'Dangerous Liaisons', *Marxism Today*, May 1990, pp26-27.

29. Jon Cruddas, *Race, Class and Migration: Tackling the Far Right*, May 2007.

30. Paul McGarr 'Show red card to nationalism', *Socialist Worker*, 22.6.02.

31. Martin Smith, 'Nothing to Reclaim', *Socialist Review*, November 2006.

32. Martin Smith, 'Houmous and kebab on St George's?', *Socialist Worker*, 24.4.04.

33. Private correspondence with the author.

34. Neil Davidson, *The Origins of Scottish Nationhood*, Pluto 2000, p17.

35. Neil Davidson, *The Origins of Scottish Nationhood*, p11.

36. Arthur Aughey, *The Politics of Englishness*, Manchester University Press 2007, p31.

37. Neil Davidson, 'In Perspective: Tom Nairn', in *International Socialism Journal (ISJ)*, 82, March 1999.

38. Neil Davidson, *The Origins of Scottish Nationhood*, pp202-203.

39. Neil Davidson, 'Scotland: almost afraid to know itself?', *International Socialism Journal (ISJ)*, 109, February 2006.

40. Eric Hobsbawm, 'Falklands Fallout', *Marxism Today*, January, 1983, pp13-20

41. Gregor Gall, *The Political Economy of Scotland*, University of Wales Press 2005, p108.

42. Tommy Sheridan in *Guardian*, 3.5.03, quoted in Gregor Gall, *Radical Scotland*, p158.

43. Gregor Gall, *The Political Economy of Scotland*, University of Wales Press 2005, p128.

44. Billy Bragg, *The Progressive Patriot*, Black Swan 2006, p350.

45. George Schöpfin, *Nations, Identity, Power: The New Politics of Europe*, quoted by Arthur Aughey, 'The Challenges to English Identity', in Robert Hazell, *The English Question*, Bantam Press p58.

Postscript to Britain: England's turn?

Tom Nairn

Henry V holds an incomparable place in what Michael Herzfeld has called the 'cultural intimacy' of English identity – the reference points that define nationality, and help make it into patriotism. The climax of Shakespeare's history plays, Henry V glorified Elizabeth's reign through a 1599 retrospect on her Tudor ancestors. The Crown that had emerged from generations of factional and then religious strife was by the end of the century much stronger, and its nation was growing in confidence. Both the romanticized hero-king and his great cadences on the Agincourt battlefield were giving voice to this new England. Naturally, those have been the things that later literature and cinema have turned to – definitions of a later English (then British) nationalism. Theorists of nationalism such as Liah Greenfeld have played their parts too, perceiving Shakespeare's imagined community as 'God's First-born', the pioneer of all later nation states.

Today, more caution is called for, regarding both Englishness and the idea of nationalism. And this isn't a question of multicultural correctness, or of giving less offence to England's present-day neighbours. Shakespeare himself employs artful distancing devices, both at the beginning and the end of the tale – a feature of the play captured rather well in Laurence Olivier's famous 1944 film version. His Chorus, the abstruse arguments of Act 1, and the comedy-like last act frame the main action, naturally hoping to sway spectators, but (it has been argued) by inviting them to pass judgement. He was not merely inviting the Globe public to celebrate genetic superiority, or a nationism destined to conquer others. The '-ism' didn't arrive until centuries later. It was more a question of reassuring them that the English (especially their upper classes) were as good as anybody else – and could claim their rightful place as equals against a resistant feudal world.

As Germaine Greer has pointed out, Shakespeare was addressing an

'Elizabethan audience, hungry, responsive, unselfconscious ... [that] did not outlive the old Queen'. It was this molten, questing enthusiasm of a society in formation that stirred Shakespeare's imagination, and has gone on firing that of later generations. But, inevitably, misunderstandings have arisen in this process. The early-modern identity voiced in Henry V was not at all typical of later nation-states. 'Ethnicity' in the later, harder sense was the by-product of populations with disputed land frontiers, who often defined themselves by war, and always by competitive struggles. In this sense the English population of the archipelago differed in a striking way from the rest of Europe: although internally as diverse as other countries, its external frontiers appeared fixed by nature. In Richard II – an earlier history play – they are famously depicted as this 'sceptred isle ... this precious stone set in a silver sea'.

The English did of course have minor border problems, above all with the Scots – the 'weasels and mice' of Act I, Scene 2. However, the Welsh border is given centre stage in the play with the character of Llewellyn (phoneticised as 'Fluellen') – and also a very positive meaning. Keen to support Henry V's partly Welsh Tudor dynasty, Shakespeare allows his hero a Welsh-aristocratic blood-line. Class transcended genes, as it were, allowing the promotion of Wales as an auxiliary of Englishness – particularly in the context of a war of justified overseas expansion. Only four years after the play's first performance, a suitably weasel-like Scot succeeded to the English throne as James I; but auxiliary-promotion would prove more difficult with Scotland. Indeed, it took over a century, concluded provisionally by the 1707 Treaty of Union.

Has that provisional era now ended? Two striking features of the 1599 play suggest as much: its obsession with class, and the acceptance that England was somehow more herself outside of herself – expanding, leading the way. 'No king of England if not king of France', Henry says in Act 2, Scene 2. He declares that his strength lies in God – plus the virtual certainty of 'a fair and lucky war ... with every rub smoothèd on our way'. In 2007, one doesn't have to search so far back for similar ideas: the confidence of a country most itself when out of itself, bestowing its values upon others. By the time of Shakespeare's death in 1616, England's (then Britain's) expansiveness was of course established far beyond France, in the North Atlantic arena and then all round the globe. And the need to redefine any more limited – or ethnic – identity appeared unimportant: 'little England', as it was called derisively in the 19th century.

As for class, military historians have shown that Agincourt was won by commoners. It was another victory for the deadly long bow, whose infernal hails of steel broke up the French mounted charges, and gave tactical superiority to a far smaller English force. But one would never guess this from the play, where Westmorland, Salisbury, Exeter and the other toffs proceed to celebrate their triumph and Henry is rewarded with the girl, Catherine of France. An early-modern class structure would in such ways be borne forward over centuries to come, alongside earlier assumptions about empire. Perhaps Greer's point about the transient character of the Elizabethan Globe public still needs to be expanded, and deepened. The national 'intimacy' of Englishness has suffered from the archaic splendour of Shakespeare's verse, at the same time as being incomparably nourished by it. The poet may in fact have contributed too much to England's contemporary identity, in the sense of lessening the need for other modes of identification – political, constitutional, republican – which have none the less ended by reasserting themselves.

Surely no post-expansive Commonwealth or 'Special Relationship', no surrogate for Henry's God who 'fought for us', no over-emphasis on some post-modern 'Britishness', should deter the straightforward wish for an England – at least 'devolved', and possibly independent, defined by democracy rather than mainly by a coastline? It's England's turn, for a renewed identity that can acknowledge the Bard of Avon, yet with a soul less in thrall to the time-bound legacy of Henry V.

English literature: readings and resources

Imagined Nation draws on a wide variety of sources and influences for inspiration. 'English Literature' is a guide for readers who want to hunt out the origins, and more recent developments, of the ideas and arguments in our authors' contributions.

Break-up of Britain by Tom Nairn was first published in 1977 and, although written from a Scottish perspective, remains the starting point for any consideration of the democratic case for devolution for all parts of Britain. Tom's *After Britain: New Labour and the Return of Scotland* and *Pariah: Misfortunes of the British Kingdom* updates the analysis following the 1997 and 2001 General Elections. His *Bard of Britishness*, published by the Institute of Welsh Affairs, is Tom's critique of Gordon Brown's speeches on Britishness in the build-up to becoming prime minister.

Imagined Communities by Benedict Anderson is a classic text from the New Left which examines the history and significance of the formation of nation states. Perry Anderson's *English Questions* is a collection of key essays relating this mode of understanding specifically to the British state, culture and class relations. Patrick Wright's *On Living in an Old Country* is a superb collection of essays which explore how our sense of the past impacts on the present and future of Englishness.

Imagined Nation begins with an essay that questions whether football's 'ninety-minute nationalism' represents anything more than a summer burst of flag-waving. For an examination of the significance of England fan culture read Mark Perryman's *Ingerland: Travels with a Football Nation* and the collection he also edited on the subject, *The Ingerland Factor: Home Truths from Football*. A historical perspective on the place of football in the making of the English is provided by David Winner's *Those Feet: A Sensual History of English Football*.

Billy Bragg's *The Progressive Patriot: A Search for Belonging* brings together all of Billy's considerable thinking on the subject with an admirable depth of research to provide a brilliant read. Richard Weight's *Patriots: National Identity in Britain 1940-2000* is all-consuming in its 866-page detail and is the definitive account of post-war Britishness and how the break-up has impacted upon this once united Kingdom. Philip Dodd's *Battle over Britain*, Mark Leonard's *Britain: Renewing our Identity* and David Goodhart's *Progressive Nationalism: Citizenship and the Left* should be read as responses to this thematic from the centre-left. From the right two key texts are Simon Heffer's *Nor Shall My Sword: The Reinvention of England* and Roger Scruton's *England: An Elegy*, which make their case for England. For a right-wing populist case against Labour devolution and all it represents read Peter Hitchens' *The Abolition of Britain* and *Littlejohn's Britain by* Richard Littlejohn.

Julia Bell and Jackie Gay's edited collection *England Calling: 24 Stories for the 21st Century* brought together novelists from all across the country to record their imagined England. Kevin Williamson's collection *Children of Albion Rovers* did something similar for Scotland.

Race, Sport and British Society, edited by Ben Carrington and Ian McDonald, combines academic analysis with popular writing to provide a very clear understanding of why sport matters in most discussions about racism's connection to national identity. Specific to football, yet with a currency that could be applied to most sports, three books that add enormously to any serious study of the experience of race in sport are Dave Hill's biography of John Barnes, *Out of His Skin*, Daniel Burdsey's *British Asians and Football*, and *The Changing Face of Football*, by Les Back, Tim Crabbe and John Solomos.

Andrew Gamble's *The Decline of Britain* charted the socio-economic background to the Thatcher-Major years, including the reasons for their triumph and eventual downfall. Andrew's *Between Europe and America: The Future of British Politics* develops this long view in the context of Blair's, and now Brown's, problematic positioning of Britain as somewhere in-between Atlanticism and the European Union – a triangulation that remains central to any consideration of England's eventual place in the world. On the inconsistencies of the Union Anthony Barnett's *This Time: Our Constitutional Revolution* is an optimistic reading of the potential that the 1997 Blair landslide uncovered. Although the hopes might have been mostly dashed, the case

Anthony makes for these ideals remains as important as ever. Andrew Marr's *The Day Britain Died* records the fallout of Labour's devolution settlement in a highly readable account. *Bring Home the Revolution: The Case for a British Republic* by Jonathan Freedland puts the monarchy at the core of any argument over a future British state; it is not specifically addressed to devolution but the republican argument is bound to feature as the breaking-up gathers pace .

Park and Ride: Adventures in Suburbia is written by one of the best chroniclers of the peculiarities of everyday life around, journalist Miranda Sawyer. Add Hanif Kureishi's *Budha of Suburbia* and Gautam Malkani's *Londonstani* for fictional observations and you'll never crack a joke about chintz-curtain conservatism again.

The best book on the post-war British far right remains Martin Walker's *The National Front*. Though the organisation has now been overtaken in terms of significance by the BNP, Walker's account of the late 1970s NF is a textbook example of rigorous research to both expose, and aid, an understanding of fascism. *Hurrah for the Blackshirts* covers the rise and eventual fall of Oswald Mosley's British Union of Fascists. *Very Deeply Dyed in Black* by Graham Macklin continues the story after the war and the short-lived revival of Mosley's political career. For an in-depth study of the BNP vote see the Democratic Audit report *The BNP: The Roots of its Appeal* by Peter John, Helen Margetts, David Rowland and Stuart Weir. The best resource for updated analysis of the changing fortunes of the Far Right is the monthly anti-fascist magazine *Searchlight*, and its excellent website, www.searchlightmagazine.com.

Originally published in 1935, George Dangerfield's *The Strange Death of Liberal England* is the classic account of the factors that brought a cataclysmic end to one early twentieth-century political era and helped to shape the outcome of its successor. Robert Tressell's novel *The Ragged Trousered Philanthropists* tells the story of an early twentieth working-class socialism framed by its English origins, uncompromisingly internationalist in its vision. EP Thompson's *The Making of the English Working Class*, Krishan Kumar's *The Making of English National Identity* and Peter Ackroyd's *Albion: The Origins of the English Imagination* provide useful historical accounts to help an understanding of whatever became of Labour England.

Pies and Prejudice is a great travelogue from the North of England written by Stuart Maconie. Simon Armitage's *All Points North* combines the personalised observation of the poetry Simon is best known for with great prose to provide humour with meaning. Dave Haslam's *Manchester, England* concentrates on one great city to tell us so much about life without London.

Edited by Gerry Hassan and Chris Warhurst, *Tomorrow's Scotland* is a comprehensive introduction to the politiics of post-devolution Scotland. Also edited by Gerry, *Scotland 2020* outlines the long-term future for an independent Scotland. For a rounded assessment of the impact of nationalist values on Scottish culture read *The Scots' Crisis of Confidence* by Carol Craig and *Stone Voices* by Neal Ascherson. A highly readable account of the Welsh devolution settlement is *Wales Says Yes* by Leighton Andrews. Beatrix Campbell's *Agreement! The State, Conflict and Change in Northern Ireland* covers not only how the peace agreement was formulated and eventually secured but the manner in which self-government in Northern Ireland has developed out of this process. In blogland there are some fine independently-minded commentators on Scottish and Welsh politics. Kevin Williamson's blog www.kevinwilliamson.blogspot.com is one to recommend from Scotland. Obviously partisan, the website and blog by left-wing Plaid Cymru Assembly Member Leanne Wood is an insight into a progressive-patriotic politcs at work, www.leannewood.org

Jeremy Deller and Alan Kane's Folk Archive project can be viewed online at www.mini-host.org/folkarchive. The work is also chronicled in the book *Folk Archive: Contemporary Popular Art from the UK*, co-authored by Jeremy Deller and Alan Kane. Colin Irwin's *In Search of Albion* is an enjoyably funny travelogue of England's extraordinary variety of town and village festivals. For a musical version of how to mix old and new traditions and call it 'folk' visit www.imaginedvillage.com, the website of Simon Emmerson's project *The Imagined Village*. Sue Clifford and Angela King's *England in Particular* is an A-Z from Abbeys and Allotments, to Yew Trees and Zigzags, an encyclopaedia of everything that adds up to England in the face of global corporate stan-dardisation. The book arises out of the hugely impressive campaign Common Ground, website www.commonground.org.uk.

David Downing's *The Best of Enemies* is a comprehensive history of Anglo-German football rivalries. *Who Cares about Britishness?* by Vron Ware is a global survey of attitudes towards Britain's national identity.

Paul Gilroy's book *There Ain't No Black in the Union Jack* is a definitive text for understanding linkages between debates on race and national identity. His most recent book *After Empire* revisits these linkages in the context of arguments over the future of multiculturalism. Contributions to that argument include Yasmin Alibhai-Brown's *Who Do We Think We Are* and Arun Kundnani's *The End of Tolerance*. Sarfraz Manzoor provides an outstanding insight into the everyday impact of these arguments with his autobiographical *Greetings from Bury Park: Race, Religion and Rock N' Roll*. Michael Collins' *The Likes of Us: A Biography of the White Working Class* is an evocative historiography of the London borough of Southwark, a book that needs to be read to engage with the discontents that arise from the racialisation of Englishness. For a policy-led response to debates on multiculturalism and national identity read The Runnymede Trust's 'Parekh Report' *The Future of Multi-Ethnic Britain*. The Institute of Race Relations has a website, www.irr.org.uk, and publishes a quarterly journal, *Race and Class*, essential resources towards a better understanding of the politics of race.

Real England: The Battle against the Bland by Paul Kingsnorth is one of the first books to bring together environmental activism with a progressive patriotic politics; it is a refreshingly inspiring read. *Tescopoly* by Andrew Simms makes a not dissimilar case though in this instance looking specifically at the impact of the global supermarket on the local high street, and the consequence which he terms 'clone towns'. This theme is regularly visited also by the New Economics Foundation, website www.neweconomics.org. The relationship between rural and urban England is debated in a collection of essays, *Town and Country* edited by Anthony Barnett and Roger Scruton.

George Orwell's *The Lion and the Unicorn* remains the starting-point for most considerations of a political imaginary for an English Left. This book and Orwell's other writings on an English socialism have been usefully brought together in a Penguin collection *Orwell's England*. Gregory Elliott's *Labourism and the English Genius* was written at the low-point of Labour's defeats at the hands of Thatcherism yet remains an insightful commentary on the potential for a politics beyond Labourism. A critique of Orwell's brand of English socialism from a feminist perspective is brilliantly provided by Beatrix Campbell's *Wigan Pier Revisited*. For examples of a neighbourly political imaginary of some considerable relevance to the English Left look north of the border. Gregor Gall's *The Political Economy of Scotland* is just the kind of book English socialists should be writing about their own country. The collection edited by Gregor, *Is There a Scottish Road to Socialism* is the sort of debate their friends in south should have. The latter is published by the impressive journal *The Scottish Left Review*, see their website www.slrp.co.uk One of the few places a political imaginary for an English Left is debated is the Socialist Unity website, www.socialistunity.com with many useful links too for sources of similar ideas.

Notes on Contributors

Mark Perryman is author of *Ingerland: Travels with a Football Nation*. Convenor of the LondonEnglandFans supporters group, Mark has been a leading figure in building a positive reputation for England fans home and away for the past twelve years. A regular commentator about England fan matters on TV and radio, he is also a Research Fellow in sport and leisure culture at The University of Brighton, and co-founded the self-styled 'sporting outfitters of intellectual distinction' Philosophy Football. He has written widely on the issue of Englishness, including for the journal *Soundings*, the Institute for Public Policy Research, *Red Pepper* and the collection *The Politics of Heritage*.

Nicola Baird is an environmental journalist and co-author of *Save Cash & Save the Planet*. She is the Editor of Friends of the Earth's membership magazine, *Earthmatters*. In 2007 Nicola travelled with her partner and two small children round Britain for three months in an effort to uncover the potential for stay-at-home family holidaying. A subject which, along with a wide variety of other green subjects, Nicola blogs about at http://aroundbritainnoplane.blogspot.com.

Julia Bell is a novelist writing mainly for young adults. Her latest book is *Dirty Work* and deals with issues of human trafficking. In 2001 Julia co-edited with Jackie Gay *England Calling*, a unique collection of short stories from the cities and counties of England that explored our cultural landscape. Julia lectures in on the Creative Writing MA at Birkbeck College, London. Her website is www.juliabell.net and she also blogs at http://culturalcringe.blogspot.com/.

Billy Bragg is a singer-songwriter and political activist. His first album, released in 1983, contained the song *New England*, which proclaimed 'I don't want to change the world, I'm not looking for a new England, I'm just looking for another girl'. He then spent the next twenty-five years doing just the opposite. His book *The Progressive Patriot: A*

Search for Belonging was published in 2006, and his latest album *Mr Love and Justice* was released in March 2008.

Stephen Brasher is an amateur Labour historian and has been a member of the Labour Party for twenty-five years. He was a Haringey councillor 1990-2002 and is currently Chair of Governors at Bruce Grove Primary school in the borough. Stephen is a member of the Electoral Reform Society and campaigns for proportional representation in the Labour Party.

Daniel Burdsey is Senior Lecturer in Sociology at the University of Brighton. The author of *British Asians and Football: Culture, Identity and Exclusion*, he has written for a range of academic journals on aspects of racism, identity and multiculturalism in sport. He is currently undertaking major research projects on British Asian football fans and British Asian professional cricketers.

Ben Carrington teaches Sociology and is the Associate Director of the Center for European Studies, at the University of Texas at Austin. He is also a Visiting Research Fellow at the Carnegie Faculty of Sport and Education at Leeds Metropolitan University. He has written widely within cultural sociology, the sociology of popular culture and the sociology of race and is regarded as one of the leading international authorities on the cultural politics of race and sport. Ben is the co-editor with Ian McDonald of *Race, Sport and British Society* and *Marxism, Cultural Studies and Sport*.

Anne Coddington is Senior Lecturer in Sports Journalism at the London College of Communications. Sports Correspondent for the magazine *Red Pepper*, Anne was formerly editor of the fortnightly newspaper *New Times* and co-edited in 1998 the book *The Moderniser's Dilemma*. Author of *One of the Lads: Women who Follow Football*, Anne has spoken at British Council seminars around the world on gender, popular culture and nationhood.

David Conn writes a weekly column of investigative sports journalism for the *Guardian*. He is the author of *The Beautiful Game: Searching for the Soul of Football* and *The Football Business: Fair Game in the 90s*. In 2005 David won the highly prestigious Sports News Reporter of the Year award.

Andrew Gamble is Professor of Politics at the University of Cambridge. His books *The Decline of Britain* and *The Free Economy* *and the Strong State*, alongside Andrew's regular essays in the magazine *Marxism Today*, were hugely influential in developing an understanding of the politics of Thatcherism. Currently he is joint editor of journals *The Political Quarterly* and *New Political Economy*, as well as a Fellow of the British Academy. His most recent book *Between Europe and America: The Future of British Politics* won the 2003 W.J.M. Mackenzie Prize for best book in political studies.

Paul Gilroy wrote in 1987 *There Ain't No Black in the Union Jack*, which remains one of the most important texts towards an understanding of race and culture in Britain. Currently the first holder of the Anthony Giddens Professorship in Social Theory at the London School of Economics, Paul's books include *The Black Atlantic* and *After Empire*. In 2007 he edited and provided the text which accompanied the images in the widely-acclaimed book *Black Britain: A Photographic History*.

Gerry Hassan is a Demos Associate and was Head of the Scotland 2020 and Glasgow 2020 programmes; he produced two books published by Demos: *Scotland 2020: Hopeful Stories for a Northern Nation* and *The Dreaming City: Glasgow 2020 and the Power of Mass Imagination*. Gerry is author and editor of a number of books on Scottish and UK politics and policy, most recently, *After Blair: Politics after the New Labour Decade*, published by Lawrence and Wishart. His forthcoming research projects include Gordon Brown and Britishness, the SNP in power and the crisis of Scottish Labour post-devolution.

Markus Hesselmann is the London correspondent for *Der Tagesspiegel*, Berlin's daily newspaper, and previously was the paper's Sports Editor. Markus co-edited with Christopher Young the book *Der Lieblingsfeind. Deutschland aus der Sicht seiner Fußballrivalen* (The Favourite Enemy. Germany as seen by its Football Rivals).

Rupa Huq is Senior Lecturer in Sociology at Kingston University. Author of *Beyond Subculture*, Rupa has also been a music journalist and DJ as well as a Labour Party parliamentary candidate in General and European Elections. A contributor to the *Guardian* at 'Comment is Free', Rupa also blogs at http://rupahuq.wordpress.com. She is currently writing a book on Englishness and Suburbia.

Graham Macklin has since September 2007 been engaged on a Leverhulme Trust funded project based at Teesside University entitled 'The Rise of White Racial Nationalism'. Author of *Very Deeply Dyed* *in Black: Sir Oswald Mosley and the Resurrection of British Fascism after 1945*, Graham has written widely on the nature of British fascism for a wide range of academic journals and general publications, including the *BBC History Magazine.*

Andy Newman is a trade unionist and socialist activist. He is on the Southern Regional Council of the GMB trade union, an associate national council member of Respect Renewal and a member of the national steering committee of the Stop the War Coalition. Andy runs and regularly contributes to, the hugely popular left blog site www.socialistunity.com.

Tom Nairn is the author of *The Break-Up of Britain*, first published in 1977. Following the Labour government's devolution settlement of 1997 he wrote *After Britain: New Labour and the Return of Scotland*; and in 2002 he revisited the issue in *Pariah: Misfortunes of the British Kingdom.* A major figure of the post-war New Left, with Perry Anderson Tom Nairn pioneered a hugely important debate on British decline in the 1960s. He later played a key role in introducing concepts such as the 'national-popular' and 'hegemony', from the Italian Marxist Antonio Gramsci's work, to a wider intellectual and political audience.

Richard Weight is the author of *Patriots: National Identity in Britain 1940-2000* and co-author with Mark Garnett of *Modern British History: The A-Z Guide.* A Fellow of the Royal Historical Society and of the Royal Society of Arts, he is a contributor to *The Times* and makes television and radio documentaries for a variety of broadcasters, including *Analysis*, which he presents for BBC Radio 4.

Index